STÉPHANIE DE GENLIS

THEATRE FOR CHILDREN

By WINIFRED WARD

Director of the Children's Theatre of Evanston; Assistant Professor of
Dramatic Production, Northwestern University; Supervisor of
Dramatics, Elementary Schools of Evanston, Illinois

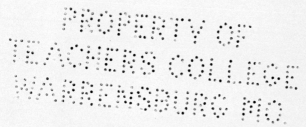
DRAWINGS BY CHARLES VANCE

. . . .

D. APPLETON-CENTURY COMPANY
INCORPORATED
New York   *London*

1939

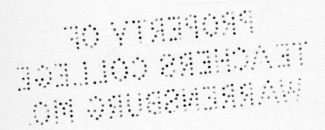

TO

AGNESS LAW

WHOSE INSPIRED TEACHING
HAS MADE MY WORK A JOY

PREFACE

THE VERY gracious reception given my *Creative Dramatics* has encouraged me to write this sister volume, which has as its objective, not the development of children through the creating of original dramatizations, as did my former book, but rather the production of artistic and beautiful plays for the joy of child audiences.

Much has been written concerning the directing, producing, and managing of adult drama, but very little about children's theatres. Because of the rapidly growing interest in this field, which has caused the establishment of hundreds of theatres for children in the past few years, a book such as this would seem to be greatly needed.

In writing *Theatre for Children* I have had in mind those who were inexperienced in the production of children's plays, whether for theatre, school, camp, or any other purpose. Experienced people do not need it, for they have worked out their own ways of doing things.

Beginning directors, however, can avoid many mistakes if they have some guidance from those who have learned by wide experience. Even if it is only a matter of reassurance, it is worth something to know that people who have been long in the work have the same ideals as they do.

First of all, then, the book has been written for the young person who would direct plays for child audiences, whether the actors are adults or children. Because such a very large proportion of these persons at the present time are women, it has seemed consistent to refer to the director as "she." It is encouraging to note, however, the growing number of young men who are becoming interested in children's theatre work either from the directing or the producing angle. There is no reason why they should not find great opportunity in the field. Even the hard-headed professional producer has for many years considered the children first in the elaborate pantomimes produced each holiday season in London.

Teachers, too, I hope, will find the book helpful. Though only a section of one chapter is exclusively devoted to school plays, a large part of the book is intended for teachers in public and private schools and studios. The same might be said for auditorium directors, recreation leaders, settlement workers, camp counselors, workers in church schools, Y.M.C.A., and Y.W.C.A. leaders, and all others who produce children's plays.

Because an entire volume could be written on almost every phase of the material covered in the book, it has been necessary to consider not the general aspect of the subject, but rather that which pertains directly to child audiences. For this reason the short Selected Bibliography at the end of this volume is very important for those who have not had adequate training in the general field of directing and producing plays.

Among the many people who have helped me in the preparation of the book are Harold A. Ehrensperger, who has been my valued adviser and critic; Geraldine Brain, whose work on the Play List has been of inestimable service; Charles Vance, who did all of the drawings; William McCreary, who is responsible for some of the production material. I have benefited by the suggestions of Berneice Prisk in the chapter on costuming; Louise Lambert has helped on research; Hazel Easton on proof-reading. I am indebted to Charlotte Chorpenning for her generous contribution of the first act of her play, *Alice in Wonderland*.

I deeply appreciate the fine coöperation all of these people have given me. If my book proves useful to those who produce plays for child audiences, I feel that a large measure of the credit will be due my colleagues and friends who have been so ready with their time and help.

WINIFRED WARD.

CONTENTS

CONTENTS

ILLUSTRATIONS

TEXT FIGURES

THEATRE FOR CHILDREN

CHAPTER I

WHERE THE CHILDREN'S THEATRE CAME FROM

THE YEAR is 1784; the place, a handsome country estate near Paris, belonging to the Duke of Chartres. The occasion, a play presented by children in a beautiful theatre set in the midst of a garden. It is a performance in the first known theatre for children.

The audience which has gathered for the entertainment this evening is a distinguished one. In it are the Duke and Duchess and a group of their friends from the Palais Royal; David, the noted painter; many of the families of the nearby countryside; and the household of this estate. More adults there are in the audience than children, yet unlike all theatres which have gone before, this is unquestionably a theatre for children.

In front of the curtain, at one side of the stage, are two harps, one large, the other quite small. Every one knows who will play them, for Madame de Genlis has long been recognized as a skilled harpist, and the little daughter of the Duke is her talented pupil. They make a charming picture as they enter, the handsome woman in her softly flowing gown and the attractive little girl, and the audience greets them with enthusiastic applause. The composition they play is a delicate pastoral air, the little girl proving remarkably proficient for so young a child. One would wonder at her accomplishment if he did not know that for almost as long as she can remember, her indefatigable teacher has given her two lessons every day!

When the curtain rises there seems a strange unreality about the picture which is revealed. The misty, far-away appearance of the three figures in the pantomime is due to the gauze curtain through which they are seen. The story is that of Psyche and her persecution by the jealous Venus. Throughout the action of the story there is soft music from the harps, heightening greatly the effectiveness of the pantomime. The two daughters of Madame de Genlis, aged fourteen and fifteen, are playing Venus and Psyche this evening, with a little English girl as Cupid. Of this pantomime Madame de Genlis writes in her *Memoirs,* "Never will there be again seen three faces together so full of beauty, charms, and graces. David was enraptured with that pantomime, which realized, so he said, the perfection of the *beau idéal.*" [1]

Following this part of the program comes the boys' play, *The Traveller.* The actors in this piece are the three little princes, sons of the Duke and Duchess of Chartres, one of whom is later to become King Louis Philippe. The boys and girls seldom play together in this theatre, for constant association in rehearsals is considered not quite delicate.

Now comes the last and most ambitious production of the evening, *The Effects of Curiosity,* a moral treatise on the evils which the excessively curious person is sure to bring upon himself and others. The curtain rises upon a rather remarkable garden scene. Instead of a painted setting, the audience sees a real garden! For the stage of this surprising little theatre can be opened on to the out-of-doors, and the players may walk down the long path of the garden and directly on to the stage. Since this performance is given at night, the garden walk is brightly illuminated, so that the audience can easily see the characters some time before they enter. The effect is quite

[1] Mme. de Genlis, *Memoirs,* Vol. III (Colburn, 1825).

lovely and as the scene of the play is supposed to be the garden of a country estate, this unusual stage is especially suitable.

The Effects of Curiosity tells the story of Helen, the younger daughter of the household, whose besetting sin is prying into the affairs of others. Because she determines to find out the secret which her mother and sister are keeping from her, she pieces together all the stray bits of information which she and Rose (the gardener's daughter) can collect. Not realizing the significance of what she discovers, she nearly brings disaster upon the family by imparting her news to the very person from whom they are trying to conceal it. Stopping short of tragedy, the little play ends with the repentance of Helen and the forgiveness of the mother she idolizes. Madame de Genlis' daughters play in this piece also, and she herself acts the part of the mother, being an experienced actress as well as a musician. Two other girls and the oldest of the princes have parts, though the boy appears only at the end and has no lines to say.

To a modern audience all three plays on this program would seem singularly unfitted for children. Not only are they stilted and wordy, but they are also moral to the point of sermonizing. One can scarcely imagine an audience of children listening attentively to such speeches as Sophia's when she says to Helen, "I am certain you never intentionally do a bad action; but, sister, excessive curiosity always draws after it the most dangerous indiscretions. Mama has told you this so often." Or Helen's repentant lines, "Alas! I will justify her hopes, and from henceforth will live only to atone for those faults of which I am made doubly sensible by her kindness. Come, dear Sophia, lead me to her that I may throw myself at her feet!"

MADAME DE GENLIS

The author of these and all the other plays performed in this children's theatre was no other than the versatile Madame de Genlis, already mentioned as a musician and actress. Having educational theories so advanced for her era that she would have been known as a leader in "progressive education" if such terminology had existed, this amazing woman wrote her own text-books when she disapproved of those which were available, and believing that the drama offered great opportunity for moral training, she wrote a whole series of plays for her children.

LE THÉÂTRE D'ÉDUCATION

These plays, with many others, were published in 1779-80, in four volumes entitled *The Theatre of Education*. Some of them were based upon Bible stories, *Hagar in the Desert* being one of the most effective. The moral lessons which are characteristic of all the plays are indicated by such titles as *The Spoiled Child, The Dangers of the World, The Generous Enemies, The False Friends,* and *The Truly Wise Man*.

Strangely enough, the popularity of *The Theatre of Education* was enormous. The first edition was entirely sold out in six days, and within a year the plays had been translated into no fewer than six foreign languages. Already the author's daughters had played in them at the Palais Royal; they had gained for their author the approval of the king-critic, La Harpe, who, in his complimentary verses, "adored at once, the author, the work, and the actresses." [2]

[2] Austin Dobson, *Four Frenchwomen* (Dodd, Mead & Co., 1928).

HER FRIENDSHIP WITH ROUSSEAU

At the time of her marriage, Stéphanie de Genlis knew little about Jean-Jacques Rousseau except that he was considered a great man. She had read none of his works and probably was entirely ignorant of his revolutionary theories about education. One day a friend told her that her husband was planning a joke on her in which he would pass off an actor as Rousseau. M. de Genlis, as it happened, forgot about his plan and some time later brought Rousseau himself for a call. Scarcely able to restrain her mirth, Stéphanie conversed in the most natural manner about everything that came into her head. In the course of the evening she sang and played for him, proving so genuine and delightful that Rousseau actually promised to dine with them next day. When he left, Stéphanie, ready to laugh at her husband's expense, had the laugh turned on her when she found out that her guest had been no counterfeit but the great Rousseau himself!

For five months after this meeting Rousseau dined with them nearly every day. He was always friendly and in good spirits, conversing freely and enjoying their company. It was only when M. de Genlis sent him a case of a certain wine he had praised that his hatred of patronage caused him to send back the wine with a note breathing flames and fury, in which he renounced the donors forever.

Just how advanced would have been Madame de Genlis' educational philosophy if she had not known Rousseau, it is, of course, impossible to say, but it is generally assumed that she was strongly influenced by the ideas in his *Émile, a Treatise on Education*. Her writings and her methods of teaching bear out her sympathy with Rousseau's doctrines concerning the rights of the child. She, too, believed that children should be regarded as individuals, that their intellectual and spiritual needs should be studied and provided for.

The education of her own two daughters gave her an opportunity to experiment with her ideas, and when the Duke of Chartres, in 1782, gave her the position of governor of his three sons (such a position for a woman being unprecedented, even though she was already in charge of his daughter), the opportunity of her life was at hand. For Stéphanie de Genlis was a born teacher, and thenceforth she gave up everything else in life to devote herself to the education of these royal children.

That she was successful is conceded even by her critics. From early morning until bedtime, everything they did contributed to their education. They rose early, took their morning walk in German, dined in English, supped in Italian. In her *Memoirs* she avers that she was the first governor who taught languages by conversation. She had magic-lantern slides painted for teaching history, and her young pupils dramatized stories of famous voyages and acted them in the park of the estate. The whole household took part in these performances. They had a wardrobe of costumes, ponies for the processions, and a number of pretty little boats for their fleets.

Madame de Genlis, unlike most educators of her day, believed that children would learn more readily if they enjoyed what they were doing. She ridiculed the idea that nothing is known well except what is learned with difficulty. The idea of making even their amusements instructive she believed to be so evidently advantageous that she could not conceive how it could be neglected. To this end she caused a little portable stage to be erected in the great dining-room, upon which they performed historic and mythological pictures. Those who were not performing were obliged to guess what the pictures represented. She saw to it that the children's recreation was never mere amusement!

All such activities were in reality a part of her educational theatre. True, they were intended more for the benefit of child-player than for child-audience, and they were for a very limited group of boys and girls. Yet, heretofore, there had been no theatre designed purely for the benefit and the entertainment of children, either as players or audience. In order to appreciate the significance of this children's theatre, it may be well to glance back over the years and see what had been provided for child audiences up to this time.

WHAT THE FAR EAST OFFERED CHILDREN

As early as 2000 B.C. the Chinese are believed to have had dramatic religious festivals, jugglers, sword-dancers, and other forerunners of legitimate drama.[3] The art of the shadow-play had reached a high degree of perfection by 1000 B.C. When we read of this type of entertainment, we know that children must have been in the audiences which witnessed such shows, and without doubt have been a part of the festivals. Later, in the professional theatre, the boy's part became that of an apprentice to a theatrical director who put him through the severest kind of training for six or seven years in preparation for an acting career.

No one knows how far back the shadow-puppets of Java go, but they are thought to be of great antiquity. Originally they were manipulated by the head of each household, the spectators being members of his family. Later, however, shadow-plays became professional entertainments. Curious, indeed, to a person in the western world are these flat, conventionalized

[3] Glenn Hughes, *The Story of the Theatre* (French, 1928).

figures controlled by wooden sticks attached to the arms! Sitting on a mat between screen and lamp, the operator holds the puppet above his head as he manipulates the arms. The attention of the audience is drawn, not to the puppet, but to the moving shadows on the screen.[4]

Open-air festivals connected with religious worship have been cultivated by the Hindus for several thousand years. Though dancing, music, and poetry predominated in such rites, they were often dramatic in character, especially when they celebrated the lives of deities.

According to some authorities, India was the birthplace of the puppet. A very old Indian tale gives an account of a basketful of marvelous wooden dolls presented by the daughter of a celebrated mechanician to a princess. "One of these could be made to fly through the air by pressing a wooden peg, another to dance, another to talk!"[5] It is said that large talking puppets were even used on the stage with human actors.

The "doll-theatre" has long entertained the Japanese, though it has been used primarily for the entertainment of adults. Accompanied by a stringed instrument called a samisen, ballad-dramas were enacted by puppets, the story being chanted by a minstrel.

The large dolls used in this theatre, which is still popular, are so elaborately made that sometimes each joint of each finger can be articulated, eyes move from side to side, eyebrows can be raised to express scorn or surprise.[6] Curiously enough, the operators who control the puppets work in full view of the audience, two or three sometimes being required to manipulate one puppet. It is interesting to note that these doll-theatres were the first to use revolving stages.

[4] *Ibid.*
[5] Helen H. Joseph, *A Book of Marionettes* (Huebsch, 1920).
[6] *Ibid.*

GREECE

In the search for children's drama, we turn, naturally, to Greece in that first great period of drama, the fifth century B.C. Prior to this time we find that children took part in religious processionals which were of a dramatic nature, and there were many children in the audiences. Boys and probably girls, it is thought, were taken later to the great dramatic festivals, and they saw the plays of Æschylus, Sophocles, Euripides, and Aristophanes.

But these were adult plays, all of them, and children took only what they were able to understand and let the rest go. In all the plays of a five-day festival, not one was ever intended for children.

THE ROMAN THEATRE

The Roman theatre held still less for child audiences than did the Greek, unless the lavish spectacles which were characteristic of the Roman stage can be considered childlike. Like every other people, the Romans had long held religious festivals which were dramatic in nature, and the whole population participated. But their plays, given in huge theatres during the first five hundred years A.D., degenerated into sensuous displays which were elaborate beyond all reason, and though children and even babies were taken to them, nothing could have been more unsuitable for them to see.

From the sixth to the eleventh centuries no organized theatre existed. Jugglers, tight-rope walkers, dancers, singers, tumblers, buffoons, and their like afforded the only kind of entertainment even approaching the dramatic. Children were always in the shifting out-of-door audiences which witnessed

most of these shows, just as they were later in the crowds
which laughed at Punch and Judy.

By the eleventh century a new entertainer had emerged—the
minstrel. Best known as a man who composed songs, and sang
or recited them to the music of some instrument, he was
often accomplished in other arts as well. But entertaining as
he was to old and young, he seldom attempted characterization
and, therefore, does not belong in the theatrical category.

FOLK DRAMA

In every European country, however, the people from early
times had found an outlet for their dramatic impulse in festivals and folk plays. Most of the festivals were of pagan origin
and had as subject-matter the changing seasons. The Easter,
May Day, and Christmas festivities were the most important
of these celebrations, and many were the rites and customs
attendant upon them.

One of the most interesting developments connected with
May Day is that which originated with the sword-dance.
Every country had some type of sword-dance, and though the
form of the dance differed, the symbolism was usually the
same. It was a celebration of the death of winter and the birth
of spring. There is always a conflict of two forces in the dance,
with the triumph of one of them, followed by a joyous dance
of victory. In some countries this idea developed into the
Sleeping Beauty story, the hundred years' sleep signifying
Winter from which Spring is kissed awake by the Prince.

In England the morris dance, which is practically the same
as the sword-dance, became the most popular amusement during the fourteenth and fifteenth centuries. It is a dramatic
dance in which national and legendary heroes are characterized

by the dancers, and country clowns are used for the comedy they can supply.[7]

Finally, dialogue was added, and the sword-dance grew into the Mummers' Play, one of the liveliest and most popular folk plays in history. It was a country product, with farmers and villagers for actors, and the lord of the manor and his family and friends as audience. Beginning as a May Day feature, it finally came to belong to the Christmas Eve festivities, and it has since been retained along with the ceremonies connected with the boar's head, the Yule log, and the Christmas carols. Such drama as this is thoroughly childlike in character, simple and naïve enough for the youngest.

MIRACLE AND MORALITY PLAYS

Alongside of the folk festivals was that form of religious drama known as the miracle, mystery, and morality plays. Growing up in the Christian church, these plays were a development of the dramatized Bible lessons by which the priests taught the people, so that the subject-matter was known to children and adults alike.

The terms, miracle and mystery, were both used for plays based on Bible stories of the lives of the saints. The moralities dealt with virtues and vices as characters, with such names as Knowledge, Good Deeds, Greed, Anger, and Meddlesome. Such plays were intelligible to children though they were not always suitable in subject-matter.

In a dramatic ceremonial, *The Slaughter of the Innocents in Bethlehem,* the child choristers, dressed in white and headed by a lamb, walked around the church in procession, after which they were supposed to be murdered by order of Herod.

[7] Glenn Hughes, *The Story of the Theatre* (French, 1928).

They were then called by an angel to heaven, and they pre-
tended to ascend by rising up and walking into the choir.[8]

Children doubtless witnessed the miracles and mysteries in
the church, and afterwards in the church-yards and on the
double-decked wagons known as pageants. These sometimes
included the entire scope of Bible history, from the Creation
to the Day of Judgment. On the festival days when these
pageants rolled through the streets, each pausing at intervals
to enact a scene from Bible history, the whole town and
countryside came to see them. In those plays which treated
of the lives of saints from birth to death, children were used
to represent their youth. They also played a pictorial part
as angels, and the older boys often represented women.

THE BOY KING'S PLAYERS

According to the *Royal Dramatic Record*,[9] which lists the
theatrical entertainments at the English Court, the boy king
Edward VI (1537-1553) maintained a regular establishment of
players, as his father, Henry VIII, had done, the Christmas
entertainments being kept up with great pomp. Mention is
made of a play called *Æsop's Crow* which was performed by
the King's Players at Court, in which most of the actors were
dressed as birds.

During the short reign of Edward VI, the Princess Elizabeth,
who was four years older than Edward, evinced a fondness
for the drama which was to be characteristic of her as a queen.
In the account of her household are items of sums paid for
plays and interludes which were performed especially for her.
The taste of the age was still barbarous, however, and the

[8] Mantzius, *History of Theatrical Art,* Vol. II (Duckworth, London, 1903).
[9] Edited by J. K. Chapman (Mitchell, London, 1849).

plays contained so much that was coarse and crude that they must have been absurdly inappropriate for the entertainment of a little girl.

THE BOY ACTORS

An exceedingly important part was played by boys in the formative period of English drama, when trained actors were few and the acting profession discreditable. At first they were amateurs, students in boys' schools or in the choir schools. Believing that performance in plays was valuable in the practice it offered in speaking the Latin tongue and in giving an easy, assured bearing, Eton and Westminster, at least, made dramatic performances a part of their curricula.[10]

Schoolmasters wrote plays for their students, and they "were no more afraid of spicing their dramatic works with exceedingly strong jokes than of directing the sharpest attacks against the highest authorities."[11] *Ralph Roister Doister,* written by Nicholas Udall, Master of Eton, was one of many plays to be given amateur performance. Though numerous adult plays were produced for visiting notables, a considerable number of plays must have been given for school audiences. These would scarcely be considered commendable for children to-day, but they must have been well thought of at the time, since there was so strong a sentiment in their favor.

In 1566 a comedy called *Palemon and Arcite* was acted by students before Queen Elizabeth in Christ Church Hall. An incident is related in which some of the boys who were on the stage, hearing a cry of hounds, were so much taken by surprise, supposing it to be real, that they cried out, "There, he's caught! He's caught!" The Queen, who was highly amused

[10] Hildebrand, *The Child Actors,* University of Illinois Studies (1926).
[11] Mantzius, *History of Theatrical Art,* Vol. II.

61555

to see them so carried away by it, exclaimed, "Oh, excellent! These boys are in very truth ready to leap out of the windows to follow the hounds." [12]

The students in such choir schools as St. Paul's and the Chapel Royal gave dramatic performances which began by being amateur but later became professional. In about 1600 the boys from St. Paul's were established in a private playhouse near the cathedral, while the Chapel Royal Company occupied a new theatre in Blackfriars. They entertained, too, at the court of Elizabeth, in the masques and pageants which were given in the castle halls or out of doors. That such playwrights as Lyly, Chapman, Dekker, Marston, and Jonson wrote for the boys' companies is proof enough that their acting was superior; and that for a time they won audiences away from the adult companies convinces us that they were highly popular.

As soon as able adult actors appeared on the English stage, the boy companies declined. They had played an important part in the theatre, but it was an adult theatre in spite of the fact that children were the players. When at the present time the question arises as to whether a children's theatre implies a playhouse in which children act, let the inquirer look back at the boy companies to be convinced that it is the play and the audience rather than the actors that make a children's theatre.

THE CHRISTMAS PANTOMIMES

Beginning early in the eighteenth century English theatres have each year during the Christmas season presented elaborate spectacular entertainments which have come to be known

[12] The Royal Dramatic Record.

collectively as "the pantomime." The whole family goes to this glorified vaudeville. It is an English institution. Consisting of ballets, songs, dances, topical jokes, Harlequin and Columbine acts, what not, instead of the wordless entertainment one would expect from the name, it has a fragile connecting link of nursery tale or fairy lore, the favorite of which is "Cinderella." "Dick Whittington," "Babes in the Wood," "Robinson Crusoe," and "Jack and the Beanstalk" are other stories which have been much used.

Julian Wylie, an authority on provincial pantomime production, averred that in spite of the popularity of the pantomime among adults, he considered them last when putting on his shows. Experience taught him that if he could please the children, the success of the pantomime was assured. He considered them discerning critics, jealous guardians of the highest traditions. If he tampered with a story, he said, the children wrote him letters of protest.[18] One could wish that American children would guard their favorite stories as jealously from the changes made by the radio and the moving-picture producers!

WHAT ITALY AND FRANCE OFFERED CHILDREN

The favorite source of theatrical entertainment for Italian children since the Renaissance has been puppetry. Introduced into the country no one knows when, both the outdoor Punch and Judy show and the highly artistic marionette plays and operas have delighted children and adults.

Punch, of course, had his beginnings in the old Italian comedy, and in the puppet show he is garbed like his ancestor, Punchinello. The lusty old *Commedia dell' Arte,* though

[18] A. E. Wilson, *King Panto* (Dutton, 1935).

broad and full of action, was not for children, whether or not they went to see it. Punch, himself, brutal and dishonest through and through, is, for all his comedy, a preposterous hero for a play which has been presented for children these hundreds of years.

Marionettes have long been popular in France, too, but French children have many more types of drama than do little Italians. Operas, ballets, pantomimes, and stage plays are the heritage of boys and girls in the country where the children's theatre was born. The Christmas season, especially, brings many plays for them, and the clever pantomimes of the winter circus have been an institution for years.[14]

GERMANY

Mediæval drama was not lacking in Germany, where miracle plays, farces, folk drama, and religious processions were a part of the lives of young and old. Around Nuremburg, in particular, the amateur drama flourished, Hans Sachs (1494-1576) alone writing two hundred plays, many of which he himself produced.

During the sixteenth century a slapstick type of play developed, which was centered about a low-comedy character called *Hanswurst*. For a long time the *Hanswurst* plays were popular with German audiences, the children sharing the delight of their elders in his clownish antics.

"THE CHILDREN'S RECKONING"

Among the folk festivals which have long been given annually in Germany and may still be seen to-day is the pic-

[14] Mackay, *Children's Theatres and Plays* (D. Appleton-Century Co., 1927).

turesque *Kinderzeche* or *Children's Reckoning* at Dinkelsbühl, in Bavaria.

This festival commemorates the debt the people owe to the children for saving the town years ago. At a time when it was besieged by the Swedes and no help was forthcoming, the burghers met to decide whether they would capitulate or fight to the finish. The debate waxed hot as a messenger from the Swedes was brought into the room by the young daughter of the burgomaster. Remaining to hear him demand immediate surrender, the girl found out that the Swedish commander besieging the town was sorrowing for his little son who had just died.

Before the burghers had decided upon their answer, she had gathered together a large company of children who begged that they might be allowed to go out and appeal to the Swedish commander not to burn their village. At last the burghers were persuaded to give their consent, and the children went out from the town singing. The story goes that the general's heart was softened, and, consequently, the village was saved.

The Reckoning, as enacted each year, is a touching play. The whole town is turned over to the children, and the celebration begins early in the morning with the music of a boys' band which marches through the streets. Next comes the inevitable sword-dance performed by youths in the village square, followed by folk-dances accompanied by fife and drums.

The *Rathaus* or town-hall is the scene of the burghers' meeting, and here the big audience of villagers gathers to see this famous event in their history reënacted by their *Kinder*. Hardly a dry eye is to be seen in the house when the children march out into the square, singing, and as the audience follows to see the last part of the play, one knows that these fathers and mothers have been deeply moved.

Now the Swedes approach to take the town, and the singing children, led by the burgomaster's daughter, go out to meet them. Up to the general himself the girl advances, holding by the hand a handsome little boy. A moment more and she has made her plea; and when the tiny boy is lifted up, the general shows how deeply he has been affected by taking the child in his arms and kissing him.

What wonder that Dinkelsbühl keeps alive by this charming festival the memory of that day when children won by peaceful means what their hard-headed elders believed could only be gained by force!

DENMARK

Birthplace of Hans Christian Andersen, Denmark might be expected to take more than usual interest in children's drama. And, indeed, this is true. Plays for children have long been given at the Christmas season, as well as many notable performances in out-of-door theatres.

Copenhagen has in recent years established a school theatre which presents a series of very fine professional plays each season, many of the actors coming from the Royal Theatre. It is managed by the school theatre association which is governed by a committee elected from the teachers' organizations. Other children's theatres are scattered throughout the country, the whole movement having real significance in children's theatre history.[15]

[15] McFadden, "Europe Challenges American Parents," *National Parent-Teacher* (1937).

RUSSIA

More adequately than any other country in the world, Russia has provided drama for her children. In addition to the many folk and religious festivals, dramatic dances and puppet-shows common to most countries in early times, Russia for many years produced plays in the professional theatres which were delightful for children to see.

Then, in 1918, the Moscow Theatre for Children was founded, with a gifted and far-seeing artist of the theatre, Natalia Satz, as director. Becoming a state-supported institution, it was later moved into an imposing playhouse on Theatre Square. Though there are other children's theatres in Moscow, and many throughout the Soviet Union, this one has been outstanding in reputation and achievements.

These Soviet theatres are professional, each with its own company of artists and technicians. The Moscow Theatre for Children has had an acting company of as many as fifty artists, with a staff of directors, scenic artists, and electricians, as well as an orchestra of its own.

In addition to these workers which are usual in all theatres, are psychologists, child specialists, educators, and authors. Believing in the theatre as a potent educational force, the Russians work systematically in the study of their audiences, that they may learn child interests and thereby make their plays both entertaining and "activizing." Testing a play with one audience after another, the authors and directors cut and change and elaborate until it suits the age level for which it is intended; or, if it seems too young or too old for this audience, it is sometimes tried with children of a different age. For Moscow theatres have different productions for the six- to nine-year-olds, ten to thirteen, and fourteen to sixteen.

Some of the plays offered in these theatres contain Soviet propaganda, others are purely artistic and entertaining. *The Emperor's New Clothes,* which seemed to a visitor who did not understand the language merely a capital dramatization of the Hans Andersen tale, was explained as a story which proved there was no place in this world for kings! *The Negro Boy and the Monkey,* a humorous and popular pantomime, showed the senselessness of race prejudice.

Whatever one may think of the type of education which goes on in the Russian children's playhouses, he must award the theatre the highest honor for its artistic achievements. Its plays are beautifully acted and staged, with an entertainment value which it would be difficult to surpass. Instead of scattered plays such as are produced for children in other countries, Russia has a self-respecting schedule of production so complete that in Moscow, at least, a child would have a choice of plays *any day in the week,* with an admission price low enough to assure even the poorer boys and girls the opportunity of attending the theatre.

OTHER EUROPEAN COUNTRIES

Drama for children in other European countries has not been notable. All had picturesque folk and religious festivals during the Middle Ages, and school drama has flourished for a time in some of them.

Many children's plays have in recent years been produced on the professional stage of practically all European countries, especially at holiday time. There has been little concerted action, however, to provide good drama for children, and to provide it consistently. There is without doubt a growing interest in children's theatres throughout the world, and the next twenty years is likely to see much history made in European child drama. Whether it will come through the amateur or professional theatre, whether it will be state-supported or maintained by altruistic organizations of adults, it is impossible to say.

THE UNITED STATES

The children's theatre in the United States is of very recent origin, but no country, perhaps, has at the present time more widespread interest in developing such a theatre. The movement has been chiefly in the amateur field, the professional theatre having as yet contributed little to the cause.

THE CHILDREN'S EDUCATIONAL THEATRE

First to recognize the need for child drama were the social settlements. In about 1892 they began to present simple versions of nursery tales with child players and child audiences.[16] In 1903 the first significant theatre for children was founded by Alice Minnie Herts at the *Educational Alliance* in New York. It was called The Children's Educational Theatre.[17] With Emma Sheridan Fry as dramatic director, such plays as *The Tempest, The Fairy Ring, Little Lord Fauntleroy, Snow White, The Little Princess, Editha's Burglar,* and *The Prince and the Pauper* were presented by and for children. A definite educational policy governed the productions of this theatre. Standards in plays, staging, and acting were kept high. Children were encouraged to work out their own interpretations of the characters they played. In the case of *The Tempest,* neighborhood families who had never read a page of Shakespeare

16 Mackay, *How to Produce Children's Plays* (Holt, 1915).
17 Herts, *The Children's Educational Theatre* (Harpers, 1911).

in their lives were inspired by the enthusiasm of their children to acquaint themselves with the play before they came to see it. Sometimes a lecturer explained the plays in the language spoken by the parents of the children. Every effort was made to bring about a general appreciation of the drama which was produced in the theatre.

So valuable an institution was this educational theatre that it is a pity it existed only six years. In a poor neighborhood which boasted only cheap picture-shows, it was a source of great happiness to children, bringing beauty and fineness into lives that were drab and commonplace. One cannot help wondering how far and how deep the influence of that theatre went, and whether to-day there are not still many people who think of their connection with it as one of the loveliest experiences of their childhood.

Since the short life of the Children's Educational Theatre, there has been an ever-increasing number of plays for children all over the country. Hull House in Chicago, Christadora and Neighborhood Houses in New York, and many other social settlements have significant achievements to their credit. Some of the most skilled directors in the country have worked with the children of our foreign-born population, and the loveliness of their productions in the settlement theatres has surpassed in many ways anything else which has been done. In bringing the picturesque beauty of the folk festival and the fairy-tale play to children who live amid the ugliness of factory and slum districts, these settlement workers fill a far greater need than do the producers of plays for more fortunate children.

THE CONTRIBUTION OF THE DRAMA LEAGUE

The Drama League of America, under the leadership of Mrs. A. Starr Best, made an outstanding contribution to the children's theatre movement in this country. With Cora Mel Patten as chairman of the junior department, children's leagues were established in many cities, and a great number of plays and pageants were presented. Lists of plays suitable for children were sent out to interested groups, collections of children's plays were published, and help was given in the direction and production of child drama.

On the Municipal Pier in Chicago, the Drama League conducted each summer an extensive recreation program under the supervision of Bertha Iles. Plays, pageants, and folk dancing gave an outlet to the dramatic impulse of children from immigrant families, and provided interesting entertainment for the crowds who frequented the Pier.

In the awakening of general interest and the dissemination of knowledge concerning children's plays, the Drama League deserves highest credit. The history of the children's theatre in America really had its beginning in this pioneer organization which made ready the ground and planted the seed from which it has grown.

CONSTANCE D'ARCY MACKAY

A name which will go down in children's theatre history in the United States is that of Constance D'Arcy Mackay, the woman who has made a more distinguished contribution to the cause of good drama for American children than has any other one individual.

Without well-written plays there can be no theatre worthy the name. At the time when the Drama League was arousing interest in the production of children's plays, the lack of good material was a serious problem. Most of the juvenile plays listed in the publishers' catalogues were distinctly third-rate, and the teacher who was unwilling to sacrifice her standards was very likely to become discouraged.

To such a person the plays of Constance Mackay were truly a godsend. With a beautiful simplicity and dignity, with a worthy idea at the heart of each one, they stood out above the mass of child drama with almost a royal air. No artisan was this author, but a real artist, an artist with a sense of what was fitting for children, an understanding of what was charming to them.

When a school wished an exquisite little Christmas play, there was *The Christmas Guest* and, later, *The First Noël;* when a play long enough for a full program was needed, what more delightful than *The Silver Thread?* Camps of little girls have enjoyed the pageant-like *Forest Princess;* junior high schools could find no finer play for their graduation program than *Youth's Highway.*

THE JUNIOR LEAGUE

When the Chicago Junior League presented its first children's play in 1921, it probably had no idea that this was to be the beginning of a great work undertaken by its national association. The enthusiasm and the success of the young women who presented *Alice in Wonderland* [18] in Chicago led to the production of children's plays by the Junior Leagues of other cities, until by 1938 an ambitious program of plays for children was carried on by the one hundred forty-eight Leagues in the United States, Honolulu, Canada, and Mexico.

No single policy is followed in the number or type of plays

[18] By Alice Gerstenberg (French).

produced in a season by the various Leagues, nor in the players used in the productions, though the League members more often than not make up the casts of their productions, and sometimes write their own plays. They reach many thousands of children each season in their regular productions and in those they give for underprivileged groups.

CLARE TREE MAJOR

A pioneer in the professional theatre for children, Clare Tree Major established in New York City, in 1921, a Saturday morning theatre in which the actors were young professionals. After a few years her companies began touring the country, giving in many cities a series of several plays each year. Mrs. Major herself manages and directs her companies, besides writing most of the plays which they present. She has awakened in a large number of communities an interest in theatre for children.

EMERSON COLLEGE

Among the earliest children's theatres established by professional schools was that founded in 1920 at the Emerson College in Boston. Students of college age were the actors, and they often directed the productions as well. Original dramatizations of stories were much used, in addition to well-known children's plays. Performances were for some years given every Saturday afternoon.

THE CHILDREN'S THEATRE OF EVANSTON

The School of Speech of Northwestern University, in 1925, founded a children's theatre for the boys and girls of Evanston and the North Shore. Two years later the Board of Education and the Parent-Teacher Associations of the Public Schools joined the University in sponsoring the theatre and it became a community institution. The casts for the four plays given each season are drawn from the creative dramatic classes of the public schools, the School of Speech, and the town. Adult rôles are filled with students of college age, children's parts with boys and girls. Backstage work is done by students in the children's theatre and stagecraft classes of the School of Speech. Four performances of each play are given in public school auditoriums, with some additional performances at the University.

THE CHILDREN'S PLAYS OF THE GOODMAN THEATRE

The same year in which the Evanston theatre was founded saw the first children's plays at the Goodman Theatre in Chicago. Here, each Saturday afternoon, students in the School of the Theatre have been presenting plays for children during the winter season. Both players and crews are young adults, the work in the Children's Theatre being a part of their school training. Four or five different productions with several performances of each play have made up their schedule for the season.

THE KING-COIT SCHOOL

Not a children's theatre, but a school which has done distinctive work in occasional children's plays, is the King-Coit School of Acting and Design of New York City. Here young children from six to twelve in addition to acting in the plays have for some years designed and helped to make the most exquisite scenery and costumes to be found anywhere in children's productions. Some of their plays have been based on old Persian, French, and Hindu stories—not at all the kind of material which could be used in a children's theatre, but

*NALA AND
DAMAYANTI*

Hindu play,
King-Coit School,
New York.

nevertheless interesting for the type of production which the school undertakes.

JUNIOR PROGRAMS

One of the hopeful developments of recent years in the field of professional entertainment for children has been the launching of Junior Programs of New York. This organization sends out touring companies to many cities and towns over the country, presenting entertainments of excellent quality for child audiences. The ballet of *Pinocchio,* the operas *Hansel and Gretel* and *The Bumblebee Prince,* and the play *The Reward of the Sun God,* based on an Indian legend, are examples of the interesting productions they bring to boys and girls.

OTHER TYPES OF THEATRES

A volume of considerable proportions would be necessary to give a complete history to date of the children's theatre in this country alone. If such a volume were forthcoming, it would be outmoded to-morrow, so rapidly are children's theatres springing up—and, alas, sometimes dying down. The theatres which have been mentioned are representative of the many types of production which have been going on throughout the country in the field of child drama. Some are pioneers, others, like Junior Programs, are hopeful signs for the future.

Children's theatres sponsored by municipalities are only just emerging. Palo Alto, California; Milwaukee, Wisconsin; Duluth, Minnesota, were among the first cities to recognize their value by making them a regular part of their recreational program. Those under the wing of civic or little theatres are as yet very few and very young. San Francisco's experiment with a theatre program to which various groups of the city contribute has met with marked success. Individuals, like

Marie Agnes Foley of Chicago, have built up theatres from their own students. And, very recently, some of the federal theatres have produced plays for children.

All of this activity in children's theatres as such is only a small part of the wide production of children's plays going on all over the country. Recreation associations have been struggling for years to improve the caliber of the plays and pageants produced on public playgrounds. They have worked against great difficulties and have made gratifying progress.

Public and private schools have been constantly advancing both in the quantity and the quality of their productions. Churches here and there have done exceptional work. Camps and clubs take much greater pride to-day than they took yesterday in presenting good plays.

Optimism about the future of the children's theatre cannot but be justified in view of the great advance which has been made in the past twenty years and the sound basis on which so many theatres are being built to-day. Both in Europe and the United States there are signs that the children of the future will have a real theatre of their own, a theatre where they can see plays suited to their age and interests instead of trying to satisfy their hunger with the crumbs of adult drama which was their only fare in ages past.

The time is still far off when all children will have this opportunity. Vast numbers of boys and girls grow up without ever having seen a real play. Even though there are now hundreds of children's theatres, a very small percentage of the millions of American children are reached as yet. We have a long way to go before we shall have provided in any adequate way for the hunger of our children for real plays; but that we are moving toward such a day there can be little doubt.

CHAPTER II

AS WE THINK OF A CHILDREN'S THEATRE

WHENEVER you watch a group of brothers and sisters circled about the family radio in the evening, ostensibly doing their home-work while listening to their favorite dramatic program, or pass a moving-picture theatre on a Saturday afternoon when a long line of children is inching up to the box office to get tickets for a dramatization of *Heidi, Tom Sawyer, Little Women,* or another of the stories so dear to the hearts of children, you are impressed anew with the fascination which drama holds for young people.

Millions of children know no other theatre than the moving picture and the radio, and these, of course, are not really theatre at all. With an intense natural interest for the dramatic, they grow up without ever seeing a play in flesh and blood. They do not say, "Go to, let's have a real theatre!" because, having no basis of comparison, they cannot realize the lack of complete satisfaction in the plays of radio and picture-show. To say, "Well, if they do not know the difference, why do anything about it?" is like suggesting that because children can play in vacant lots there is no point in providing playgrounds, or because they seem satisfied with cheap adventure stories they need not be given better books.

Grown-ups are in a position to satisfy their own need for drama. If enough of them desire a civic theatre they can establish one. When the organization becomes strong enough to warrant a campaign for a playhouse they can plan a drive for contributions. But to conceive of children founding a theatre for themselves requires a great stretch of the imagination. Just as boys and girls depend on their parents and other adults interested in their welfare to supply homes, schools, playgrounds, and clinics so must they count on grown-ups to provide for their need of those enriching experiences which come through the arts.

America, so far ahead of the rest of the world in standards of living, so rich in material things, so awake to social responsibilities, has far to travel along the cultural way before it even catches sight of the shining towers and crimson banners which mark the first milestone of its journey. Long years of utilitarian effort are necessary in any new country before it is ready for the fuller life which is made possible by the arts. Love for music, drama, literature, and appreciation for the beauty of gardens and trees, of dwellings and pictures, grows slowly. Not until people have leisure do the arts flourish, and not until then is any considerable value placed on those gracious qualities of character and personality which are the essence of culture.

Encouraging signs that we are going in the direction of the "shining towers and crimson banners," though, are on every hand. Note the thousands of people of every class who gather each night of summer in the cities to hear fine orchestras play the world's great symphonies, the tremendous interest in public school music, the excellent quality of creative art done by young people, the steadily increasing appreciation of beauty in houses and gardens.

Music is making far more significant progress at the present time in America than any other art. The love for really good symphonies and operas has spread from the few to the mass of people, so that Beethoven, Wagner, Tschaikowsky, and other composers of their caliber, have millions of appreciative listeners to-day where only a few years ago they had thousands.

THE RADIO'S CONTRIBUTION

One has not far to look to find the reason for this. The radio has educated the country by offering on its programs the greatest music of all time played or sung by the best artists of their day. One has only to dial the right station on the almost universal radio and this music is his! Familiarity with great compositions brings the appreciation which could not possibly come with the first hearing.

The radio has carried its education much further than this, however. Looking to a future in which good music shall be the well-loved heritage of all, it is not neglecting to educate the children. Many of the most gifted musicians of the country feel that they can give no greater service to their art than to have a share in the music appreciation hours for young people. Because of such education, hundreds of thousands of boys and girls are growing up with an intelligent understanding and appreciation of the world's great music.

When one considers that this is only a supplement to the very fine musical education of children which goes on daily in public and private schools in even the smaller towns of the country, one does not wonder that the generation which is growing up is far more musically minded than any that has gone before. Orchestras, bands, glee clubs, and instrumental classes, in their concerts, recitals, contests, and demonstrations of creative music, are constantly reaching new heights, even the youngest of them amazing audiences of the older generation.

Music is the most universal of the arts, but life is not so rich that we can afford to lose the soul-satisfying experiences which come from the other arts: from painting and sculpture, from literature, from the dance, and from the art of the theatre. What has been accomplished in music education can be done in the other arts. Leaders in music have had vision and courage. Their imagination has led them to see what could be done, and they have taught so well and so consistently that their work has been accepted everywhere. How many schools in which the other arts are neglected have superior music departments! How many citizens of how many towns speak with pride of the music in their schools and in their communities!

Cities to-day are finding that they can support symphony orchestras as well as baseball teams. The time is coming when they will discover that a municipal playhouse, too, can be an integral part of community life. But the time for a real theatre will not come until our children are educated in drama as they are now being educated in music. No art can become a vital, moving force in a country unless the children grow up in it; unless it is a part of their lives from the time they are very young. And so, if we are to build a theatre in this country, with appreciative audiences who will bring their interest and their support to what is good, we must expose our children to the best plays in the same way that they are exposed to the finest music.

THEATRE FOR CHILDREN

A hopeful indication that we are faced in the right direction is the great and growing interest throughout the country in providing a theatre for children. From the little handful of children's theatres of fifteen years ago have grown many hundreds; some scarcely worthy of the name, it is true, but many, many others which are bringing joy to children by the thousand. With a new one springing up every day or so in Oregon, Virginia, Texas, or one of the middle western states, and with others ceasing to function after a season or two, it may be well to pause for a moment to take stock of the whole movement.

Just why should people the country over be founding theatres for children? The boys and girls haven't asked for them. Why do children need theatres anyhow? Why not let them play freely and naturally just as they have always done, and wait until they are grown up to go to the theatre? Those who want to see plays now can go to the moving-picture shows!

Whether or not such questions are asked, the people who are fired with the zeal to found such a theatre should know the answers and believe in them. If their purpose is merely to give their pupils a chance to act, it is not a real children's theatre but a laboratory or a demonstration of work, worthy enough, but mistaken in terminology. If the idea which prompted it is the amusement of children for an hour or more in return for twenty-five or fifty cents, it may be a theatre, but it is not a particularly valuable one.

MARK TWAIN ON THE VALUE OF A CHILDREN'S THEATRE

"It is my conviction that the children's theatre is one of the very, very great inventions of the twentieth century," wrote Mark Twain, "and that its vast educational value—now but dimly perceived and but vaguely understood—will presently come to be recognized. . . .

"It is much the most effective teacher of morals and promoter of good conduct that the ingenuity of man has yet devised, for the reason that its lessons are not taught wearily by book and dreary homily, but by visible and enthusing action; and they go straight to the heart, which is the rightest of right places for them. Book-morals often get no further than the intellect, if they even get that far on their spectral and shadowy pilgrimage; but when they travel from a children's theatre they do not stop permanently at that half-way house, but go on home." [1]

WHAT DOES A CHILDREN'S THEATRE CONTRIBUTE TO THE COMMUNITY?

Greatest of all reasons for a children's theatre is the never-ending joy it can bring to the boys and girls. We who are grown up have only to look back to our own childhood and think what a deal of happiness a children's theatre would have added to our lives to estimate what it would mean to young people of to-day. What glorious fun it would have been to see *Peter Pan, The Blue Bird, The Sleeping Beauty,* and *Cinderella* on the stage!

The joy that a children's theatre brings, however, though quite enough reason for its existence, is only one part of what it can mean to the children of a community. Woven into the fabric of nearly every play for young people are ideals of loyalty and courage, of honesty, good sportsmanship, and justice. Because such ideals are made concrete in characters the children love, and because these characters hold the sympathy of the audience throughout a plot in which good and evil clash, it is inevitable that something worthy must come of it. What children tell about after seeing Rosemary Musil's *Seven Little Rebels* is their delight in seeing the little colored girl, Letta, sit in the jello, and in the equally funny episode

---

[1] From a letter to a teacher, published in a Chicago newspaper.

in which she pretends to be a snake-charmer. What they get from the courage and loyalty of the "little rebels" they do not talk about. But their sympathy for Miss Baker and the children as against the hypocritical Miss Proudfoot is very evident, and sympathy worthily aroused has always lasting value.

HORIZONS

Without vicarious experiences any individual, whether child or grown-up, would lead a very narrow existence. The craving for new experiences, many of which would be impossible in reality, is a universal characteristic. Most of us are hemmed in by horizons which would be limited indeed if they could not be pushed out by the stories we read, the plays and moving pictures we see, and the people we meet.

A children's theatre is a way of bringing new and delightful experiences to boys and girls—experiences which broaden interests and bring about a finer understanding of people. To a great extent books fulfill this purpose. But Rip Van Winkle's experience with the dwarfs on the lonely mountainside could never be so alive and so thrilling to boys and girls in the reading as it is when well played on the stage. The awakening of the Sleeping Beauty by the Prince after a hundred years has far more romantic glow in the play than in the story hour.

One evidence of the greater impressiveness of drama is the fact that cruel or violent deeds read or told about do not frighten children as they do when seen on the stage. Every child who goes to see *Jack and the Beanstalk* has been told the story. He knows all about the giant and his cruelty, and he has heard of Jack's narrow escape. Then he comes to the play, and even though the giant is made rather ludicrous in order not to be too frightening, he often shrinks down behind the row of seats for safety, rising up occasionally to peer timidly at the stage until it seems safe to emerge. Of course a child so young and timid should not be taken to the theatre at all, for the kind of plays he would really enjoy would be insipid for the majority of the audience.

It is useless to ignore the longing for adventure which is a part of every boy's make-up. Both radio and moving picture have taken advantage of this interest by offering one thriller after another, the quality of which is often very cheap. The flood of mystery and detective stories, too, has increased the demand for the exciting, the sensational, until normal life is in danger of seeming dull and lifeless. What should the children's theatre do about it? Try to educate the children away from lurid tales of gangster hideouts and thrilling exploits of G-Men? Hope to win them by plays in which Freddy and Dottie dream of a trip to the moon? Or in which Billy is cured of laziness by little Brownies who do other people's work?

No, the way to win boys to the children's theatre is to give them adventure stories with suspense and excitement. Not cheap tales of adventure, but good ones like *Tom Sawyer, Treasure Island, The Prince and the Pauper,* and for a very modern one, *Radio Rescue.* Boys can be counted on to like such plays as these, and in presenting them the theatre is not only giving them satisfying experiences but is also doing something constructive in improving their taste. Girls enjoy another kind of vicarious experience. By empathy they live through Jo's fascinating experiences in *Little Women,* Katrinka's career as a dancer in the Imperial Ballet, Eleanor Lytell's thrilling adventures as an Indian captive.

EDUCATION FOR ADULT DRAMA

Just how important is it that the children's theatre educate audiences for the future? What assurance can we have that our plays *are* educating children? What effect can such education have?

Ask a producer of adult plays why he thought it worth while to stage a cheap or salacious play, and he will tell you, "It is what the people want. Look at the way they flock to see it. You can't expect me to produce plays that are over the heads of the audience." Allowing for all the bad plays which he thrusts upon the public and builds up by advertising, there is, of course, truth in what he says. It is the audience which makes the theatre. If people are satisfied with frothy or meretricious drama, the playwrights will have no incentive to write better. If good plays cannot attract audiences they become fewer and fewer.

Those who are concerned for the theatre, who believe in its inherent cultural and social value, recognize the need for audiences which shall demand better drama than they are now getting. They know that support of good plays encourages the writing of more good plays, and that even commercial producers will stage better drama if they are reasonably sure of audiences.

In the world's two greatest periods of drama: the fifth century B.C. in Greece, and Elizabethan England, audience enthusiasm ran high. Whole cities saw the plays of Æschylus, Sophocles, and Euripides, and the crowning of the playwright whose work was adjudged finest was accompanied by excitement comparable to that aroused in this country by a World Series baseball game! Interest in the theatre was great, too, in Shakespeare's day. People flocked to the plays in huge numbers, and though they were an unmannerly crowd, they were not lacking in enthusiasm. The result of the exalted place which the theatre held in the lives of the people was a drama which is immortal. The incentive to write was stronger than in any other period in the world's history, and as a consequence, greater plays were written.

If the children's theatres of this country, by presenting only superior plays, can develop in the boys and girls who will be the adult audiences of to-morrow a more discriminating taste in drama than their parents have, they will have made a distinct contribution to American life. For if, as Hughes Mearns says, "Nothing so surely disgusts one with poor work as a goodish experience with something better," [2] then it surely follows that experience in seeing the best child drama will create a taste for better adult plays. Dramatists will be found to supply these plays, then, and the level of drama will be higher.

Only when people regard the theatre as a challenge to fuller living rather than as a means of escape from life can drama reach a high peak. Always demanding that the entertainment quality of the play be high, the future audience will not resent drama which causes them to think. If a generation of children grows up with a more intelligent interest in good plays than its parents and grandparents had, the theatre will not have to depend on the "tired business man" as audience. Indeed, many of his kind, having been exposed to good drama in their early years, will no longer be satisfied with the type of play which requires that "brains be checked in box-offices," but will enjoy good theatre as they now enjoy good music. Some playhouses there will always be to cater to the people who refuse to think, but if great numbers of children grow up

[2] Mearns, *Creative Power* (Doubleday, Doran & Co., 1929).

with an educated taste in drama, there will be plenty of support for really good plays.

The condition of the American stage at the present time is critical. Its salvation will not come through the commercial drama nor from the little theatres of the country. If we are to have a generic theatre in the United States, it must come through the intelligent education of our young people. Just as the dramatic festivals of olden days, and of some European countries to-day, have brought drama into the daily life of the people, so it must be made a vital force in the lives of our boys and girls if we are to build an American theatre which will endure.

THE PROBLEM OF LEISURE

What to do with leisure time has never until very recently troubled American people. Long hours of work for men and burdensome household duties for women formerly made leisure an incidental thing. Children of pioneers and, even now, children of farmers, have always had plenty of work to do, so that little time has been left for play.

Most Americans to-day, however, have many hours of free time each week. How they use it is only beginning to be a problem. Parents' concern for the leisure activities of their children is evident in their patronage of music and dancing classes, of play clubs, Y.M.C.A. and Scout activities, summer camps, and in innumerable other ways. Schools offer many activities in athletics, music, dramatics. A few of them expose their pupils to all kinds of interests by offering fascinating electives in such things as metal-work, clay-modeling, stage-craft, journalism, camp cooking, glee clubs, and orchestras, some of which are carried into after-school hours. Outside of school the radio and the moving-picture show occupy a large share of the leisure time of children, both offering some good programs, and a much greater assortment of unsuitable ones.

To most children nothing has so much entertainment value as plays. The almost universal dramatic impulse takes them to adult picture-shows time and again because this type of recreation comes nearest to the thing they crave. If the picture relates the story of an artist's model who inveigles a silly old millionaire into marrying her, or a husband who deserts his wife for a much more attractive mistress, the children (especially the boys) may not be pleased with the picture as a whole but may be interested in some of the details. Then there are always the comedy, the news-reel, and half a dozen more possibilities for mild amusement.

Even if the time should come when there are moving-picture houses for children in America as there are in Russia, when really suitable pictures are available for children, they will still fail to take the place of real theatre. They have their place, and it is a significant one, but they are merely one aspect of an adequate program for children, to which every art should make a contribution.

THE CHILDREN'S THEATRE OF THE FUTURE

Saturday afternoon. Boys and girls walking or skipping along the street towards an interesting-looking building before which stands an exquisite bronze figure of Peter Pan. A bus from the next town drives up in front of the theatre and disgorges its load of laughing children. "Come back at about half past four," one of the chaperons calls to the driver. It is nearly two-thirty now, and children are arriving in large numbers from every direction, some of them being brought in cars by parents or older brothers, many more walking or running. They have come to the regular Saturday afternoon performance at The Playhouse, in the theatre wing of the Art and Recreation Center, which is dedicated by the city to the happiness of its children.

They enter a large, attractive foyer where many children are buying tickets at the box-office or waiting to be joined by other members of a theatre party. A woman who has brought several tiny children is turned away by a sign which reads, "The Performance This Afternoon is for Children Over Eight. Younger Children Not Admitted." Disappointing as this ruling sometimes proves, it is based on a knowledge of the wide variation in interests of different age levels. Little children would be restless and distracting if they were allowed to come to this production, whereas the puppet show of *Little Black Sambo* offered in the series of plays for younger children would have been delightfully entertaining to them.

Most of the children who are coming in, being the proud possessors of reserved season tickets which they bought at a surprisingly low cost, do not pause in the foyer but go first to a check-room where all wraps are left. Then, passing through the softly lighted and carpeted halls to the curtained archways which lead into the auditorium, they are shown to their seats by ushers in attractive uniforms.

A charm which never seems to diminish pervades this lovely theatre. It is not rich nor elegant, but its gaiety and imaginative beauty transport all who enter here to the enchanted land of Make-Believe. Grown-ups as well as children are held in its magic spell, so that they are always to be found in large numbers, shepherding groups of borrowed or underprivileged children if they have none of their own to bring.

On the walls of the auditorium in soft colors are large murals of favorite story-book people. Snow White wakes to see the Seven Dwarfs gazing at her in astonished admiration, Cinderella waves to her Fairy Godmother from the pumpkin-coach as she departs for the ball, Pinocchio rides over land and sea on the back of the Pigeon, Alice sits at tea with the Mad Hatter, the March Hare, and the Dormouse, Robin Hood competes with the king's archers before good Queen Eleanor.

If this theatre were one of the playhouses in which productions were given for young people of high-school age as well as for younger children, the decorations would not so definitely suggest childhood, but since most of the plays here are for children under fourteen, these lovely murals help to create the mood for the kind of plays they will see when the velvet curtains open. Some of these theatres of the future have no murals, the walls being plain but attractive in color, and all the originality concentrated in the curtain. Here in soft, lovely colors like a tapestry is the picture of a favorite old tale. Or appliquéd on the handsome blue background, is perhaps a symbol of the afternoon's play. (Figure 1.)

The floor of this ideal auditorium is inclined more than would be necessary for adults, so that the audience has no need to rise to its feet in a body to see a piece of business on the floor of the stage. The seats are comfortable and there are rods on which the younger children can rest their feet.

THE STAGE

The stage is a flexible one because of the nature of the plays which are given here. Instead of the regulation proscenium arch and a single stage, there are several playing areas on varied levels. The four or five shallow steps across

PINOCCHIO

Ballet presentation of Junior Programs, Inc., New York.

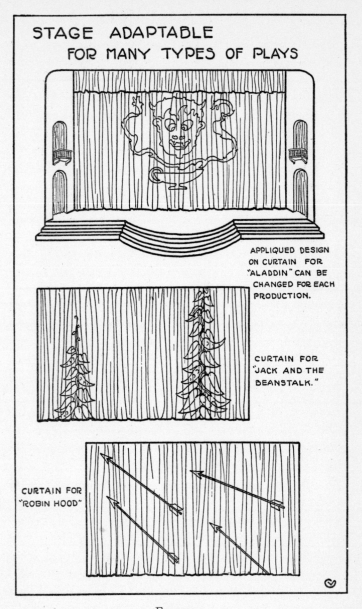

STAGE ADAPTABLE
FOR MANY TYPES OF PLAYS

APPLIQUED DESIGN
ON CURTAIN FOR
"ALADDIN" CAN BE
CHANGED FOR EACH
PRODUCTION.

CURTAIN FOR
"JACK AND THE
BEANSTALK."

CURTAIN FOR
"ROBIN HOOD"

FIGURE I

the front of the stage make it possible for the players and audience to meet at times, and the arched doorways on either side with balconies over them afford opportunity for interesting street scenes. The action sometimes progresses from the stage proper to the street and then to the steps without waits, lights being focused first on one area and then on another.

There is an unusually festive feeling in the air to-day, for the program is to be an elaborate play, Edgar White Burrill's dramatization of Bennett's *Master Skylark*. Last Saturday it was a moving picture and the Saturday before a marionette show. Once a month there is a play, presented usually by a town group, occasionally by professional actors. To-day's cast includes some of the most skillful adult actors in the community, with a few children in youthful rôles. An entirely different series of entertainments is offered for little children on Saturday mornings. During the week there will be several more performances of the play, as well as shorter programs which are given by the children themselves. These programs are often informal creative dramatic plays, sometimes marionettes or shadow-plays. No charge is made for them and they last not longer than an hour.

A series of fine concerts for children given by an adult professional orchestra has many subscribers during the winter, and the children enjoy them the more because of stories of the composers and their works which are told during the intermission. Operettas and ballets are also on the schedule of the year's program.

But now the house lights begin to dim and all attention is centered upon the leader of the children's orchestra who is standing in a lighted area before the curtains, ready to tell them about the overture. This composition, like all the others which are played here, is in key with the story which is to come. An interesting fact or two about the composition, with the playing of a certain motif, and suggestions which will awaken their interest in watching for it to appear first in the wood-wind section, then in the strings, causes the audience to listen in a way that would put their elders to shame.

The Elizabethan music, chosen for to-day's performance, sets the mood for the play as nothing else could do, for the story of Master Skylark takes place in sixteenth-century England, and the plot is built around the beautiful singing voice of a little lad. When the overture ends and the applause dies away, there is a stir of eager expectancy, for the play is now about to begin! The Prologue, who is one of the minor characters, now appears before the curtain and announces the play very cleverly, making programs unnecessary; but he does not announce the cast, for that would detract so greatly from the illusion of reality.

Through six scenes the audience follows the exciting adventures of one Nicholas Atwood, "Master Skylark." They admire the Lord High Admiral's Players, and they cannot help liking Gaston Carew even though he does take Nick to London against his wishes. They are introduced to Will Shakespeare as a man before they know him as a playwright, and they take him to their heart on this their first acquaintance with him. The girls, living the part of charming little Cicely, are carried out of themselves by the romantic glamour of the play. Shakespeare's England comes alive for all of them.

Even though the production is elaborate, the revolving stage makes the changes almost instantaneous, and only one intermission breaks the spell of the play. This is the time for real relaxation, for standing and stretching cramped muscles, for talking with one's neighbors. In one corner of the auditorium under a sign which reads, ASK ME IF THERE IS ANYTHING YOU

DO NOT UNDERSTAND, stands a young girl in Elizabethan costume, ready to answer questions about the play. A group of children gathers around her bursting with such queries as, "Did the things in this play happen in history?" "Was there really a Master Skylark?" "How could you find a boy who was such a fine singer to play the part?" "Oh, I know him," brags a little girl. "He lives just two blocks from us."

Many of the children are in the foyer talking with friends, or in the recreation room looking at the new art exhibit or at the stage models and pictures of former plays. A large group of eight- and nine-year-olds is being taught by the orchestra leader a bit of the madrigal which Nick sang in the first act, until, at the sound of a trumpet, the movement toward the auditorium begins, and soon the children, refreshed and eager, are in their seats waiting for the last part of the performance. The orchestra is heard again, the Prologue makes his announcement, and the play is on!

As the interesting story draws to a close, with Master Skylark reunited at last with his mother, hearty and prolonged applause voices the approval of the big audience. The boys haven't needed crime and mystery for their enjoyment. The girls have reveled not only in the story but in the Elizabethan scenery and costumes as well. It has been one of the most satisfying plays of the season and will be remembered and talked about for many a week to come.

This is a picture not of a theatre that exists now in America, but of one that is to come. It is a far cry from the theatre of Madame de Genlis' day to this. Eighteenth-century children would have opened their eyes wide at such a playhouse. They would have been amazed to see so entertaining a play.

When one pauses to reflect on the vast change in the attitude of adults toward children since the time that Rousseau propounded his revolutionary theories, he expects almost anything to happen. In place of gloomy literature warning children of punishment after death, we have books like Eloise Lownsbery's *The Boy Knight of Reims,* and Evaleen Stein's *Gabriel and the Hour Book,* which are inspiring at the same time that they are entertaining. The school dominated by the birch rod has given place to one in which children work happily together, growing by experience and learning to live by living.

In view of the great changes brought about in recent years by the enlightened attitude toward children, it is perhaps not too much to hope that in the not far-distant future, art and recreation centers similar to the one described here may be found in many American cities. In the development of the appreciation of beauty in art and in life it could do a lasting service to the youth of the land, bringing a happiness and a cultural value which would enrich the life of every community in which it existed.

CHAPTER III

ORGANIZING FOR ACTION

W E SHALL TAKE for granted in discussing the organization of a children's theatre that the need for one exists in this particular community. The preceding chapters have presumably established the reasons why such an institution would be of value, and we are supposing that no opportunity to see good plays is at present being offered the children.

SPONSORS

The enthusiasm for a theatre may originate from one individual who is trained, perhaps, as a director of children's plays, or it may arise within an organization which has no members experienced in children's work. A parent-teacher association, discouraged about the quality of picture shows and radio programs available for its boys and girls, may decide to take matters into its own hands in order to raise the standard of children's entertainment in the town. A Junior League or other altruistic group of women may undertake such a project as a service to the community. Professional schools of the theatre are in a position to accomplish two purposes by the establishment of a children's theatre: experience in acting for their students and the fulfilment of a community need. A city may be progressive enough to sponsor such a theatre as a part of its recreation program. Theatres representing all these types of organization and sponsorship are to be found in the United States.

Civic theatres have been surprisingly slow in realizing their opportunity to build for the future by establishing children's departments. Well organized and equipped for such work, they should be foremost in the field. By enlisting the schools to coöperate, they could do not only a fine thing for their communities, but they could also strengthen their own position by the many additional people who would become interested in their work. Only recently have such theatres begun to awaken to their responsibility in the junior field. As they become stronger more of them will doubtless enlarge their activities to include children's plays.

IF ONE INDIVIDUAL HAS THE SPARK

What is the best way to go about the founding of a children's theatre if an individual rather than an organization first becomes imbued with the idea? May he or she undertake the project independently if experienced or well-trained in children's dramatics? May it be a means of livelihood, a profession?

A children's theatre is a large-sized undertaking even in its simplest form. It involves both art and business. Even though this individual may thoroughly understand children, though she may know how to choose and direct plays, make costumes, design and build settings, do the make-up for a cast, publicize her production, manage the business of a theatre, sell tickets, and manage the house—though she may be expert on all these, she is only one person. It is physically impossible to do adequately so many jobs. The financial risk, too, is great. Business firms who would be willing to supply lumber, paints, costume materials, and other production necessities to a well-established organization might insist on a cash basis if an individual were taking the responsibility alone. She must have much help. Where will it come from if not from members of some institution or organization?

Individuals have undertaken the sole responsibility of children's plays—teachers, mainly, in private studios. But in such cases they have done one of two things: either they have staged and managed the plays so crudely that they were not worthy the name of children's theatre, or else they have enlisted volunteer or hired workers to help with the productions. By means of an imposing list of patrons and patronesses, such individuals have sometimes built up a large following which has put their theatre on a near professional basis.

WHAT ORGANIZATIONS TO INTEREST

Suppose this individual, instead of attempting to work alone, decides to try to interest one or more organizations to shoulder the responsibility. Which are the most likely ones? Will it be better to win over one or several to this work? Would it be feasible to build up an independent children's theatre association from interested people in the town?

If she decides that it will be wise to begin with one sponsoring group which is already established, with the idea of expanding later, she will consider which organization of the town is most likely to make a success of a children's theatre. Among the questions she will ask herself and others are the following:

1. What groups can be counted on to have children's interests at heart?
2. Which are interested in the drama?

3. Who would care most about enriching community life?
4. Which are the strongest organizations? The most influential? The most highly respected?
5. Which are most permanent?
6. Have any similar groups in other cities undertaken children's theatre work?
7. Does any one of them have a stage and auditorium to offer?

All towns of three thousand or more inhabitants can be counted upon to have several of the following organizations: boards of education, parent-teacher associations, civic theatres, drama clubs, Junior Leagues, American Association of University Women and other women's clubs, men's and women's service clubs, municipal recreation departments, and chambers of commerce. Religious education departments of churches, Young Men's Christian Associations, Scouts, and many other groups would be more likely to coöperate with rather than to sponsor a children's theatre.

If an individual sets out to win over a certain organization to the founding of a children's theatre, she will, of course, talk it over with various members first, especially with the officers. If they are interested and she is asked to present the matter to the whole organization, she will do well to spend long and prayerful sessions in marshaling her ideas into such form that they will be convincing, that they will stir people with real enthusiasm. She will need also to make a definite plan for the working out of these ideas.

Suppose the members of the organization were interested but cautious about committing themselves to any great obligation. Fear of the financial risk, and greater fear of the work involved, would quite possibly lead them to say, "We see that it is a worthy plan and we should be glad to coöperate, but we already have enough work to do."

Most projects of any size do not spring up overnight. If they have a mushroom growth, they are likely to die out as suddenly as mushrooms, for they have not had time to take root. A children's theatre requires education. It may be introduced this year and accepted next if the idea is so timely and so well presented that it fires the leaders with enthusiasm.

BEGIN BEFORE THE BEGINNING

Wouldn't it be a wise move on the part of the originator of the idea to suggest that an interested group, instead of committing itself to a children's theatre, agree to take the responsibility for one good children's play? This should not be very difficult, especially if an auditorium is available and she can direct the play. If this much is conceded, it behooves her to put every ounce of the intelligence, taste, and imagination she possesses into this production, organizing it carefully and giving very freely of her time and energy. If she sees to it that the play is wisely chosen—and "wisely" in this case means the best possible dramatization of a favorite child's story—that it is carefully cast with people who will make it live for the audience, staged charmingly, and publicized effectively, it will unquestionably arouse so much interest that the cause will gain great momentum. Then, before the first flush of enthusiasm fades, it is time to strike for a real children's theatre, a permanent institution which will continue to bring joy like this to the children of the community.

THE BOARD OF DIRECTORS

By this time the organization which sponsored the play is convinced, let us say, and eager to go ahead, believing it of sufficient importance to justify them in giving up some other activity, perhaps, in order to have the time to devote to it. The first move is to be the appointment of a board of directors to formulate policies and govern the theatre. This is a group of intelligent and public-spirited women who have some prestige in the community but no auditorium or equipment. Some of their members are much interested in the theatre and more are lending their support because of their concern for children's recreation. None of them has had any training or experience in producing plays for children. They are willing to launch the enterprise, hoping to make it a real community institution after they have proved its worth. How shall they proceed?

The board of directors, elected by the organization, may consist of:

1. A general chairman who, being at the head of the board, should have much executive ability. It is her duty to supervise every department, the heads of which she may or may not be expected to appoint.

2. A business manager, whose duties are described in Chapter XII.

3. A publicity manager. Chapter XI.

4. A playreading chairman. As the director is not permanent in this particular situation, the playreading committee is very important, having the responsibility of choosing all of the plays. It is necessary that the chairman of this committee have real knowledge of children and their interests in literature and drama. She should also be a good judge of what constitutes a suitable play, though the person who is to direct them should always be consulted.

5. The chairman of casting. The casting committee in some instances actually chooses the cast, but more often as-

sembles those who are to try out, the director making the actual decision on the players.

Great care should be taken in choosing this board member that she may be a person who will not be swayed by any pressure exerted to get certain actors into a cast. The policy of casting according to social prestige is fatal to any theatre. It may appear to be successful for a time, but it has proved disastrous to innumerable little theatres. If this board member is known as a thoroughly sincere person, she may have a few unpleasant experiences with those who press her to cast people who live "on the north side," or, if children are used, the offspring of ambitious mothers; but if she holds consistently to her principles, she will soon win respect for the merit system.

6. The production chairman. Whether or not this person actually supervises the building of the scenery, it is her duty and that of her committee to see that it is done. She may recommend a technical director and work with him in the designing and building of settings and properties, or she and her committee may do the work themselves.

7. The community chairman. Since only one organization is sponsoring the theatre, this chairman of a committee-at-large should be appointed to make contacts with parent-teacher associations, schools, municipal recreation departments, clubs, settlements, children's hospitals, orphanages, and other agencies interested in the welfare of children. The purpose of such a committee is not only to find audiences, but also to arouse the interest of future possible sponsors.

In addition, the officers of the sponsoring group—the president, the vice-president, the secretary, and the treasurer—may be directors *ex officio*. The executive committee of the children's theatre association may be made up of the general chairman, the business and publicity manager, the production and the community chairmen, and the director.

IF A THEATRE HAS SEVERAL SPONSORS

The pioneer group, having proved the worth of a children's theatre through several seasons, may now believe that the time has come to make it a community institution. So much interest has been manifested in the theatre, so many children have come to count on it, that there is a general feeling that it should be made permanent.

The three or four plays a year which have been presented by the theatre, though always anticipated with great joy by the boys and girls, supply but a small fraction of their entertainment each season. It is believed that in order to be adequate, performances should be given as often as once a week, with outside entertainments as well as the amateur plays.

Unless the theatre is taken over by the city as a regular part of the recreation program, with a paid director and an assurance of support, one of two proceedings might be followed. Several producing groups might contribute one play each, thus making up a season of amateur productions which could be enlarged by a few professional entertainments. If this plan were carried out the play chairman of the board, in consultation with her committee and the various directors, would have to come to an agreement concerning a well-balanced program for the season.

The danger in this type of organization is that the standard of production might be very uneven. Granted that each group does superior work, such an arrangement is very excellent. At all events, the unifying force must be strong and the insistence upon high standards maintained throughout.

The other plan is for an organization to be formed, say, by five or six strong associations or institutions, one of which should be the Board of Education. What other groups should be asked to join the pioneer organization in sponsoring the theatre will depend upon their interest in children and in the drama. The producing staff, in this case, would be centralized and paid.

There are dangers in multiple sponsors, it must be admitted—dangers which may bring disaster upon the venture unless there is a strong permanent director to act as a guiding hand. They may not pull together, they may have different ideas for the theatre, they may try to dictate in matters which only the executive committee should decide. It cannot be urged too strongly that the permanent director be allowed much freedom in such a theatre—freedom in choosing plays and casts, and in guiding the policies of the theatre. The board should choose a director in whom it can have confidence, and then coöperate in every way to help him or her make it a success. Many a board has ruined a little theatre by petty bickerings and jealousies, by division into factions and holding of personal grudges.

Suppose that two members have been appointed or elected by each organization to make up a board of directors. Within this group the officers of the children's theatre may be elected. As in the smaller organization, there will be a general chairman; business and publicity chairmen, unless a person outside the sponsoring groups is paid to do this work, in which case the board member may be the treasurer,[1] a playreading chairman, a chairman of casting, who will not cast the plays but will be responsible for assembling those who try out, a produc-

[1] See Dean, *Organization and Management of Little Theatres* (D. Appleton-Century Co., 1927).

tion chairman, who may supervise the technical end of the productions, though probably not having anything to do with the actual building, and a community chairman. The executive committee may be made up of the general chairman, the director, the technical director, the business and publicity manager. Some of the board members will not have active duties in the theatre, but will help to determine general policies and choose the workers, as well as take their part in placing the theatre on a sound financial basis.

The length of office for the board members should be so planned at the beginning that the terms will expire in different years. Thus, if there were twelve members, the terms of four of them might expire in one year, four in two years, four in three years. The advantages in this plan are that there would be continuity in policy, with fresh points of view each year.

A CHILDREN'S BOARD

Adults, in managing a children's theatre, can keep more closely in touch with the children's point of view if they provide for a child board of directors to supplement the direction of grown-ups. Such a board is valuable in contributing ideas about the choice of plays, the kind of staging the children enjoy, the use of *entr'acte* time, and many other aspects of the children's theatre. They may be a very valuable aid in publicizing plays in their respective schools and in helping during the ticket campaign. If several children are needed to assist at performances, they will take great pride in carrying messages, giving information, taking care of the ventilation, and other needed duties. The fact that they are having a part in the management of the children's theatre is a source of pride to them, and if one or two are appointed each season

by the principal of every grade school they will be representative of every part of town.

Regardless of whether or not the members of the staff are
paid, they must expect to work very strenuously if the project
is to succeed. It is no slight task that can be done between
motor trips, and it would seem formidable if it were not so
fascinating. In a children's theatre of any size, the chief workers
are specially trained and paid.

Most indispensable staff members are director, technician,
business and publicity managers and costumière. Under these
heads (who should be permanent if possible) are the assistant
director, electrician, construction and stage crews, house manager, and ushers.[2]

Psychologists, teachers of children, and authors of children's
books and plays should also be workers in a children's theatre
if it is to make a scientific study of the children's reactions.
Only by thorough expert study of children, with the conse-
quent adaptation of material to their needs and tastes, can
the theatre be of high educational value in addition to its
function of providing recreation for leisure time.

This organization may seem over-elaborate to a beginning children's theatre, and, indeed, few existing theatres are
so complete as to be able to make a real study of their audience.
Beginning in a small way as most children's theatres do, some
of the crew heads may be the whole crew. Many people are
needed, however, to operate a theatre which gives ambitious
productions, and it is well to start out with a carefully organ-

[2] Their qualifications and duties are discussed in Chapters VII, IX, X, XI,
XII, XIV.

ized staff instead of expecting two or three more or less distracted people to manage the whole show. By distributing responsibility, more people will work in the theatre and consequently more will be interested; and together they can build up a theatre of which the whole community will be proud.

AN ENDOWED THEATRE

After a children's theatre has won recognition as one of the valued institutions of the city, it is time to begin plans for endowment. For the reasons given in Chapter XII, a children's theatre should not be a money-making institution. If well managed, it can pay its way; but it should be put on a permanent basis instead of left to a precarious existence from year to year. Just as the playground for physical well-being has become an institution in every progressive city, so may the children's theatre be as valuable in providing healthy recreation of another kind.

One of the great functions of the board of directors may be the work of building up an endowment for the theatre. Community or art centers, whether housed in new school buildings planned for the purpose, or, better, in buildings of their own, could well include a theatre for children. It may be a long time before children's theatres have their own buildings, if, indeed, that is even desirable. But the time is past when any plan for a city's recreation can overlook the children. In the meantime, it behooves all those adults who believe in the need for a children's theatre to work so well that when the time is ripe for a community center, this theatre for children cannot possibly be ignored.

CHAPTER IV

WE DECIDE TO WRITE A PLAY

SINCE Stéphanie de Genlis published her *Théâtre d'Éducation* in 1779, a large number of children's plays have come into being. Playwrights began to write for them as soon as the desire to produce plays for young audiences created the need. The supply of really good drama, however, has not nearly kept pace with the demand, so that the author who can write effectively for children is sure of having his plays produced many times.

Aside from the joy the creative artist always finds in an original piece of work, a director who can write for his own theatre may take additional pleasure in being able to provide the kind of plays which are peculiarly adapted to his audiences. If he wants a dramatization of a popular new book, he may be able to get the publisher's permission for a local production even though it might be withheld for a play which was to be published. If he needs a new modern play, he may be able to supply it himself without waiting for some one else to write it for him. The royalties which make so many plays prohibitive, especially for schools and clubs, may thus be avoided, and if his work is really good he can be a valuable person on the staff of any organization to which he belongs.

Financially, the writing of children's plays has in recent years come to be worth while. Most producing groups in the past considered the payment of royalties impossible, but many of them have now become educated to the idea that only good plays are worth doing, and that if an admission is charged, they owe it to their audience to pay the reasonable royalty required for most children's plays.

With innumerable schools, clubs, and children's theatres producing drama for young people, the market for first-rate plays is excellent, so that the writer who can learn what children like will find a real opportunity in this field. There is a constantly growing need for short plays suitable for assemblies, clubs, and church groups, and full-length plays for children's theatres. Many such plays are proving remunerative for their authors even though the royalty on a single performance is small.

These statements are not intended to encourage young people to go into the field of playwriting as a means of earning a living. Almost anyone can put a story into dramatic form. Even children can make charming little plays from literature, and they often entertain audiences by acting them. But such plays seem very crude when considered in the light of production by other groups. Plays written by pupils in schools are sometimes published, but they are interesting only as illustrating what a group can create. That it is not easy to write a good play is evidenced by the flood of poor and mediocre ones to be found in most play publishers' catalogues. When one reflects that only a small proportion of the plays written find publishers, he cannot but be impressed by the inference that most plays which people write must be very bad indeed.

How, then, can the person who has some gift for writing learn to do really good plays for children? Who can hope to succeed in this field?

First of all, he must have creative imagination. Without this gift he can contribute nothing better than the prosaic plays which are to be found on every side, cluttering catalogues and making common what should be rare and beautiful. Every grown person who has done any 'writing must have discovered whether or not he is creative. Let him not presume to enter the field of children's playwriting without imagination! Along with this indispensable qualification is an enjoyment and a facility for writing. Both imagination and effectiveness in putting down one's thoughts grow with use, but there is no question that each is prerequisite to successful playwriting.

That one must know and respect children if he is to write for them has been proved again and again. Many a clever adult, incapable of getting the child's viewpoint, belittles the dignity and intelligence of young people by refusing to take his play seriously. Others shoot over their heads by satire and symbolism which are meaningful only to adults.

The grown-up who likes children can learn to know them by study and association. It is not enough to know individual boys and girls, though this is important. Whoever would write plays for them should study audiences made up of children. He should learn what it is that absorbs their attention so that they are oblivious to all else, what it is that causes a breathless hush, a wave of sympathy, a burst of merry laughter. He should talk with them between scenes, note what they say when the play is over, find out what remains with them the next day.

A knowledge of dramatic technique is obviously a requirement of the person who would write for any audience. The reading of good books on technique such as are to be found in the Bibliography of this book and a study of the best children's plays will be one excellent kind of preparation for such writing. To know what has already been done in child drama is an advantage, and the reading of the best plays which have been written is often stimulating. An occasional creative writer may be limited rather than inspired by wide reading of plays, but the majority of people profit by it even though this preparation is not to be compared in value with the study of child audiences.

A thorough knowledge of children's literature is a more necessary foundation than an acquaintance with many plays. Because of the indisputable fact that drama based on literature is dearer to children's hearts than any other kind, a playwright who knows his Grimm, Andersen, *Arabian Nights,* his *Robin Hood* and *King Arthur, Alice in Wonderland, Peter and Wendy,* Christopher Robin, and all the rest of the fine traditional and modern stories, has the strongest of foundations on which to build.

Experience in directing plays enables an author to avoid many mistakes which are made by the writer who knows nothing about stage business. If he has ever directed he will not resort to soliloquies for his exposition, nor send a character a quarter of a mile away on an errand and bring him back five speeches later, nor expect the audience to see an important piece of business beyond a window, nor any of the other things which the director knows will seem absurd to an audience.

MATERIAL FOR A PLAY

Suppose we have decided to write a play for children's theatre use. No limitations such as a special occasion, or the necessity of a one-scene play, or a definite cast are imposed, so that we are free to write whatever we choose. It is to be a long play, which means from an hour and one-half to an hour and three-quarters in length, counting the scene changes.

What material shall we use? A novel? An original plot? We consider carefully all possibilities in order to find something which has not already been done well, something that is likely to appeal to children, that holds the charm for us which is needed for long and concentrated work. It must be no slight story such as offers only enough material for a one-act play. It must be meaty enough to provide several good episodes which will build to a real climax. Finally, it must have the universal qualities which will give it lasting value.

FOLK AND FAIRY TALES

It is natural that our first thought should be of those beloved traditional stories which we catalogue as folk- and fairy-tales. Innumerable lesser stories have been lost all along the years in which these have been coming down to us. The timelessness of "Cinderella," "Snow White and the Seven Dwarfs," "Hansel and Gretel," "The Sleeping Beauty," the *Arabian Nights* tales, "Rumpelstiltskin," "Jack and the Beanstalk," must be conceded whenever we sit in a child audience and feel the spell in which these old stories hold all modern children. If we discard this great folk literature it is because we find that other authors before us have dramatized it so well that there is no reason for our attempting to do so.

MYTHS

A search among the great number of myths, especially the Norse and Greek, reveals many dramatic stories. Some of them are so bound up in a complexity and maturity of relationships as to make them impossible for children's plays. Others concern gigantic feats and magic transformations which eliminate them at once. The two Midas stories, including "The Golden Touch" and "The Judgment of Midas," can be woven into a good play; "Baucis and Philemon" is possible, also the Persephone stories; and the two Norse myths, "Thor's Quest of the Hammer" and "Sif's Golden Hair," [1] have unusually good dramatic values.

BALLADS

Ballads may next be considered as our material. Plays based on either traditional or modern ballads are rare, and it might be wise to look into their possibilities. Children of ten or older who have had the opportunity to take part in creative dramatics have doubtless dramatized "Get Up and Bar the Door," "King John and the Abbot of Canterbury," "The Miller of Mansfield," and a number of other ballads. Sometimes they have made plays of considerable length from these short ballads, reading between the lines and enlarging upon the concise plot. But since most ballads concern but one incident, they will make better short plays than long ones.

An occasional ballad such as "Lizzie Lindsay" (which Eva March Tappan has expanded into a delightful story); [2] the "Robin Hood" ballads, out of which many plays have been written; "King Wenceslas," "The Legend of William Tell," Browning's "The Pied Piper of Hamelin," and Longfellow's "King Robert of Sicily"—these and other traditional and modern ballads have been or could be used as material for full-length plays.

HERO TALES

Both legends and modern tales built around great heroes and heroines are significant sources of material for children's plays. The majority of boys and girls in children's theatre

[1] Brown, *In the Days of Giants* (Houghton Mifflin Co., 1902).
[2] In *Old Ballads in Prose* (Houghton Mifflin Co., 1901).

audiences are hero-worshipers, and if stories of great heroes, both real and legendary, are dramatized, they are likely to prove both interesting and inspirational.

Up to the time of this writing no good full-length play based upon the Arthur cycle has been forthcoming, in spite of the fact that children like the stories and often ask for such a play. It is true that many of the Arthur tales do not lend themselves to the children's theatre stage, being concerned with tournaments, battles, and romance. There is such a wealth of material, however, that a first-rate Arthur play could most certainly be written.

Whoever is searching for a hero around whom to build a play will perhaps read carefully the stories of Ulysses, Siegfried, Charlemagne, Roland, Marco Polo, Columbus, and other heroes and heroines both ancient and modern whose stories have an appeal to children. Robin Hood, most fascinating of heroes, is already the central figure of so many plays that it is better to turn from him to other heroes. Pioneer stories, being of great interest to children, may inspire plays concerning less widely known heroes and heroines, such as Eleanor Lytell in *The Indian Captive*. If they are true stories they have an additional appeal to the realistically minded boys and girls from nine to twelve.

MODERN PLAYS

The need for good modern plays, whether original or dramatizations of stories, is great. At least one play in modern dress each season is highly desirable both for the sake of variety and because children like them. Up to the present time very few of good quality have been written. *Mr. Dooley, Jr., Radio Rescue,* and *Seven Little Rebels* are examples of original

*THE INDIAN
CAPTIVE*

Junior League
Children's Theatre,
Nashville, Tennessee

modern plays which have proved very popular with child audiences.

Simpler to write than original plays, and more sure to appeal to boys and girls, are dramatizations of favorite novels. Each year a few books which are published offer good material. Dramatic rights are difficult to get, however, and whether or not a playwright hopes to sell his work, he will have to apply to the publisher for permission to use the story. Sometimes this is granted for a local production, but a special arrangement must be made if the author expects the play to be used elsewhere. Until the copyright expires, the publisher can forbid dramatic rights, sell them outright, or require that all royalties be divided. Before beginning any dramatization, therefore, even for local use, the writer should seek the publisher's permission.

PLAYS CONCERNING SOCIAL QUESTIONS

A clear field exists for the person who can write children's plays around vital social questions. Practically nothing has yet been done in this country by plays in the way of developing right attitudes toward race differences, social inequalities, true versus narrow patriotism, war and peace, and many other acute problems of the modern world. In order to determine exactly what questions can effectively be brought before children in dramatic form, how these problems may be made concrete and childlike without losing their essential meaning, and, finally, how the play may at the same time be made highly entertaining, an author needs a rich background of information and experience. If the presentation is too adult, it will leave children cold; if it teaches too obviously, they will be suspicious. The idea must be so imbedded in an interesting plot that the children themselves sit in judgment on what is done. Without apparently trying to sway the audience, the author so constructs his play that true values stand out clearly, and sympathy is never misplaced.

Plays of this sort should be forthcoming for our American children's theatres. We are past our infancy, ready to do a little thinking. Not for worlds would we give up our rich heritage of imaginative literature. But along with it we need drama that will awaken our young people to thoughts and emotions regarding urgent questions of the modern world. Before narrow prejudices have had time to fix themselves upon children, good drama might do much to bring vividly before them a larger view of many questions, provoking independent thought instead of docile acceptance of their elders' opinions. Who will write such drama for the children's theatres of America? It is an opportunity and a challenge.

A PLAY BASED ON A NOVEL

Because this book is intended for the inexperienced, and because it is advisable to begin writing children's plays by basing them on good stories rather than by attempting at once the difficult task of originating one's own plots, the proceeding here given concerns the former plan. After one has had successful experience in dramatizing children's stories, he should venture into original plots, but in most cases not until then.

Let us imagine that we have chosen to base our play on a novel which is well liked by children. We have been greatly interested in it at first reading and are convinced that it would make a good play. Before making a final decision, we re-read it with the idea of a play in mind. We visualize the episodes as scenes, try to get the author's idea back of the story, become better acquainted with the characters. Yes, this has material for a full-length play, we think. It is both dramatic and charming, with characters which are well drawn and an idea which will make the whole thing worth doing. Unlike the episodic stories which we have discarded, stories such as *Little Men, Five Little Peppers, The Dutch Twins,* this one has a series of related incidents which build to a strong climax.

With the decision made, we lose no time in finding out whether we can get permission to use it. Possibly the publisher allows us to use it locally, but forbids our publishing the play unless he and the author approve it. If the copyright happens to have expired, however, no permission need be asked. Such a story is a wise choice for an inexperienced writer. Next we get to know plot and characters better. We read the novel until we are familiar with everything that is implied as well as written. The characters become more and more real as we note whatever throws light on them. We come to know what they do and think outside the book as well as in the written scenes.

Nothing is put on paper until a great deal of thinking has been done. During this preliminary work we discover that the technique of playwriting differs so greatly from that of novels that much rearrangement will have to be done. The novel is not limited by time or space, but the play must be condensed into an hour and three-quarters or thereabouts, and have some regard for the unities of time, place, and mood. Because fewer changes of scene can be made, some episodes will have to be telescoped or omitted.

The novelist uses any number of characters, and they may change greatly or grow up in the course of the story. Though this is possible for the dramatization, it is more difficult to make plausible because of the limited time at one's command

and the practical difficulties of an unlimited cast. Characters are described by the omniscient novelist so that we may know their innermost thoughts and motives. No such opportunity offers itself to the dramatist unless he resorts to the artificial soliloquy, and he must make his characters known objectively.

On the other hand, the dramatist can save pages of descriptive matter by what his audiences actually see and hear. Settings, costumes, lights, business, and intonations of voice tell in a flash what the novelist needs pages to describe. The very expression on an actor's face may push off the imagination so that the audience guesses what the novelist could never effectually make clear.

Throughout this preliminary study we shall discover and keep always before us the author's purpose in writing the story. Is the development of a central character the most important thing in the novel, as in *Mary Poppins?* Or is it the picture of an historical period such as is painted in *Gabriel and the Hour Book,* or *He Went with Marco Polo?* Did he write this story concerning a foreign people in order to help build a friendly feeling for them, as in the *Twins* books? Or is it intended to be just a good story, like *Treasure Island,* interesting for its own sake? Whatever we decide is his real purpose we should plan to emphasize in our play.

As we think through our dramatization we keep always before us the climax of the novel, for it helps us to decide which scenes are essential. Those episodes which prepare for and lead steadily up to the climax, each heightening the interest and developing the characters, are the essential ones in any play. Other fascinating incidents there may be, but by leading into some ramification of the plot they may give an emphasis which is not intended. It is better to use fewer scenes and develop them well than hurry from one to another.

Always there will be incidents in the novel which, while not necessary to the working out of the plot, will make extremely interesting scenes. Because they contain comic or dramatic situations they will heighten the effectiveness of the play, and even though they do not advance the plot, their absence would disappoint the children who know the story. Such scenes are often to the play "what the twinkling eye and the smiling countenance are to the human being. Life without them is possible; but life with them is fuller, deeper and more beautiful." [3]

"THE BOY KNIGHT OF REIMS"

If we chose, for instance, to base our play on Eloise Lownsbery's very fine novel, *The Boy Knight of Reims,* and were fortunate enough to secure the publisher's permission, we should find such rich material for a play that the selection of incidents would be exceedingly difficult. Fascinating as a novel, it contains enough story for several plays, and only by the most careful study can we determine what to select.

In the story of the little boy, Jean d'Orbais, one of whose ancestors planned the Reims Cathedral, whose family has worked on it every generation since, there is a wonderfully fine and authentic picture of mediæval life in France. Pages, squires, and knights, apprentices and masters of the guilds, live before us in the moving story, the Maid of France herself figuring in the later episodes of the book.

The novel begins about the time that young Jean is apprenticed to a goldsmith. The boy soon finds that Master Anton is dishonest, puts alloy in his gold. Resolved to leave his master, he is dissuaded by Colin, who works with Anton. Colin

[3] Wilde, *The Craftsmanship of the One-Act Play* (Doubleday, Doran & Co., 1928).

promises to teach Jean all he knows, and says that sooner or later Anton will be found out without their having to tell.

In spite of his fear and distrust of his master, Jean leads an interesting life. He and his friend Marcel are sent one day to a château seven miles away to deliver a gold platter to the Countess, and they have a fascinating afternoon. On their way home they are surrounded by brigands, and barely escape being robbed of the gold pieces they have been paid.

As the boys grow older they set up an atelier in an old shack and begin to model secretly, for they can work only on Sunday, and that would not be allowed if any one knew. But Marcel, falling in with bad company, leaves Jean to chisel the stone after they have made their model, and when it is finished, in a fit of anger and jealousy, Marcel smashes its head. Nearly beside himself with rage and disappointment, Jean rushes to the cathedral to find the Bishop. But once there he sinks down beside a great pillar, and, in a vision, he sees his ancestor, the first Jean d'Orbais, who planned the cathedral. From him young Jean learns its secret: "Men learn of God through beauty," and as the vision fades away, a great peace comes over him.

Meanwhile, the goldsmith's guild discovers Master Anton's guilt, expels him from this craft, and frees Jean from his apprenticeship. Working now with his father, Jean is completely happy, for his gift is that of a sculptor rather than a goldsmith. When, later, he shows promise of being a fine artist, the Countess, in an impressive ceremony, makes him a knight whose service is to beauty, and Jean pledges to devote his whole life to work for the cathedral.

Now great news comes. The Maid of France is bringing the Dauphin to be crowned in Reims Cathedral; and Marcel, who has been fighting in her army, sends Jean sketches of her, with the message that Jean will know what to do with them. What Jean does is to make a glorious statue of Jeanne d'Arc, which is placed in front of the cathedral only the day before the Maid herself enters the city. Then comes the coronation with all its splendor, and afterward the moment when the Maid meets Jean and tells him that she has heard of his knighting. And just before she wheels her horse to leave Reims, she bends down and drops her glove into his hands as a symbol of knightly trapping.

What is at the heart of this dramatic story, so permeated with spiritual beauty, so full of movement and color? Which of its high moments is the highest? What episodes will most directly lead to it?

Three very high peaks, each so dramatic that we are reluctant to give up any one of them, may confuse us as to which is loftiest, until we remember the title, *The Boy Knight of Reims*. At once the exquisite little chapel in the château comes before us. At the ceremony in which the young squires are knighted by the Count, there comes a surprise. The Countess steps forward, a silver chisel in her hand in place of a sword, and calls Jean to come forward. Overcome by amazement and awe, Jean comes and kneels before her.

"You others have taken the oath of chivalry," she says, smiling down at the young knights, "but Jean will take the oath of service to Beauty, for a great ideal started for him by the first Jean d'Orbais more than two hundred years ago, the ideal continued by his uncle who made the windows for this chapel, and by his father and mother." And administering an oath which dedicates his life to the cathedral, she touches his bowed head with the silver chisel and dubs him knight.

This must be the climax of our play in spite of the fact that the story goes on to tell of the coronation, with Jeanne, the

Maid, as the central figure; for though Jean's statue is placed before the cathedral, and though he is honored by the Maid, he seems a minor figure in all the magnificence of the coronation.

We know that if the knighting is to be the climax, we must omit this last elaborate scene. We are loath to let go so striking an episode until we realize that too many impressions will be confusing in a play, and besides, that few productions could do justice to so tremendous a scene.

Knowing our climax, we must select carefully among the many earlier scenes for those which will lead up to it most naturally. Unless we do this well, we are in danger of reaching a climax in the scene which must precede this one: the cathedral episode in which the spirit of the first Jean d'Orbais seems to speak to our Jean. So impressive and compelling did that scene prove in one dramatization of the story that the young boy playing the part of Jean was emotionally stirred to the point of tears, and could scarcely be persuaded to finish the play. It is a beautiful scene, and a necessary one, but it must not be the climax.

To avoid the possibility of an anti-climax, the knighting scene must be built high by careful preparation. Striking the note of knighthood early, the dramatization might sound it again and again. Beginning with a boyhood wish which had no hope of fulfilment, emphasized by the Countess' order from the goldsmith of what might be a goblet to be used in the ceremony, and its delivery by Jean and Marcel; repeated in the boys' conversation on their way home; and then built up by the suspense connected with the ceremony in the chapel, it might culminate in a scene of wonderful beauty and meaning because it was the fulfilment of a great desire. This would, of course, have to be reconciled with Jean's great wish to help in building the cathedral, but that would be possible without great difficulty.

Having a single view, it is easier to choose the incidents which precede. In any play, if the opening is too far from the climax, it is difficult to sustain the interest. On the other hand, the audience should actually see the significant episodes which bring about the crisis. In *The Boy Knight,* the first really dramatic scene is the one in which Jean begins his work for the goldsmith whom he discovers to be dishonest. The decision about the second scene will not be so easy, for it might be one of several incidents. Perhaps we may decide on one which could be played before the curtain: the episode in which Jean and his friend Marcel are returning from the castle after having delivered the goblet which the Countess had ordered in the first scene. This episode is not necessary to the structure of the play, but it is dramatic and full of suspense, and may develop the interest in knighthood. The third is a necessary scene, for it shows Marcel's terrible deed, the destruction of the statue which the boys had made, which forms the crisis of the play. Jean's wild rage when he sees what has happened causes him to rush from the shack to pour out his woes to the Bishop. This brings us to the cathedral scene in which Jean learns the secret of the cathedral, and it leads directly to the final episode in which he is knighted.

Much has of necessity to be omitted, though it is especially hard to give up Anton's trial by the guild. A great deal of thought is required to determine how much must be explained in the exposition, how much detail can be ignored, and how the scenes are to be linked so as to make the play flow smoothly.

THE SCENARIO

By this time we should have arrived at the place where we are ready to put our play on paper. We have, perhaps, already jotted down certain notes about scenes and characters, but we have made no plan. Now we begin to make a scenario or outline of the play which we expect to write. There is no set form or length for a scenario. No two writers make it in the same way. Some write without any division of scenes at all. But in order to clarify one's thinking about the nature of his play, the sequence of scenes, and the relations of his characters, it is strongly advisable to outline the play in considerable detail.

A scenario is based upon action. It tells whether the play is a comedy, tragedy, melodrama, historical play, or still another type of drama. After listing and describing the characters, it gives the number of acts and scenes, and describes the settings. If these are intended to suggest the mood of the story that, too, is indicated after a short preliminary exposition. Everything that happens in the play is described, as well as the causes of the happenings and their effects. At least a part of the action is illustrated. Some dramatists include bits of dialogue which they intend to use in various scenes, others include none at all.

It should be clearly evident from the scenario where the emphasis is to be. The reader should know who among the characters are most important, which events are significant, what is the real point of the play.

THE WRITING OF THE PLAY

At last we have come to the actual writing of the play. Many dramatists consider that their biggest work has been done before they arrive at this point. All important questions having been decided, the detailed scenario being ready, only the dialogue remains to be written. This, however, to an inexperienced writer, is a big part of the play, for unless there is much dialogue to be taken over from the novel, he finds it exceedingly difficult to give his people lines which shall express character as well as forward the plot.

As in the scenario, the play opens with a description of the setting, with an indication of the mood if it is intended to express a certain feeling. Next, the characters are introduced, and we must lose no time in identifying them by the dialogue. Even though the novel upon which the play is based is well known, we must not take for granted that the audience will recognize the people. Not only must the characters be known, but their relationships must be made clear. The dramatist must not depend upon the programs for this identification; the play itself should show it.

EXPOSITION

Innumerable devices are used for conveying to the audience the information which should be known concerning characters and situation. The conventional prologue and the artificial soliloquy, both of which quite openly tell the audience what the author wishes them to know, are at one extreme; while the natural conversation of the characters, which reveals it bit by bit, is at the other. Besides these, settings, costumes, names and appearance of characters, all tell much about the story.

When one character tells another what the audience needs to know, it is very important, of course, that it seem the natural thing for him to do. If the audience wonders why the second person should not already have known what he tells, the illusion of reality will be gone and every one will see it as a trick. A stranger in the play provides a motive for giving information, though this device has been greatly overdone. The more subtly and swiftly it can be told, the better. Not all of it needs to be given at once. In a children's play it should be delayed until actually needed. But there must be enough to make the audience understand why the characters do and say what they do. Certainly the audience ought not be made conscious that the characters are talking to give them information.

THE DRAMATIC SITUATION

At first the audience is interested in the settings and the characters; then something happens and there appears on the horizon a "cloud no bigger than a man's hand." [4] This is the beginning of drama. From now on the audience should look ahead, wondering how this thing will affect the characters, speculating as to what the outcome will be.

In *The Prince and the Pauper* the first dramatic situation arises when the pauper is thrust away from the gate and the little prince angrily rebukes the guard for his cruelty. In reading the play, one knows at once that this will cause any audience to lean forward with interest, intent on knowing what will come of it. There has been little time to prepare for this situation, but sufficient to make it clear that a group of curious people has gathered at the gate in the hope of seeing royalty. When we see a little waif peer through the iron gate, eager to see the Prince of Wales, we feel sorry when he is thrown roughly to the ground by the guard.

A dramatic situation which is clear when it occurs is much more effective than when explained afterwards. We are not

[4] Wilde; *The Craftsmanship of the One-Act Play* (Doubleday, Doran & Co., 1928).

surprised when Tom is dragged away, for we expect the guards to keep the populace at a respectful distance. The interference of the prince is unexpected, but we can easily imagine that his attention would be drawn by the noise.

THE COMPLICATION

Dramatic situations alone do not make a play. Other factors are added in drama as they are in life to make the solution more difficult. In the case of *The Prince and the Pauper* the first complication comes when, having invited the pauper into the palace and discovered that he was hurt, the prince rushes out to have the guard punished and is himself thrust out of the gate. Many other complications arise until the audience is following two dramatic stories, each full of adventure and suspense.

SUSPENSE

Suspense, according to George P. Baker, is "a straining forward of interest, a compelling desire to know what will happen next." [5] It can be aroused only when we are in sympathy with one or more characters. If we do not care what will happen to any one, there can be no suspense. Sometimes it is only sympathy for the underdog, often it is sympathy for some one who is denied what he is quite clearly entitled to have. It always involves the emotions. Both Cinderella and Snow White are denied the positions which they should have in their households. Both are made drudges when they should be enjoying the happiness which would result from right treatment by their families. We are sorry for them, and our chief interest in the plays of which they are the central figures is in seeing them win this happiness.

[5] Baker, *Dramatic Technique* (Houghton Mifflin Co., 1919).

A play without suspense would be no play at all. Something must be continually held back by the dramatist, and the desire to know how things are going to work out must become more and more intense. This does not mean that the audience should be kept in ignorance of what is going to happen to the characters. In fact, a dramatist heightens the interest by letting the audience in on the secret. The suspense in that case results from the desire to know how the characters will react when they learn what has happened.

According to Archer,[6] "... The essential abiding pleasure of the theatre lies in foreknowledge. In relation to the characters of the drama, the audiences are as gods looking before and after. Sitting in the theatre we taste, for a moment, the glory of omniscience. With vision unsealed, we watch the striving of purblind mortals after happiness and smile at their blunders, their futile quests, their misplaced exultations, their groundless panics. To keep a secret from us is to reduce us to their level, and deprive us of our clairvoyant aloofness."

In *Peter Pan* the foreknowledge which the audience has about the children's return is sweet to them. All the time the mother is sitting by the window, sorrowing for her lost children, the audience is chuckling over the knowledge that Wendy, John, and Michael are safe in bed, and in another moment will pop their heads out and run to throw themselves in her arms.

How can there be any suspense in the dramatization of well-known stories unless it is brought about by intense interest in seeing just how the characters will work themselves into and out of the crisis? The boys and girls in the audience may be entirely familiar with the outcome of the story of *The Scotch Twins,* but they recapture all their first thrill by watch-

[6] Archer, *Playmaking* (Small, Maynard & Co., 1912).

ing the actions and reactions of the characters who do *not* know.

THE DEVELOPMENT

Every scene in the play should contribute its share to the development of the plot, each increasing the interest and entertainment value. When one imagines an act divided into the many small scenes which compose it, scenes divided usually by an entrance or exit, he may think of these little scenes as contributing many different values to the play. Some are needed for exposition, others for furthering the action, still others for development of character. Several will be needed to give time for something to happen offstage, as in *The Prince and the Pauper,* when the Lord St. John goes to the palace to look for the great seal. These last are called "cover scenes" and they should never be mere padding. Even though they may have been used to allow for the passage of time, they should possess interest in themselves, and should be of value in furthering the plot. In Charlotte Chorpenning's dramatization of *The Prince and the Pauper,* this cover scene is used to unravel the tangled skein of events so that by the time the Lord St. John returns, much has been made clear to both boys.

The amateur author is far too likely not to write a cover scene at all. He often sends his people on errands with the speed of lightning, bringing them back long before they could possibly accomplish their errand. Time can be condensed on the stage, it is true, but it is absurd to have people consume an entire meal while three lines are being spoken, or have them send for the caretaker of the estate and then bring him on with a rapidity which could only mean that he was waiting outside the door.

Some events are talked about rather than shown, and it requires exceptionally good judgment to determine which may happen off stage, and which must be shown in full view of the audience. If a scene in which great interest has been aroused is omitted, an audience feels cheated. During the time which is supposed to elapse between acts a dramatist often has important events occur, but there are some things which are too significant to take place then. Chief of such scenes is the one up to which the drama has been built. It is called the *scène à faire* or obligatory scene, and as the name implies, it is the scene in the play which the audience *must* see. Not to show them Cinderella actually trying on the glass slipper or the Sleeping Beauty awakened by a kiss, or Rumpelstiltskin routed by the guessing of his name would be the playwright's unpardonable sin.

CLIMAX

In a play written for child audiences, the climax or highest moment should come either at the very end or within a few speeches of the final curtain. What the nature of the climax is to be varies with the play. It is not always accompanied by "fireworks," though more often so than in one designed for adults.

Whatever point in the play arouses the most intense emotion is the climax, and it is not always the same for different people. It grows out of the crisis, the scene in which matters are most complicated, when suspense is at its height. Some resolution must come speedily. This may be the highest peak of all, or it may lead to a still greater one. Wherever this highest peak comes, it is the climax.

In the short play, *Youth's Highway,* the crisis comes in the scene where the master of the apprentices discovers first that

THE BLUE BIRD

Community Playhouse, Pasadena, California.

Michael has corrected his (Griffo's) drawings, and, immediately afterwards, that Michael has with him a marble faun's head which he claims to have made himself. He rushes to the door calling to the guard to arrest Michael, and to the amazement of all, Lorenzo the Magnificent appears, asking, "Who calls the guard so loudly?"

Griffo then accuses Michael of stealing the faun's head. But Lorenzo's art spy is with him and loses no time in identifying Michael as the boy whom he considers the worthiest apprentice in Florence.

Now comes the climax. Lorenzo invites Michael to come and live with him in the ducal palace, to eat with his sons, work with his artists, and, with his arm about Michael's shoulders, he leads the boy out to a great opportunity, leaving Griffo and the other apprentices staring after him in amazement and chagrin.

CHARACTERIZATION

At the heart of every play are its characters. These people should seem real. We can sympathize with them. If they are mere puppets used by the dramatist to carry forward the plot, we do not care what happens to them.

In dramatizing a story which already has interesting characters, it should not be difficult to individualize them in our play. Yet beginning playwrights often change flesh and blood people into paper dolls because they are so intent on getting the story told that they forget the importance of the characters. One of the signs of the mature playwright is his ability to individualize his people. Some of the minor characters may be types, for they only supply a background of life, but the people who make a play immortal are always living, breathing characters, as real as any of our friends.

To write such people into his play, a dramatist must have a deep insight into human nature. But if a novelist has already created them, the playwright's task should be an easy one. If he understands the characters, if he really appreciates them, he can make use of the novelist's descriptions and dialogue so that the people will live in his play as they do in the novel.

Economy in the number of characters is desirable in a play, both from the practical standpoint of costuming (one need not consider the cost of a large cast unless he is writing for the professional theatre), and because the stage should not be cluttered by actors who have nothing to do.

Whether or not the play is a story dramatization, the characters should be consistent throughout. If a person is made to do or say something which is contrary to what the audience has been led to think about him, they will not accept him as a real person. When, in dramatizing a story, incidents must be inserted for cover scenes or for any other purpose, the playwright should be most careful not to force characters to do anything which it is hard to imagine them doing.

It would be entirely illogical, for example, for Jo of *Little Women* to take to gossiping, or Hans Brinker to complain of his poverty. To have a character suddenly turn against a friend whom he has always had every reason to trust is unconvincing. When a third person tells him that his friend is deceiving him, we expect our character to defend his friend and demand proof of his guilt instead of weakly believing all that he is told.

DIALOGUE

A dramatist who bases a play on a novel uses all possible dialogue from the novel itself. Even when there are insufficient lines for any given scene, he may find characteristic dialogue in some section of the book which is not being used in the play. In this way a large proportion is sure to be absolutely true to the characters. Only when really necessary does he invent his own dialogue, and this he writes as nearly like the other as possible. When one attempts to add to the dialogue of Mark Twain he finds himself at a loss to write lines which can in any way compare with the inimitable dialogue of *Tom Sawyer, Huckleberry Finn,* and the others.

Dialogue, like plot, must be selected and condensed. Only the essentials of a conversation are presented. All the inconsequentials are dropped unless they have a reason for being, in that they make the characters more real. A garrulous person must be shown as he is, but even his dialogue is made less boring in a play. Dialogue must do three things: clarify the situation, tell the story, show the character. If, in addition, it has some literary quality, if it is poetic, charming, witty, so much the better, so long as one can believe that it really belongs to the characters.

When the dramatist writes original dialogue, he needs to hear his lines spoken as he writes. Only in this way can he avoid writing speeches that no actor can say naturally. If he hears them or tries them aloud, he will be more likely to avoid the fault into which so many playwrights fall—the fault of writing speeches that are too long. In children's plays, especially, it is a mistake to write lengthy ones. Short, natural conversation which gets to the point at once is the only kind of dialogue which is successful. If writers of such plays would only bear this in mind, directors would not be forced to do so much cutting.

Now at last our play is written! We have spent many more hours on it than we had considered possible. The most telling and interesting episodes of the story have been selected and fitted into a scene sequence which builds with plenty of suspense to a strong climax. The characters talk and act like real people—the people whom the novelist created. We believe that the children who see our play will sympathize with our heroine, will care what happens to her. We are sure that they will be satisfied with the outcome.

It has been a big task, this making of a play. We did not realize all its difficulties until we tried it. We shall be more appreciative of good drama in the future, and our next play will profit by the experience of writing our first. But with all the time and work and vitality expended on it, we shall feel well satisfied if, when it is finally produced, we can be in the first audience and see children sitting forward in their seats to drink in every word, feel a hush of suspense when their sympathies are aroused, hear the refreshing laughter which tells more plainly than words that our play is meeting with some measure of success.

CHAPTER V

DISCOVERING THE STRUCTURE

HAVING DISCOURSED for many pages on how to make a play from a story, suppose we examine one which has been written. We are searching, let us say, for a good opening play for our children's theatre season. It must be popular and of good quality. We find a new dramatization of *Alice in Wonderland* and *Through the Looking Glass*. They have been favorite stories of ours, so that we shall be more than usually critical in judging such a play. We shall watch jealously to see whether the author has used the episodes we most enjoy, and, more important than all else, whether she has held to the child's point of view in writing the play.

ALICE IN WONDERLAND

by

CHARLOTTE CHORPENNING

ACT I

At the bottom of the rabbit hole. It is a narrow tunnel, of which one side runs along the back, and the top disappears in shadow. A shaft of daylight falls in, obliquely, as if from the opening above. A tiny door, rather high in the back wall, stands open, and the light from the garden (magic, not daylight) shines in through it and gleams on a dainty glass table. The White Rabbit hurries on, takes a watch from his waistcoat pocket, and stops in the shaft of light to read it.

RABBIT. Oh dear, oh dear, I shall be too late!

[*He moves into the light from the garden and stops in astonishment.*]

Oh, my dear paws! The door to the garden is open!

[*He fetches a stool, reaches up, shuts the door, gets a little key from the glass table, locks the door, draws a curtain over it. and returns key to the table. A shadow falls across him from something that has blocked the opening above. He snatches up a flashlight, turns it on, and throws it toward the entrance.*]

Oh, my ears and whiskers! Something has fallen into my rabbit hole! I'd better put out the lights!

[*He does so. There are little squeals from above.*]

It sounds like a little girl.

ALICE [*off*]. Down, down, down. I wonder where I'm falling to?

RABBIT. It talks. It is a little girl.

[*He wriggles his ears, listening.*]

ALICE. After such a fall as this, I shall think nothing of falling downstairs. Why, I shouldn't say a word even if I fell off the top of a house!

RABBIT [*nodding*]. Which is very likely true.

ALICE [*nearer*]. I wonder how many miles I've fallen. I must be getting somewhere near the center of the earth. I suppose I'll fall right *through* the earth, and come out among people who walk with their heads downward.

RABBIT. I do nothing of the sort!

ALICE. The antipathies I think they call them. No, that doesn't sound at all the right word. I'm glad there's nobody listening.

RABBIT [*his ears going stiff with surprise*]. Glad nobody's listening! Now, how can she be glad of a thing that isn't so? I must think that out. [*He wriggles his whiskers between his hands as if they were the edge of a hole.*] Of course, she's got to be glad about something. And she hasn't any whiskers to let her know all sides of everything. So she can't be too particular what she's glad about.—Oh, my fur and forepaws! How dark it's getting!

[*He jumps back in alarm and turns off his light as Alice bounces out of the rabbit hole. She shows only in silhouette in*

the faint light coming from above. She curtsies as soon as she
can get to her feet.]

ALICE. Is this the end?

RABBIT. The question is: Is there any such thing?

ALICE [*indignant*]. Of course there is. Everything comes to an end
sometime.

RABBIT. It might be a beginning, you know.

ALICE. I don't see what you mean.

RABBIT. Of course, you can't see in the dark.

ALICE. It isn't my fault it's dark. I don't like it at all.

RABBIT [*turning on his light*]. Then why don't you make a light?

ALICE. I didn't know there was one.

RABBIT. That's because you didn't look for it.—Oh, my tail and
toe-nails! I shall be late.

[*He scurries toward exit.*]

ALICE. Wait!

RABBIT. Who told you you could order me about?

ALICE. I didn't mean to be rude—

RABBIT. Then don't be! It doesn't work down here.

ALICE. I only wanted to ask you. Will you please tell me where
I'm going?

RABBIT. That depends on which door you go through.

ALICE. I don't see any doors.

RABBIT. That's because you don't look where they are.

[*Lights come up on a row of doors in the back, one at a time.*]

ALICE. Oh, there's one! And there! And—how many doors are
there?

[*The rabbit puts his watch to his ear and counts, his ears, eyes,
and tail keeping time.*]

I asked you how many doors there are.

RABBIT. I heard you.

ALICE. Then why don't you answer me?

RABBIT. I have to count them first.

ALICE. You don't count doors by a watch.

RABBIT. I do. There's a new door every second.

[*There is a pause during which the rabbit gets more and
more vigorous in his counting.*]

ALICE. How long will it take you to count them?

RABBIT. Forever.

ALICE. I—I don't think I can wait that long.

RABBIT [*putting away the watch*]. Oh, very well, if you don't want to know.

ALICE. There are quite enough doors for me here, anyway. Which one shall I try first?

RABBIT. That depends on where you're going.

ALICE. That's what I want to find out.

RABBIT. You'll never know where you're going till you've been there.

ALICE. Then I think I'll just go back—back where I came from.
    [*Behind her, an invisible door swings shut over the entrance to the rabbit hole.*]

RABBIT. It's one thing to think so and another to do it.

ALICE. I wish you wouldn't contradict me all the time.

RABBIT. I wish you'd mind your manners.

ALICE [*looking for the opening*]. I came down a rabbit hole. It was here a moment ago. It must be somewhere. I was almost an hour falling through it.—Oh, Rabbit, if you please, I want to go back.

RABBIT. It's no use whatever to want that.

ALICE. Why not?

RABBIT. Every hour is a one-way road. It will take you wherever you choose, but it will never take you back again.

ALICE. I want to see the sky. I want to see my kitten. Isn't there any way to get out of here?

RABBIT. Dozens of ways.

> There's a way for me
>   And a way for you,
> And one for Johnny
>   And one for Sue.
> But you can't go back,
>   And you walk alone,
> For every Jack
>   Has a way of his own.

Now *your* way is through the garden. But you'll have to be the right size to get into it.

ALICE. The right size?

RABBIT. If you're too large, you can't get through the door.

ALICE [*illustrating*]. I can make myself small—see? I can even go on my knees. I can go on all fours.

RABBIT. If you're too small you can't reach the keyhole.

ALICE [*illustrating*]. I can stretch up, ever so.

RABBIT. You might not reach, for all that.

ALICE [*turning to the doors*]. Then I think I'd like to try at once, please.

RABBIT. Try what?

ALICE. Whether my size will let me into the garden.

RABBIT. One of them will.

ALICE. That's a silly thing to say. I can't be more than one size at a time.

RABBIT. Your foot has a size, hasn't it?

ALICE. Yes.

RABBIT. And you change your shoes to fit it.

ALICE. Yes.

RABBIT. And your hand has a size. And you change your gloves to fit that.

ALICE. Yes. But it changes every once in a while.

RABBIT. Exactly. And your Self has a size, and *it* changes every once in a while. And down here you change your skin to fit that. It can happen very quick. Why, there are places down here where you have to run as fast as ever you can just to stay where you are. And you can shut up like a telescope quick's a cat can wink its eye. Or you can open out like the biggest one you ever saw, before you know it.

ALICE. Could I shut up to be smaller than this?

RABBIT. Oh, my whiskers, what a question! Ever and ever and ever and ever and ever and ever and *ever* so much smaller.

ALICE. As small as I was when I was a baby?

RABBIT. You could shut up so small that you'd go out altogether, like a candle.

ALICE. What should I be like then, I wonder?

RABBIT. What *does* the flame of a candle look like after it's blown out? Think hard.

ALICE. I can't remember ever having seen such a thing.

RABBIT. Which is very likely true.

ALICE. It's a little frightening. Can I shut up on purpose? Can I do it whenever I like?

RABBIT. It all depends on what goes on inside of you.

ALICE. I don't know what you mean by that.

RABBIT. How do you think you got down my rabbit hole?

ALICE. I fell. I was sitting by my sister on the river bank, and I saw you run by. You were talking to yourself. That didn't seem so *very* strange, though I never heard a rabbit talk before. But then you took a watch out of your pocket, and looked at it. That made me so curious I ran after you. And when you popped down the rabbit hole under the hedge, I just popped down after you.

RABBIT. Exactly. You never stopped to think that you were too large to go down a rabbit hole, did you?

ALICE. Why, no. I just felt inside of me that I *had* to see what you were doing.

RABBIT. Exactly. And so you grew the right size to come down and find out. And you never even once considered how in the world you were to get out again.

ALICE. I wish I had.

RABBIT. It's always easier to get in than to get out.

ALICE. I suppose the only way to do now is to try— Which door? —Which door?—

[*She puts her hand on one. The Rabbit chuckles to himself so silently she doesn't hear. She takes her hand away.*]

Suppose this doesn't lead into the garden?

RABBIT. I am supposing it.

ALICE. Will I like what it does lead to?

RABBIT. That depends on how good you are at liking things.

ALICE. I wish you wouldn't talk nonsense. That doesn't mean anything at all.

RABBIT. It means a very great deal. It's much easier to like some things than others.—Oh, the Duchess! The Duchess! Won't she be savage if I keep her waiting!

[*He patters off in great haste.*]

ALICE [*running to call after him*]. Wait! Oh, please wait! Which door leads into the garden? Please tell me! Please!

RABBIT [*calling back*]. Every one must find that out for himself.

ALICE. What shall I do now? If I go through the wrong door I may never get back. Then I'd never get into the garden. Then I'd never get out of here.

[*She bursts into tears; then straightens up, and shakes a finger at herself.*]

There's no use crying about it! I advise you to leave off this minute! Stop, now, or I'll box your ears the way I did when you cheated at croquet. [*She slaps her cheeks, indignantly.*] A great girl like you! Stop crying and see what you can *do* about it.

[*As she looks around, she suddenly sees the key on the glass table, gets it, dances with delight.*]

A key! A little golden key! It must be the one. Now let me see. It looks pretty little, but it must unlock some door.

[*She tries door after door without success, and with growing anxiety. After the last one, she looks at the key dejectedly, and draws her hand over her eyes. She shakes it.*]

Your hand's all wet! Alice, I'm ashamed of you! You aren't to give up, that you aren't!

[*A light falls on the little curtain. She runs to reach for it, but it is too high. She gets the stool, draws the curtain, unlocks the door, cries out in ecstasy.*]

It's the loveliest garden in the world!

[*She tries every way to get through, arms first, feet first, shoulders sideways, etc., all in vain.*]

Oh, I wish I could shut up like a telescope, now, this minute. I think I could if I only knew how to begin. Well! You're not stupid, like some girls! You're the head of your class. You can surely find out a little thing like that!

[*A large bottle, with a huge label tied around its neck, appears on the table. Alice runs to read the label, sitting on her heels, on the ground.*]

Drink me! I'm too wise to do that in a hurry. I'll find out if it's marked poison, first.—Not on this side—nor this—
[*She tastes it in little sips.*]
Um-m-m- It tastes like cherry tart!—and custard!—and pineapple!—and roast turkey!—and taffy!—and hot buttered toast!
[*She finishes off the bottle with gusto.*]
What a curious feeling! I must be shutting up like a telescope. No—No! I'm opening out instead!
[*She unfolds from her sitting position to her greatest height, and rushes off, calling*]
Rabbit! Oh, Rabbit! I'm growing the wrong way!
[*Each time Alice tastes the bottle, the lights flicker, at first only a little, then more and more till they are dancing madly. During this the walls of the rabbit hall disappear, right and left. When the lights are steady again, the stage is dim. Alice's voice is heard off, as if far away.*]

ALICE. Rabbit! Where are you? Come here!
[*The rabbit comes pitter-pattering on, in great haste. He is throwing his flashlight about and muttering.*]

RABBIT. Oh, my whiskers! I shall be late, I shall be late.
[*His flashlight falls first on the bottom of the trunk of a tree which is the proportion of a tree to a rabbit, and then on a mushroom large enough for him to walk under. On it sits a large blue caterpillar, with its arms folded, quietly smoking a large hookah. At this moment Alice calls sharply, much nearer. The rabbit is so startled that his fan flies out of his hand. He clasps his hands over his stomach as if holding himself together.*]

ALICE [*off*]. Rabbit!!

RABBIT. Oh, my paws and paunch! What a noise!

CATERPILLAR [*looking around*]. Some one's calling you.

RABBIT [*throwing the light on the caterpillar*]. I can't stop. You talk to her, won't you?

CATERPILLAR. What about?

RABBIT. She wants to get the right size to get into the garden. You know all about it. You can tell her.

CATERPILLAR. I *can* tell her, yes. The question is: Do I want to?

ALICE [*off, peremptory*]. Rabbit!

CATERPILLAR. I don't like the way she speaks. It makes me feel contrary.

RABBIT. She's a bit upset, I think. She says she doesn't mean to be rude.

CATERPILLAR. Well, I'll try her. If she makes me feel friendly, I'll tell her what to do. If she makes me feel contrary, I'll *be* contrary. I won't tell her a single thing. She can keep any size, for all of me.

[*Rabbit starts off, beginning to fan himself. He stares at his empty hand.*]

RABBIT. Oh, my fur and whiskers! What's gone with my fan?— Didn't I have my fan in my hand when you saw me first?

CATERPILLAR. No. I distinctly remember, you held your hands like this.

RABBIT. Where could I have dropped it, I wonder? Oh, my tail and toe-nails! What if she should pick it up!

CATERPILLAR. Well, what?

RABBIT. She'd grow smaller and smaller and smaller as long as she held it in her hand. I suppose I'll have to go about and look for it. If she comes here with it, you'll have to tell her to put it down.

CATERPILLAR. I will, if I feel friendly. If I feel contrary, I'll *be* contrary. I won't say a word. She can shrink as much as she likes.

RABBIT. But she'd go out like a candle if she held it long enough.

CATERPILLAR. Then she'd better mind her manners! I'll throw things at her if she doesn't, that I will!

RABBIT. It will make me late, and I promised the Duchess to recite a poem for her guests. I'm to speak:

> How doth the little busy bee
> Improve each shining hour,
> And gather honey all the day
> From every fragrant flower!

Beautiful, isn't it?

CATERPILLAR. If you like it. It makes me feel contrary.

[*The rabbit trots off, muttering, and flashing his light about, but never catching the fan.*]

RABBIT. How doth the little busy bee—[*etc.*]

ALICE [*off, and near*]. Why don't you answer, you!

CATERPILLAR. Now, we'll see.

[*The lights are low, as the Rabbit goes with his flashlight, but shafts of it keep playing from off throughout the scene. Alice enters, seen in silhouette, larger than before and growing larger slowly but steadily, especially her neck which stretches up until she looks just like the picture. As she grows, her face comes into a beam of light. The caterpillar turns to watch her, but she is unconscious of him.*]

ALICE. Dear, dear. How queer everything is! I wonder if I've changed into somebody else. I'll try if I know the things I used to know. Let me see. Four times five is—twelve. Four times six is—thirteen.—That *can't* be right. Never mind arithmetic. I'll try geography. London is the capital of Paris, and Paris is the capital of Rome—That's wrong, I'm certain. I'll recite some poetry. I'll begin with "How doth the little—

[*She folds her hands and clears her throat.*]

> How doth the little crocodile
> Improve his shining tail.
> And pour the waters of the Nile—

I'm sure those aren't the right words! I've turned into somebody stupid. Well, at least you needn't cry about it—a great girl like you! Crying is the stupidest thing there is! I wish I could turn into somebody who could get out of here. I'm so very tired of being down here all alone. [*She sees the fan.*] I do believe that's the rabbit's fan! [*Takes it up.*] I must find him and give it to him! He'll feel sorry when he finds he's lost it.

[*The caterpillar lifts a hand, about to speak, then she continues:*]

How funny it seems, to be going messages for a rabbit! I suppose I'll be going messages for my kitten next, or some horrid little caterpillar.

[*He drops his hand, and stretches up in indignation.*]

I wonder which way he went.

[*She goes off, putting her hand up toward her head in surprise as she goes.*]

Curiouser and curiouser! Now I'm shutting up like a telescope! [*off*] I'm shutting up fast and I don't know how to stop!

[*She reënters, much smaller and still going down.*]

What if I shouldn't stop till I went all the way out! Where *is* the Rabbit! I declare it's too bad of him, so it is! Rabbit!!

[*The caterpillar, very much annoyed, throws a handful of pebbles at her. She backs away from them, behind the tree.*]

Whoever you are, stop throwing pebbles at me!

Oh, dear, oh dear, my chin will hit my foot presently, at this rate.

[*She emerges, still smaller. A puppet is used.*]

I couldn't reach the key now, even if I found the table again. I think I *am* going down to nothing. How strange that will seem. I wish I could see my Dinah-kitten first. I'd like to tell her I'm sorry I pulled her tail. I'd like to tell the rabbit I'm sorry I shouted and screamed at him. I'm afraid it wasn't at all polite— This is the curiousest thing of all! I do believe the pebbles are all turning into little cakes! This one has "Eat me" all marked out in little candies. Well, I'll eat it, and if it makes me grow smaller, I can creep under the door. Either way, I'll get into the garden.

[*She nibbles at a cake.*]

Which way, now?—I feel as if I were opening up a little—just a wee little bit. I'll find another cake.

[*She goes behind the tree, searching, and emerges larger, nibbling a cake.*]

Dear me, it makes me dizzy to keep changing so. It makes me feel gay. I want to dance. Tra, la, la!

[*She goes skipping and swaying to the music which seems to come out of the air, around the tree, emerging larger still.— It is the actress, not a puppet, this time—She stops, a bit dizzy, swaying.*]

I've only to grow a little more, and that rabbit will come when I call, that he will!

[*This annoys the caterpillar, on whom the lights have come up full. He draws himself up, feeling "contrary." Alice suddenly sees the mushroom, and walks around and under it exploring. Then she stretches up on tiptoe to see what is on top. The caterpillar stares at her, before he speaks.*]

CATERPILLAR. Who are you?

ALICE. I—I hardly know, sir, just at present. At least, I know who I was when I got up this morning, but I think I must have changed several times since then.

CATERPILLAR. What do you mean by that? Explain yourself.

ALICE. I can't explain *myself*, sir, because I'm not myself, you see.

CATERPILLAR. I don't see.

ALICE. I can't tell it any better, for I don't understand it myself. Being so many sizes in a day is confusing.

CATERPILLAR. It isn't.

ALICE. Well, perhaps you haven't found it so yet. But you'll turn into a chrysalis some day, and after that into a butterfly. You'll feel a little queer then, won't you?

CATERPILLAR. Not a bit.

ALICE [*irritated at the short replies*]. Well, your feeling may be different. It feels queer to me.

CATERPILLAR. You! Who are you, anyway?

ALICE [*in a temper*]. There's no sort of use talking to you! I want to grow larger. And I want to get into the garden. The things you say are no use to me at all. You make such very short and rude remarks.

CATERPILLAR. I don't.

ALICE. If you're going to contradict every single thing I say—

CATERPILLAR. I'm not.

ALICE. Well, you have been doing it! You can't deny that.

CATERPILLAR. I can.

[*Alice stamps her foot and turns away with a toss of her head.*]

Come back, I've something important to say.

[*Alice comes back, after a struggle, and stands waiting. He smokes a bit, surveying her.*]

CATERPILLAR. Keep your temper.

ALICE [*swallowing down her anger*]. Is that all?

CATERPILLAR. No.

ALICE. I'm afraid I was very rude just now.

CATERPILLAR. You were.

ALICE. I don't mean to be. It just comes out.

CATERPILLAR. It has to be in before it can come out.

ALICE. I'm usually very polite. But everything is so queer.

CATERPILLAR. So you think you're changed, do you?

ALICE. I'm afraid I am, sir. I don't keep the same size ten minutes together, and I can't remember things as I used.

CATERPILLAR. What things?

ALICE. Well, I tried to say "How doth the little busy bee" and it all came different.

CATERPILLAR. Try if you can recite "You are old, Father William."

ALICE. I don't know that.

CATERPILLAR. Repeat it after me. [*Very pompously he says*]:

"You are old, Father William," the young man cried;
   "The few locks which are left you are grey.
   You are hale, Father William, a hearty old man.
      Now tell me the reason, I pray."

ALICE. I'm afraid I can't remember so much at once.

CATERPILLAR. Don't interrupt.

"In the days of my youth," Father William replied,
   "I remembered that youth would fly fast,
   And abused not my health and my vigor at first,
   That I never might need them at last."

   Now repeat the whole.

ALICE. Come, I believe I can! Maybe I've not turned to somebody stupid after all!
   [*She folds her hands and recites, proudly. Part way through she begins to feel it is not quite right.*]

> "You are old, Father William," the young man said,
> "And your hair has become very white;
> And yet you incessantly stand on your head—
> Do you think, at your age, it is right?"

Some of the words have got altered.

CATERPILLAR. Try the second stanza.

ALICE.

> "In my youth," Father William replied to his son,
> "I feared it might injure the brain.
> But now that I'm perfectly sure I have none,
> Why, I do it again and again."

CATERPILLAR. That's not said right.

ALICE. Not quite right I'm afraid.

CATERPILLAR. It's wrong from beginning to end.

ALICE [*trying not to cry*]. You see, sir, I've changed a great deal. I used to be the head of my class. I think maybe it's because I'm so small that I'm so stupid. Though it was just as bad when I was very tall.

CATERPILLAR. How large do you want to be?

ALICE. I must stay small enough to get through the door, but this is such a wretched height to be.

CATERPILLAR [*angry*]. It isn't.

ALICE. But I'm not used to it. I think perhaps if I could get back to my own size, I should be myself again. Only I have to get into the garden first.

CATERPILLAR. You don't.

ALICE. I do so! It's my way out of here!

CATERPILLAR. There you go again.

ALICE. I can't help it. The creatures keep contradicting me so.

CATERPILLAR. We want to see how you take it.

ALICE. It's too bad, that it is. You act as if I were some sort of a specimen, like a bug, or a frog, or a butterfly, or something.

CATERPILLAR. You are.

ALICE [*stamping her foot and turning her back*]. That I'm not.
[*The caterpillar takes the hookah out of his mouth, gathers it up, and slides off the mushroom. He looks over the top at her and points to the sides of the mushroom as he speaks.*]

CATERPILLAR. One side will make you grow taller and the other side will make you grow shorter.

[*He starts off. Alice turns, eagerly.*]

ALICE. One side of what? The other side of what?

CATERPILLAR. If you'd kept your temper, you'd know.

[*He leaves.*]

ALICE. He couldn't have meant the mushroom. When a thing is perfectly round, it hasn't any sides. Could he have meant the underside, I wonder, and the top?

[*She walks under and breaks off a bit from above her, then out and gets a bit from the top, stretching up on tiptoes for it.*]

Now I'll try—just a wee nibble at a time, to see which is which.

[*She nibbles and waits, nibbles and waits.*]

Which way? Which way?—I'm staying exactly the same size! That's very dull and stupid, I'm sure.—He must have meant the sides. I can't make out which are the two sides of it. [*Walking around it.*] It's a very difficult question, I'm sure. Let me see.

[*She stretches her arms around as far as they will go, and breaks off a bit with each hand.*]

There! And now, which is which? I'll keep them in separate pockets till I find out.

[*She suddenly starts, peers off, then ducks behind the stem of the mushroom. A footman enters with hair curled all over his head, and the face of a frog, his eyes staring up at the sky. He looks at a watch and shakes his head.*]

FROG. Late again! That's no way for a house to behave.

[*Another footman enters, with like curls, and an envelope almost as big as himself under his arm. He has the face of a fish.*]

FISH. Will you direct me to the Duchess' House?

FROG. I'm waiting for it. It should be along any minute, now—I am her footman.

[*This interests Alice very much. She peeps farther out.*]

FISH. I am the footman of the Queen. I have a message for the Duchess. [*Bowing very low.*] For the Duchess. An invitation—

FROG. You haven't knocked.

FISH. I'd need a door, to knock.

FROG. I told you it would be here shortly. Things must be done properly. It'll be coming very soon.

[*The house appears. The Cheshire cat is on the windowsill or roof.*]

I told you so.

[*He goes to the door, and opens it. A great noise of sneezing, howling, and rattling dishes. He shouts over it.*]

You'll have to knock very loudly, or I won't hear. There's so much noise inside.

[*He goes in and shuts the door. The footman raps loudly with his knuckles. The frog opens the door and steps out, shutting it behind him.*]

FISH [*bowing*]. For the Duchess. An invitation from the Queen to play croquet.

FROG [*bowing*]. From the Queen. An invitation to the Duchess to play croquet.

[*They both bow so low that their curls get tangled. Alice laughs so hard she has to hold her hands over her mouth to keep from being heard.*]

FISH. Is some one laughing?

FROG. I'd be sorry for any one who laughed at the footman of the Duchess.

FISH. I don't know what would happen to any one who laughed at the footman of the Queen.

[*A gasp escapes Alice in spite of best efforts to choke it back. They straighten up in outraged dignity.*]

FROG. It came from there.

FISH [*very pompous*]. This way.

[*They march around the mushroom, Alice keeping on the other side.*]

You go this way and I'll go that.

[*Alice goes under.*]

It might be on top.

[*The frog goes on all fours and the fish steps on his back to look. Alice giggles in spite of herself. They start up, listening.*]

FROG. It came from under.

FISH. You stay there, and I'll look all the way round.

[*He bends down, going all the way around. Alice steps on the frog and springs up on the top. The Fish comes to the Frog.*]

FISH. No one there.

FROG. Might have sneaked around after you.

FISH. Aha!

[*He darts about under the mushroom, reversing his direction suddenly, etc. Alice nearly bursts with laughter.*]

FISH. No one, I tell you.

[*The two crawl out and stand up, backs to Alice.*]

FISH. The Queen will be expecting me.

FROG. Don't tell her any one laughed at you.

FISH [*drawing himself up and strutting off*]. She'll never guess it.

[*The frog goes into the house with the envelope. Alice nearly has convulsions of laughing. She takes some mushroom out of her pocket.*]

ALICE. Now, if only I knew which was which, I could grow as large as I liked. Then I could laugh as much as I pleased. I wouldn't be afraid of either of them, that I wouldn't— Oh!

[*She suddenly slides off the mushroom, peeping around at the Fish footman who returns. He knocks loudly. The Frog comes out.*]

FISH [*bowing*]. I forgot to tell you where the Duchess will play croquet with the Queen.

FROG [*bowing*]. You forgot to tell me where the Queen will play croquet with the Duchess.

FISH [*bowing*]. In the garden. The invitation tells you how to get there.

FROG [*bowing*]. In the garden. The invitation tells you how to get there.

[*They untangle their curls, the Fish goes off, the Frog into the house. Alice comes eagerly toward the house.*]

ALICE. In the garden! And the invitation tells how to get there! I've only to ask the Duchess! This time I'll keep my temper. No matter what happens, I'll keep my temper!

[*The frog comes out and stands at the door. He pays no attention to Alice, who comes timidly toward him. Finally she knocks on the door.*]

FROG. There's no sort of use in knocking. I'm on the same side of the door as you are.

ALICE. Please, then, how am I to get in?

FROG. There might be some sense in your knocking if we had the door between us. For instance, if you were inside you might knock and I could let you out, you know.

ALICE [*very polite*]. How am I to get in?

FROG. *Are* you to get in at all? That's the first question, you know.

ALICE. If you please, I'd like to ask the Duchess the way to the garden.

FROG. They're making such a noise in there, nobody'd hear you. [*volley of sneezes*] It's the pepper the cook puts in the soup. They ought to shut the window.

ALICE. But what am I to do?

FROG. Anything you like.

ALICE [*losing her temper*]. Oh, there's no sort of use in talking to you! You're perfectly idiotic.

[*She opens the door, ready to walk in. A large plate and then a pillow come skimming out. There is howling, sneezing, and other crashes. She backs away in alarm.*]

ALICE [*sneezing, violently*]. There's certainly too much pepper in that soup.

[*The cook strides out, pot of soup in one hand, and the pepper, shaking violently, in the other.*]

COOK. Too much? Too little! Taste it and see!

[*She thrusts a spoonful at Alice, who sneezes a perfect volley as she swallows it. The footman holds the door open, also sneezing, and the Duchess enters, singing over all the sneezing, and jiggling the baby furiously.*]

DUCHESS. Speak roughly to your little boy,
> And beat him when he sneezes.
He only does it to annoy
> Because he knows it teases.

[*The footman and cook join in a chorus.*]

Wow, wow, wow!

[*The cat's face outlined in lights, brightens. It is grinning from ear to ear. Alice looks at it with great curiosity.*]

ALICE [*as the song is finished*]. Please, would you tell me why your cat grins like that?

DUCHESS. It's a Cheshire cat, and that's why.

ALICE. I didn't know that Cheshire cats always grinned. I didn't know that a cat *could* grin.

DUCHESS. They all can and most of 'em do.

ALICE. I don't know any that do.

DUCHESS. You don't know much, and that's a fact.

> [*The cook shakes more pepper into the soup and every one sneezes—long series of them— The baby is the last, and the Duchess shakes it.*]

Be quiet! [*It sneezes again.*]

Pig!

ALICE. You shouldn't call your baby names.

DUCHESS. If everybody minded his own business, the world would go around a deal faster than it does.—Pig!! [*She sings, tossing the baby up and down.*]

> I speak severely to my boy,
> I beat him when he sneezes;
> For he can thoroughly enjoy
> The pepper when he pleases!

Be quiet, Pig!

> [*The cook begins throwing whatever is at hand at the Duchess and the baby. The Duchess is quite unconcerned when they hit her and the baby, still shaking it, while they all sneeze.*]

ALICE [*jumping up and down in terror*]. Oh, please mind what you're doing.

DUCHESS [*throwing the baby to her*]. Pig!—Here, you may nurse it if you like. I have to get ready to play croquet with the Queen. —In with the soup! The house will be going any moment!

COOK. I have finished with the pepper!

> [*The house does begin to move off.*]

FROG. Hold it! Hold it!

> [*He hangs on desperately till the Duchess is in, and the Cook rushes in with the soup. Then he lets go, and follows.*]

ALICE. Come back! You haven't told me the way!—It's very rude of you, indeed it is!

FROG [*popping back, and speaking as if it were a joke*]. Keep your temper.

ALICE. I declare, it's too bad. I'll—

    [*She goes to the edge of the stage, looking off.*]

They're quite out of sight, and not a word about how to get to the garden. [*The baby grunts.*] Don't grunt. That's not at all a proper way of expressing yourself. [*Another grunt, Alice turns back the blanket, looking at it anxiously.*] You have a very turned-up nose, my dear. It's much more like a snout than a real nose. And your eyes are getting very small for a baby! [*Another grunt.*] And that sounds more like a grunt than a baby's voice. Altogether I don't like the look of the thing at all.—Perhaps you were only sobbing, but I don't see any tears. [*A grunt and a squeal.*] If you're going to turn into a pig, my dear, I'll have nothing more to do with you. Mind, now! [*Another grunt, this time violent with kicking feet inside the baby clothes.*] There's no mistake. You are nothing more nor less than a pig! It's absurd to carry you any farther. [*She sets it down and it trots off.*] I'm no better off than I was before. I don't know where the garden is. I don't know where to find the Duchess to ask her.

    [*The Cheshire cat's face, in lights, appears above her, grinning from ear to ear.*]

ALICE [*after hesitating*]. Cheshire puss, would you tell me, please, which way I ought to go from here?

CAT. That depends a good deal on where you want to get to.

ALICE. I don't care much where, so long as—

CAT. Then it doesn't matter which way you go—

ALICE. —So long as I get somewhere that leads to the garden.

CAT. Oh, you're sure to do that, if you keep going long enough.

ALICE. I should think it must matter which way I go—[*The cat has disappeared.*] It's very rude of it to disappear while I was talking— Well, I must find some one else to ask. I'd like to find some one who isn't always contradicting or ordering one about. I wish the Cheshire cat had waited long enough for me to ask—

    [*The Cat reappears.*]

CAT. What do you want to ask?

ALICE. What sort of people live around here?

CAT. To the right lives a Hatter. To the left lives a March Hare. Visit either you like. They're both mad.

ALICE. I don't want to go among mad people.

CAT. You can't help it. We're all mad here.

    [*It disappears.*]

ALICE. Which shall I visit, I wonder?

CAT [*appearing*]. Do you play croquet with the Queen today?

ALICE. I should like it very much, because it's in the garden. But I haven't been invited so I don't know how to get there.

CAT. You'll see me there.

    [*It disappears.*]

ALICE. Come, now. That sounds as if I might get to the garden sometime. Let me see, which? I've seen hatters before. All they do is to make hats and sell them. I never saw a March Hare. He will be the most interesting.

CAT [*appearing in another spot*]. By the by, what became of the baby?

ALICE. It turned into a pig.

CAT. I thought it would.

    [*It disappears.*]

ALICE. I must see some one. I'm so tired of talking to myself. Perhaps as this is May, the March Hare may not be quite raving mad, not so mad as it was in March.

CAT [*appearing*]. Did you say "pig" or "fig?"

ALICE. I said "pig" and I wish you wouldn't keep appearing and vanishing so suddenly. It makes one quite giddy.

CAT. All right.

    [*It vanishes quite slowly, beginning with the outline of the head and ending with the grin.*]

ALICE. Well! I've often seen a cat without a grin, but a grin without a cat! It's the most curious thing I ever saw in my life!

Well, I think I'll try the March Hare first.

    [*As she turns to the left, the March Hare enters, studying the ground. Alice slides behind the mushroom to watch.*]

ALICE [*under her breath*]. Suppose he should be raving mad after all. I 'most wish I'd gone to see the Hatter instead.

HARE [*calling off*]. Here's a place. Clean as clean. Not a single crumb.

HATTER [*off*]. Help me with the table.

[*The Hare goes off.*]

CAT [*reappearing*]. Be sure to hold onto yourself this time.

ALICE. I will! I will! No matter what they say. Because I must find out which way to go.

[*The Hare and the Hatter bring on a table. It is partly littered with dirty cups and plates, and partly set with clean dishes.*]

HARE. Did you tell the dormouse to bring the stools?

HATTER. I couldn't find him.

HARE. He's asleep. I put him in the teapot.

HATTER. Then we'll have to bring him ourselves.

HARE. Be quick, or the tea will get cold.

[*They run very busily to bring in stools and one armchair for the head of the table.*]

HATTER. You'll have to help me with the dormouse.

[*They bring him in, sound asleep in a huge teapot, from which they extricate him much against his will. He continually resettles himself in new sleeping positions. They finally get him out and into a chair at the end of the table near the armchair, where he promptly drops his head on his breast, sound asleep again. They sit on either side of him, resting their elbows on him, and stirring their tea. Alice approaches, timidly.*]

ALICE. If you please, will you tell me—

BOTH. No room! No room!

ALICE. There's plenty of room!

[*She sits in the armchair.*]

HARE [*polite*]. Have some candy.

ALICE. I don't see any.

HARE. There isn't any.

ALICE [*angry*]. Then it wasn't very civil of you to offer it.

HARE. It wasn't very civil of you to sit down here without being invited.

ALICE [*polite with difficulty*]. I didn't know it was your table. It's laid for a great many more than three.

[*They stare at her, saying nothing, then drink tea.*]

If you please, will you tell me—

HATTER. Shall we tell her?

ALICE. But you don't know what I might ask.

HARE. It doesn't matter what it is.

HATTER. We won't tell you anything unless you mind your manners.

HARE [*nudging the Hatter*]. Ask her a riddle.

HATTER. [*to Alice*]. Why is a raven like a writing desk?

ALICE [*delighted*]. I think I can guess that one!

[*They look at each other, set down their teacups, look at each other again.*]

HATTER. Do you mean you think you can find out the answer to it?

ALICE. Exactly so.

HATTER. Then you should say what you mean.

ALICE. I do. At least, I mean what I say. That's the same thing, you know.

HATTER. Not the same thing a bit. You might just as well say I see what I eat is the same as I eat what I see.

HARE. You might just as well say that I like what I get is the same as I get what I like.

DORMOUSE [*sleepily, half sitting up*]. You might just as well say that I breathe when I sleep is the same as I sleep when I breathe.

HATTER [*as others push him into a cushion again*]. Have you guessed the riddle yet?

ALICE. Why is a raven like a writing desk? No. I give up. What's the answer?

HATTER. I haven't the slightest idea.

HARE. Nor I. [*Low, to Hatter*] Now watch her.

ALICE. Well!! [*controlling herself*] I should think you might find something better to do with your time than asking riddles that haven't any answers.

HARE [*taking out his watch*]. There's nothing else to do with our time but have tea. It's always six o'clock here.

ALICE. Is that the reason so many tea things are put out?

HARE. Yes, that's it. It's always tea time, and we've no time to wash the things between whiles.

ALICE. Then you keep moving 'round, I suppose?

HATTER. Exactly so. As the things get used up. I want a clean cup now. [*calling*] All move, one place!

HARE. Wake up the dormouse.

[*They punch him, etc.*]

HATTER. Punching doesn't do any good. Pour hot tea on his nose.

[*The dormouse sits up with a little squeal.*]

DORMOUSE. I always sleep at six o'clock. Is it past that?

HARE [*shaking the watch and putting it to his ear*]. It *never* is since the Hatter put hot tea in the works.

HATTER. Try some butter.

HARE [*opening it with enthusiasm*]. Hold it!

ALICE [*anxiously*]. I'm afraid butter won't suit the works.

HATTER. It's the best butter.

ALICE. That doesn't make any difference.

HARE. Did you ever *try* putting butter in the works of a watch?

ALICE. No, but I think—

HARE. Then you shouldn't talk.

[*They put their heads on one side and watch her. She keeps cool. Hatter takes butter on the bread-knife and spreads it on the works of the watch.*]

ALICE. You shouldn't do that! Won't you get crumbs in the wheels?

HARE. Do you know *why* we do it?

ALICE. No. Why?

HATTER. To make little girls ask questions.

[*They watch her.*]

ALICE. I declare—[*controls herself*] It's a very curious way to treat a watch, you see.

HATTER [*continuing with the watch*]. Take some more tea.

ALICE. I haven't had *any* yet, so I can't take more.

HATTER. You mean you can't take less. It's very easy to take more than nothing.

[*They cock their heads and watch her. The Hare shakes the watch, listens to it, and puts it down, discouraged.*]

HARE. It's no use. It's still six o'clock. He won't wake up. We'll have to move him.

[*They have difficulties with the dormouse again. When they get him on his feet he slithers to the floor. When they get him up, he leans on one and then the other of them, etc. Finally one holds him while the other pushes a chair against him. He flops to one side and the other, Alice and the Hare saving him. The Hatter pushes him up to the new place at the table. They all move to a clean place but Alice, who is left with the Hare's.*]

ALICE. This isn't very tidy.

HARE. What's good enough for me is good enough for you.

ALICE. It was clean when you moved to it.

HATTER. The rule is: Move down three places.

ALICE. But now that there are four of us—

HATTER. If you can't be civil, you'd better wait till you're invited.

[*They watch her. She finally sits down, after a struggle with herself.*]

ALICE [*pleasantly*]. It was very nice of you to take me in, I'm sure.

HARE. I vote the young lady recites a poem.

ALICE [*alarmed*]. I'm afraid I wouldn't get it quite right.

HATTER. You never get anything right.

HARE. Recite: Twinkle, twinkle little star,
            How I wonder what you are—

DORMOUSE [*singing*]. Twinkle, twinkle—

HARE. Punch him.

HATTER [*doing it, speaking to Alice*]. Begin.

DORMOUSE [*singing*]. Twinkle, twinkle, twinkle, twinkle—

HATTER. You pinch him. He doesn't mind me.

[*Hare does so. Dormouse stops singing.*]

HATTER. Now then. Recite.

ALICE. Twinkle, twinkle, little bat,
    How I wonder what you're at—
No, I'm afraid that's not quite right.

HARE. There's nothing right about it.

DORMOUSE [*singing*]. Twinkle, twinkle, twinkle—

HARE. Put him in the teapot again.

> [*Dormouse continues to sing, as they struggle to do so. As he sings the lights begin to wink to the rhythm of his singing. The struggle grows wilder, his singing louder and faster, and the lights flicker faster and faster (lobsterscope). Through it Alice shouts.*]

ALICE. If you please, how can I get into the garden?

HARE [*shouting*]. Look for the tree!

ALICE [*shouting*]. What tree? Dear me! Here's a tree with a door in it! I think I may as well go in at once.

> [*The light grows gradually quiet again, as the dormouse's song grows slower and fainter. When it is quite bright and still, the rabbit hole is back again and Alice is standing by the table.*]

ALICE [*clapping her hands*]. Here's the glass table! And here's the key! I'll manage better this time.

> [*She takes the key and sits by the little door.*]

I'm glad I brought the mushroom with me. I'll just nibble ever so little till I feel the way I'm going— Up! Now this! Yes, I feel myself shutting ever such a little bit!—I'll keep a little of this and a little of that till I'm just the right size. And *then!* I'll go into the beautiful garden.

> [*She is nibbling diligently and cautiously as the curtains close.*]

In Act II, which is, of course, in the garden, it is revealed to Alice by the Cheshire cat who continues to reappear occasionally (of course, in terms that children can understand) that the reason she finds it so hard to keep her temper is that she feels that the creatures look down on her, and when she gets this feeling she has either to cry or get angry. She goes through the act struggling against this sense of inferiority under continual fresh provocation, trying to assert herself enough to make some one tell her which path leads out to the sky. The King and the Queens pick her up on her language. For example: *Alice,* "I see nobody on the road." *King,* "I only wish I had such eyes as that! To be able to see nobody! And at such a distance, too." Tweedledum and Tweedledee contradict her steadily. "I know what you're thinking about and *it isn't so!*" They also deride her because she can't go on with certain stanzas of "The Walrus and the Carpenter," which they start, and they grow so rapid in the dance they invite her to join that she has to give up. The Mock Turtle and the Gryphon laugh at her mercilessly because she can't tell the meaning of words and sentences in "Jabberwocky," or act out the story properly. And most disheartening of all, she has to run as fast as her legs will carry her just to stay where she is. Nevertheless, she gradually finds out that if she just thinks things out herself and doesn't let their laughter bother her, she gets along better, and when she is summoned to the trial, she makes up her mind that she will follow that rule there.

In Act III, which is also arranged in the garden, she carries out this plan more and more successfully. All the creatures she has met are there, and instead of letting them make her feel good-for-nothing, therefore confusing her, she works things out in her own mind, and quietly announces the result. For example, when the King announces a rule against her, she says, "That's not a regular rule. You invented it just now." And to the King's "It's the oldest rule in the book," she answers triumphantly, "Then it ought to be number one," at which the King turns pale and shuts the book hastily. In the end, when the Queen shouts, "Off with her head," and the others cheer, she is mistress of the situation entirely. "You can't have my head cut off. You're nothing but a pack of cards!" At this there is general scurrying off. Alice looks around in triumph, and there behind her is the opening of the rabbit hole, with the blue sky above it. She runs laughing up and out, snatching up her kitten which is waiting for her.

I. ALICE *as material for a children's play.*
  A. A famous story which is widely read and enjoyed.
  B. Has already been dramatized many times, but previous versions not entirely satisfactory because they:
      1. Have no continuous thread of story, but rather, a series of more or less unrelated incidents.
      2. Avoid some of the happenings which appeal most to children (such as growing taller and shorter).
      3. Depend too much on clever dialogue and not enough on action.
      4. Do not arouse interest in seeing any certain thing happen. Do not provide "something to love, something to hate, something to root for."
      5. Have too many breaks in changes of scene.
  C. If the author has overcome these faults, a play based on these stories should be successful.

II. *The dramatic line.*
  This version has a straight dramatic line of story, made possible by injecting into the nonsense the least possible amount of sense. This is necessary for children if their interest is to be held. It is achieved in the following way:
  In Act I Alice's whole idea is to get back home. She is unable to make even a start until the very end of the act because of her disposition.
  In Act II she feels that the creatures all look down on her and this makes her cry or get angry. She is thus powerless to make any progress.
  In Act III she regains confidence in herself and succeeds. The only justification for putting sense into *Alice in Wonderland* is that a line of story is necessary for a successful

children's play. That is reason enough, so long as it does not spoil the atmosphere.

III. *The plot of Act I.*
   A. Alice falls into the rabbit hole and wants to get out.
   B. Her way lies through the garden but she cannot get through the door.
   C. The other characters refuse to help her because of her temper.
   D. At last she is able to keep her temper long enough to make herself the right size by nibbling the mushroom, and at the end of the act she is ready to go into the garden.

   This carries the audience along with no drop in the story.

IV. *The choice of incidents in Act I.*
   A. Opening scene in rabbit hole, with Alice falling in. Has especial interest.
   B. Growing and shrinking.
   C. Caterpillar scene.
   D. Frog Footman, Duchess, Pig Baby.
   E. Cheshire Cat.
   F. Mad Tea Party

   Much has been omitted, but these are the scenes the children would be disappointed not to see.

   (Note the cover scene: Alice must rush off to get long-necked mask on. The author takes this opportunity to make clear the fact that the Caterpillar will not tell Alice about the garden if she doesn't mind her manners; also, that if she finds the fan the Rabbit lost, she will shrink and shrink unless she is told to throw it down. Note, too, that when she runs off to remove the mask, she has plenty of time, for a puppet takes her place when she is tiny.)

V. *Exposition*
   The audience must be given the information necessary to understand all that happens, or the incidents will not be funny.

A. The Rabbit closes the door to the garden at first so that the audience will know where it is. This is so natural that no one would think of the author's purpose in having him do it.

B. The author has the Rabbit say, "How doth the little busy bee," correctly, so that when, a little later, Alice says it incorrectly, the children, knowing what it should be, will think her mistakes humorous.

(Note that she says it very soon after the Rabbit does, for exposition should be given near the place where it is needed.)

C. "Now *your* way is through the garden." The audience now knows that Alice must get into the garden before she can go back. This starts the line of incidents.

D. "You'll have to be the right size to get through the door." He thus prepares for the growing and shrinking.

E. The Footman says, "The house will come along any minute." When the house comes sliding in a few minutes later, the children will understand at once what it is.

VI. *Suspense.*

A. Almost at the beginning Alice is for some seconds falling down the hole. Those in the audience who have read the book will know that it is Alice, but there will be wonder as to what will happen when she arrives, and what effect her coming will have on the Rabbit.

B. There is constant wonder as to what will happen to Alice's size each time she eats anything.

C. As Alice is trying all the doors, the audience knows which is the right one and is far more interested, therefore, to see whether Alice will find it.

D. Will the Caterpillar tell her the way to the garden? Will he tell her to throw down the fan?

E. Will Alice keep her temper long enough to find out anything?

F. Will the Fish and the Frog catch Alice on the other side of the mushroom?

    G. What will the garden be like? This looks ahead to the second act.

VII. *Characters.*

    All of the characters are from the book, but there are fewer. They are a little more sensible than in the book because of watching Alice's temper. The Caterpillar becomes much more of a personality, and therefore more interesting. He was rude in the book, but she has supplied a reason for his rudeness. Note that the author has picked out one of the funniest or most dramatic traits of a character and heightened it.

VIII. *Dialogue.*

    A. Almost all dialogue is from one or the other of the books.

    B. In many cases it is taken from other places in the book, sometimes from other characters.

    C. When dialogue is added, it is so in key with the dialogue of the story that one notices no difference.

    D. A nice bit of dialogue: Alice says, "I don't mean to be (rude). It just comes out." The Caterpillar answers, "It has to be in before it can come out."

    E. Author wisely resists temptation to use a great amount of Lewis Carroll's inimitable dialogue, so delightful to read, so unwise in a children's play because not associated with action.

IX. *Action.* Much that is interesting, as:

    A. Alice falling down the rabbit hole. One can almost see her falling.

    B. Trying in every way to get through the door to the garden.

    C. Sitting on her heels to drink the contents of the bottle. It gives the impression of growing as she rises.

    D. Alice turns her back to the Caterpillar in anger. While she is turned, the Caterpillar points to the sides of the mushroom as he tells her that one side will make her taller, the other shorter.

E. Alice hiding from the two Footmen and being chased by them.

F. Bringing the Dormouse in in the teapot.

G. Actually putting the butter in the watch with the knife. Much funnier than telling about it.

After careful analysis of the dramatization, we come to the conclusion that here is a well-written play for children. It conforms to the technical requirements of good playwriting, and shows understanding of the child's viewpoint.

1. It has a good thread of story leading to a strong climax. The story is never dropped for a moment.

2. The choice of incidents has been made according to a child's interests.

3. There is never more than a minute at a time without large and definite physical action.

4. There is always a strong interest in what will happen to Alice from act to act.

5. There are only two breaks in the scene, most of the changes of setting being such as can be made without the curtain.

6. The elaborateness of *Alice in Wonderland* is to be expected from the story. With the text of this version are directions for staging it as simply as possible.

Above all other points in its favor is the fact that Mrs. Chorpenning has succeeded in retaining in her play the essence of the two Lewis Carroll stories. Her contribution lies in having made from the splendid nonsense a play with a dramatic line of story which gives every incident a greater interest for the youthful audiences who see it.

CHAPTER VI

WE FIND THE RIGHT PLAY

> THIS AFTERNOON'S PLAY
> IS FOR CHILDREN
> OVER EIGHT YEARS
> NO OTHERS ADMITTED

IF A CHILDREN'S THEATRE could hang a sign like this in its foyer, it would have taken a significant step forward. And if it lived up to all the advantages gained by limiting the age of its audiences and doing two or three separate series of plays, something very remarkable might come of it.

The wide range in the ages of children's theatre audiences offers one of the greatest problems in the choosing of plays. What is comprehensible to the five-year-old is infantile to the child of eleven. What brings a thrill to the latter terrifies the first-grader. To choose for both at once means compromise in the play and in its direction. The Giant in *Jack and the Beanstalk* must be made less terrible, more humorous; the little prince must be treated less roughly in *The Prince and the Pauper*. Suspense, which is meat and drink to the boy of ten, is often unbearable to the little girl of six.

How is a director to choose for all children when the tiny

boy and girl are in a realistic period, so engrossed in finding their way around the here and now that fairy godmothers and frog princes and leprechauns are incomprehensible; while the six-, seven-, and eight-year-olds are scorning the familiar and reaching out for the remote, the imaginative; and the older children have returned to realism, and are hungry for heroes who have exciting adventures.

AGE LEVELS

The ideal theatre for young people will have no fewer than three series of plays: the first for boys and girls from six to nine; the second, up to twelve; and the last for high-school age. A series for tiny children is unnecessary, for they do not need a theatre. Their own dramatic play is entirely satisfying, and, given wise parents and teachers to play with them, nurturing and encouraging their natural dramatic impulse, they will grow into understanding and appreciative audiences when they are older.

THE IMAGINATIVE PERIOD

Grown-ups take greatest pleasure in providing a theatre for children of the imaginative period because the old fairy-tales offer such charming material for plays. Magic mirrors and dwarfs, little men who can spin straw into gold, and god-mothers who turn pumpkins into coaches are so fascinating to the child of six, seven, and eight that adults sometimes over-look the fact that older children have reached another stage in their interests and are no longer satisfied with fairy-tales. Charming, therefore, as are *Cinderella, Aladdin,* and *Rumpel-stiltskin,* such plays should not predominate in a season's program for a general children's audience.

HALF PAST THIRTEEN

The Play House, Cleveland, Ohio.

THE HEROIC PERIOD

If one asks any boy of ten or eleven what kind of play he likes best, he will almost invariably answer, "Something exciting!" Plot is what he cares about, with plenty of action and suspense. He is thrilled by heroes who do daring deeds and have hairbreadth escapes. He loves broad humor, especially at the expense of the bully or coward. A long play with many scenes which give an illusion of reality satisfies him best. And in the end the hero must triumph and the wrongdoer must be punished—and he likes to *see* him punished! A girl of nine, ten, or eleven asks for much the same sort of thing enjoyed by the boy. But though she, too, likes realism, she is satisfied with less excitement, and she prefers a heroine to a hero. Imaginative plays, and some of those popular with older children, often please her as much as productions for her own age.

THE ROMANTIC PERIOD

Few theatres for young people offer plays for boys and girls of high-school age. Often these students act in children's theatres, sometimes are capable backstage workers. But without doubt there is a place for high-school plays in the ideal theatre for young people, where the twelve- to sixteen-year-olds may see dramas, written perhaps for adults, which delight and satisfy the young adolescent. Here the adventurous would be mingled with the romantic, the plays having less of realism and more of the idealistic than in the former period.

Since a different series of plays for various age levels is impractical without unusual facilities and great audiences, a children's theatre must do one of three things: choose plays for the age level which seems most to need them, however unsuitable they may be for the other children; vary the season's productions, alternating those for young children with those specially appealing to junior high-school age; or choose only plays of wide appeal.

ENVIRONMENT

Environment is a less important consideration than age in the choosing of plays for young audiences. The degree of sophistication becomes increasingly, almost alarmingly greater each year, due in large part, no doubt, to the moving picture and the radio. It is evident among the poor children as well as in those in better circumstances, since the influence of these two agencies is well-nigh universal.

A thin veneer this sophistication appears to be, though, when one observes an audience of children during an exciting play! Witness the breathless hush as they watch to see whether Eleanor Lytell's mother (in *The Indian Captive*) will recognize her in her Indian dress or go away and leave her a captive forever; the shouts of laughter as Friar Tuck stuffs Guy of Gisbourne into a chest and sits on it to give Robin Hood a chance to escape; the wild applause when the pirates are vanquished in *Treasure Island!*

Subtlety in plays requires not only cultural background and sophistication, but also unusual intelligence on the part of a child. Only a picked audience, therefore, can be counted on to appreciate fully such plays as Milne's *Make-Believe,* Le Gallienne's or Gerstenberg's *Alice in Wonderland,* or de la Mare's *Crossings.* Symbolism, too, is unchildlike, requiring experience and maturity for real understanding. Some symbolic stories and plays, such as *The Selfish Giant* and *The Blue Bird* are enjoyed by young people, but it is because of their story interest rather than their symbolism. Pageants representing

Faith, Peace, Democracy, and other great abstractions are seldom really impressive to child audiences.

Beauty in the play itself, and in its setting and costumes, is highly desirable for children who live amid ugly surroundings. The play should be an escape for them, an escape from sordidness, from experiences no child ought to have. For a thrilling hour and a half they may live in a delightful world where life is absorbing and colorful, and vicarious adventures satisfy their longing for excitement. It may be a dreary drop to go back to real living, but they carry something lovely with them, and the remembrance brings enrichment to their drab little lives. So let plays for the underprivileged child never fail to bring something of beauty into lives which are hungry for it whether they realize it or not.

PLAYS FOR OCCASIONS

The occasion for which a play is to be chosen often limits the director to a pathetically small amount of material. Is it for a holiday? Then one tries to find a play which suits the spirit if not the subject-matter of the day. Is it for a dignified occasion such as the exercises of the eighth grade graduating class? Or a gay "Frolics" program which must be pure entertainment—and melodrama at that? The season, the mood of the audience, the importance and size of the occasion will all condition the choice. And a wise choice is a big step toward success.

CHOOSING A CHILDREN'S THEATRE PLAY

The selection of a children's theatre play is a far more momentous undertaking than a school play which children are giving for their parents. For instead of indulgent relatives and friends who come to see their children perform, the audience is to be made up of boys and girls who come to be entertained. The occasion is ordinarily a big one, with paid admission, and consequently the expectation of a good show. If the play does not hold their interest, you may be sure that when the next production is given they will be found not at the play but in some movie audience.

The familiar has a strong appeal to children, and so they flock to see their favorite story come to life. *Snow White and the Seven Dwarfs,* which fascinated them at seven years, draws them to the theatre at eleven; and seeing it through the medium of drama, they recapture its first thrill. *Heidi* is a title which can be counted on to fill a house. So is *Hans Brinker, Rip Van Winkle, Tom Sawyer, The Secret Garden.* That is why a children's theatre is wise to open its doors as well as to open each season with a dramatization of a favorite story. Tickets must be sold in large numbers if a theatre is to succeed, and the title of a familiar and greatly loved book is the surest means of attracting both children and their parents.

In spite of the drawing power of familiar titles, however, no good children's theatre is content to offer its audiences continual dramatizations. The new, the fresh, the unusual must have their place in every season if children are to grow in appreciation and outlook. And indeed it has been proved again and again that though a new or unknown play fails to attract the crowds which come when such a title as *Pinocchio* is announced, it has quite as much chance of pleasing those who do come. Some of the most enthusiastic reactions come at the performances of new plays, and certain it is that a children's theatre has a responsibility to bring to its youthful audiences new ideas, stimulating productions, and an introduction to varied forms of art.

THE DRAMA OF IDEAS

Is there a place for the drama of ideas in the children's theatre? Can children be aroused to think about vital issues like race prejudice, peace, and democracy through plays? Should they be taught through drama?

Madame de Genlis in the eighteenth century attempted to teach morality through the little comedies in her *Théâtre d'Éducation*. As tutor of the royal children, she taught them facts concerning notable explorations by means of dramatizations performed in the garden, but it was in her comedies acted by the children that she endeavored to teach more important matters. The children of the Soviet Union are taught the ideals of a socialist republic in the children's theatre. They are shown the evils of capitalism, the dignity of labor, the senselessness of race prejudice.

American plays of this class are yet to be written, if indeed they ever will be forthcoming. Certainly the play of ideas should have its place in the children's theatre if the ideas set forth are not merely adult propaganda, but such as are applicable to the child's realm of interest. For instance, many of the implications in world peace which mean so much to adults leave a child cold because of his lack of experience. But a play which helps to build friendliness with one's neighbors at home and abroad, which exposes war and exemplifies tolerance, might conceivably have an influence on boys and girls if the plot and the characters of the play were absorbingly interesting. In other words, the preachment must be buried within a thoroughly entertaining show. The Russian theatre, intent on "activizing" its audience by the teachings in its plays, shrewdly sees to it that they are first of all good theatre.

If and when the time comes that such plays are in the market—not merely the pageants already available, which treat certain big ideas in a symbolic way, but real plays—examine them with greatest care, and if they are also good entertainment, consider yourself fortunate if you can bring them to the children.

All this is not to say that the plays to be had now are lacking in ideas. Great truths are woven into the fabric of all fine stories, and if we at present lack plays in which important modern questions are discussed, we nevertheless bring children far more than mere amusement when we present plays which help them to a better understanding of people, a fairer standard of values, a more intelligent sense of justice.

ETHICAL STANDARDS

Because ethical standards change greatly even from one generation to another, many of the old tales do not fit into present day ideas. Take *Hansel and Gretel,* for instance, one of the most popular of fairy-tales. Even though the witch is evil, Gretel by modern standards should not win our sympathy by pushing her into the oven. Nor should Robin Hood rob the rich even to give money to the unfortunate; nor the rogues in *The Emperor's New Clothes* succeed by deceit.

All three of these stories are great ones. Do their morals have an unfortunate influence on the children who read them or see them played? Are we justified in choosing plays which apparently place the stamp of approval on deeds which would never be condoned to-day?

The answer in most instances has been a compromise. True, not much can be done about Gretel's action. There it is! And from the children's standpoint it is entirely justifiable. The witch deserved such a fate, and self-preservation demanded that Gretel put an end to her. Even though a modern author would have found another way out, it is doubtful if the story has ever done children any harm.

As for Robin Hood, an understanding of the times in which he lived does much to explain the difference between his deeds and what would be classed to-day as nothing short of hold-ups. But modern stories and plays stress them lightly, telling much more of the valiant and chivalrous actions for which he is beloved.

Charlotte Chorpenning's *The Emperor's New Clothes* handles beautifully the ethical side of that delightful Andersen tale. Instead of professional cheats, the two rogues are gay young adventurers, full of the zest of living. The villain in the play is Han, the minister of the royal robes, who cheats the weavers and keeps the Emperor's gold for himself. A motive is thus supplied for the rogues' scheme to weave cloth for his robes—they will expose Han's treachery. And when their purpose is accomplished, they do not make off with the gold and jewels but scatter them to the poor weavers before they set out gaily in search of their next adventure!

IMPORTANCE OF PLOT

If you ask a group of children what they like best in a play they will almost inevitably answer, "The story!" Without asking, you have only to observe an audience of children to find this out for yourself. Granted that this is true, what kind of a story is most popular? A long and careful study of child audiences made up of all ages has led to the following conclusions concerning the plot.

1. It must be generally understood. At the very start, then, the theatre is confronted with the question, How can one possibly choose a play with a plot simple enough for young children, yet which still interests boys and girls of junior high-school age? The answer is, One cannot. This is why the teacher or chairman or director sometimes decides on the age she cares most to interest and lets the others understand what they can, or get some other sort of satisfaction from the productions. Certain plays for young children will be so quaint and humorous that the older children will enjoy them for these qualities even if the plot seems childish. Or—and this is strongly to be counted on—in the case of familiar stories they recapture some of the delight they felt when they first heard the story. If plays for young children are presented too often, however, the older children will simply stay away from the theatre.

On the other hand, tiny children may have a most unhappy time at plays which are too old for them. Unless there is enough color and action to keep them amused, they cause a real audience problem, disturbing others and making hearing difficult. "What is that man looking at out of the window?" "Why did he say that?" "I don't *like* that bad man and I want to go home!!" Occasionally a wail from a frightened child proves only too surely that this play is not a good choice for little children.

No real solution to this problem is possible when all ages see the same play. But if a director believes that it is the older boys and girls who need the theatre most, she will choose her plays for them and discourage attendance on the part of children too young to understand. Free then to choose and direct for children of eight and above, she will be able to interest them more intensely, wide though the range is from eight to fourteen. Mothers will bring tiny children less often, and the audience will not be disturbed by the restlessness which naturally follows when they cannot understand the story.

2. The plot must start out at once and involve plenty of action. The small boy who bounced up and down on his seat when things got exciting, announcing to the world in general, "I *like* that! I like a play where things happen!" only expressed what is felt universally by children. Just as they skip over the description at the beginning of a story, so do they want the author to omit the exposition and get the play going at once. In choosing a play it is well to note this carefully. There should be something which is interesting to see at the first. Because the younger part of the audience is slow in interpreting the scene, pantomime is exceptionally good. In *Seven Little Rebels* the curtains open on a large cheerful kitchen. Not a soul is stirring, but seated by the table, head resting on her hand, is the colored cook, Lizetta, asleep. Into this peaceful scene come two little boys teasing a dog with a rubber rat. When they see the cook asleep an idea occurs to them. They tiptoe over to the table, crawl under it with the dog and place the rat close to Lizetta's toe. They are just about to tickle her toe when they hear Letta, the cook's little girl, approaching. Subsiding under the table, they wait while Letta crosses with a tray of silver. As she passes the table, however, she steps on the rat, which lets out a large squeak. Paralyzed, she stands rigid, emptying all of the silver on to the floor. Her mother awakens, sees the rat, and clambers up on the chair, shrieking, while the boys roll out, shouting, "Lizetta's askeered of a rubber rat!" and then make a bee line for the door as she catches up a rolling-pin and chases them out. It is a lively

and a jolly beginning for a play, with few words and plenty of action.

If those who choose plays for child audiences will visualize as they read, they will run less risk of making an unfortunate choice. A large part of the story should be told in action, incidents being shown instead of talked about. This is imperative for little children, and it is highly desirable for boys and girls of all ages.

3. The play should build steadily and rapidly to the climax and then stop. Children will be interested in elaborate episodes which complicate the plot, but they are left confused at the end, with no pattern and no clear idea as to what the story was about. A fine simplicity and directness are significant attributes of novels like *Heidi, Hans Brinker,* and *Little Women,* whose popularity has persisted through the years. This same simplicity is characteristic of fine plays for children.

Many a director has despaired over the final curtain of a play which was otherwise very satisfactory. Either it was inconclusive, leaving the audience puzzled and wondering, or it was weak and dragged out. In choosing a play it is well to study the last five minutes very carefully as one of the factors in your decision. For the mood in which the audience leaves the theatre is no small indication of the success of the play. It need not end with "Hurrah!" or "Long live the King!" But the curtain lines, following close on the heels of the climax, should be definite, conclusive, and satisfying.

SUSPENSE

4. The moments when a child audience is holding its breath, wondering what the dwarfs will do when they discover Snow White dead, or whether the Giant will come upon Jack hidden in the oven—such moments are fraught with a silence so deep

that the very grown-up adult in the audience who knows quite well how it is coming out finds himself holding his breath, too. From seven on, children love these moments more, perhaps, than any other part of the play. Look for suspense when you read a play, and be assured that it is needed. Expectancy should carry over from one act to the next, too, and a play should ever point ahead, leaving the outcome uncertain up to the very end.

The reason that children ask again and again for a particular story is that it stirs their emotions, and no play could possibly be a success if it failed to do this. Sympathy, indignation, fear, joy, admiration, and many other emotions are awakened by good plays. If they are *worthily* aroused—and this is vastly important—the child grows in fine sensitivity and understanding. If emotions are stirred by cheap sentimentality, by false standards, or coarse humor, the harm may be great. No one has a right to arouse a child's emotions unworthily. It is worse than waste, it is sinful.

5. Comedy woven into a serious play brings needed relaxation to children, heightening their enjoyment and giving them a better sense of proportion. Examine a play well to see whether it has comedy relief. If the plot provides no comedy, some of the characters should, for not only do children like it but it has a very salutary effect on their nerves.

A play which is entirely comedy, however, is less effective with children than a serious play with a few comedy scenes. A performance of the three artisan scenes from *A Midsummer Night's Dream* offers so much comedy that children are likely to tire of it. An occasional laugh in a serious plot is greatly preferred by them.

ROMANCE

6. Let the play chairman avoid romance in choosing plays for children if she does not want her audience to scoff! The most inoffensive little love scene will seem silly to children, and many a cast has been amazed at the response evoked by a touch of romance. Why this continues to be true in spite of constant attendance at adult moving pictures is inexplicable. The surest way short of an accident to snap the illusion of a scene is to introduce love-making. Little children are not interested, from eight to eleven they scorn it, from eleven to fifteen they are self-conscious at seeing it.

All this is not to say that the Sleeping Beauty cannot marry the prince and live happily ever after. That is a satisfying conclusion. Characters may talk about love if it is kept on a dignified plane, but let a man and girl embrace, and regardless of how well it is done, a grin will go over the audience.

7. Poetic justice should characterize the ending of children's plays unless the author's object is to arouse his audience to right some wrong or to pity the unfortunate. Children have a very strong sense of justice, and a play to be satisfying to them must distribute rewards and punishments according to just deserts. Adult plays do not, of course, adhere to any such requirement, though the great majority of adult audiences prefer a happy ending. Many authors attempt to picture life as it is—and life too often is unjust.

Are we giving our children a wrong picture of life, then, if we choose plays which are characterized by an ideal justice? If so, why not have plays which will prepare them for what they will meet? Even discounting the innumerable instances when rewards are not material but spiritual, when just punishments are not seen by the world, there are real injustices on every hand. Why not give our children realism so that they will not have to be disillusioned later?

The reasons why we should not do so are very sound. In the first place, the child needs to know first what right standards of justice are before he is ready to judge right and wrong actions. If he is plunged into a situation where the worthy man is disgraced and the crook is accepted by society, he is confused. He is not ready for such injustices.

It is not necessary that a child face all the hard realities of life. Childhood is a time to grow strong in understanding, in right attitudes and appreciations, in sense of values, so that he may be better able to meet disillusionment when it comes. And to this end he should be exposed to what is fine, what is happy, what is ideal.

"We do not need too many happy endings to lull the spectator into an attitude of 'well, everything came out all right without my help,' " wrote a children's theatre director. "Every play must give an impulse to the development of the children's initiative."

Such a sentiment is thoroughly sound if the end of the play is inspiring rather than discouraging. After all, the important thing is that the sympathy is rightly placed. A sugar and water play in which there was no villain would give no opportunity of arousing sympathy for what was fine and distaste for what was wrong.

THE CHARACTERS

Character, while secondary to plot in the play we are choosing for children, is nevertheless a major interest. Indeed, such a play as *The Wizard of Oz* delights children not at all for its plot, which is a flimsy thing, but wholly because of its grotesque characters.

As in stories, the characters must be broad and obvious for the younger children, with little subtlety or complexity. They are what they appear to be, or if they are not it is very easy to see through them. Bold, courageous heroes are admired, and lovely, plucky heroines. Children like a modern kind of heroine who can do whatever her brother can, who can think of a way out of every difficulty. They like odd, comic characters and villains who *are* villains. And they want to see these stage villains outwitted by the hero or heroine and thoroughly punished.

Paper-doll characters with only one side and no red blood, who are only puppets to make the plot move, are of little consequence to children. Boys and girls want their characters to be real people such as they know in their own lives, only that they expect them to be more interesting!

It seems to make small difference to them whether or not the characters in a play include children. *Robin Hood,* one of the most popular children's theatre plays, has no child characters, nor has *Cinderella, The Merchant Gentleman,* and many others. *Treasure Island* has one youth, *The Emperor's New Clothes,* one little girl. Popularity seems not to depend on children in the story, though the majority of plays for young people do have child characters.

DIALOGUE

Brief speeches are characteristic of a play that youthful audiences enjoy, and playwrights who know children avoid verboseness. Again and again is the director forced to cut lengthy dialogue which makes the play stand still and the audience squirm. Children are right in demanding short speeches. People do talk that way. Though the adult may take delight

CINDERELLA

Clare Tree Major
presentation,
Children's Theatre
of New York

in Shakespeare's poetic lines or the lovely rhythm of the Irish plays, the child audience must be educated to them. The story lives for them far more truly if it is told graphically, with short, natural, and pointed dialogue.

This demand for short speeches might indicate pantomime as a popular form of entertainment. As a matter of fact, it is much less popular with children than plays with dialogue. After a season which included a lovely ballet of *Ali Baba and the Forty Thieves,* many children, when asked in school to write their reactions, said, "It was too silent." (It had musical accompaniment, of course.) A few even wrote, "There wasn't much action." (This in spite of the fact that it was all action!) While many wrote, "I like a play with talking better," a minority chose it as their favorite play of the season, "because it was so different," "because it was so beautiful," "because putting this familiar story on the stage with beautiful setting and lighting was a fine idea, and making it into a pantomimical dance was an even better idea."

Comedy in lines must be very broad if the whole child audience is to appreciate it. Comedy in action is much more effective. Letta, the little colored girl in *Seven Little Rebels,* sidling up to Miss Proudfoot with the garter snake around her neck scarcely needs lines, for her innocent demeanor and Miss Proudfoot's fright tell all that is needed to make the audience shout with laughter.

When searching for a play, one need not read far to know whether the dialogue is well-written or uninspired. Even the most realistic of modern plays should have dialogue which is both distinctive and characteristic of the people. The drab little one-act play, *The Fifteenth Candle,* by Rachel Field, has dialogue so beautifully written that every terse speech has implications of much emotional value.

The adult reading a play may have a delightful time chuckling over whimsical bits and clever satire. A director may produce such a play, enjoying her clever cast and anticipating the laughs of the audience. What a disappointment when speech after speech, so carefully pointed, fails to cause so much as a smile! One such experience with, perhaps, Milne's clever *Toad of Toad Hall* or *Make-Believe,* and a director will realize that much as she delights in working with such plays, she must save them for a select audience, appealing to the crowd with such broad comedy as, say, *The Merchant Gentleman* affords.

Though the number of children's plays is not as yet great enough so that the producing group has a wide choice, still both bulk and quality are rapidly improving, so that it will soon be possible to present for children only plays that meet high standards.

SETTINGS

The delighted "oh-h!" that sometimes breathes through a child audience when the curtains open on the first act leads the director to wish for a play which has a lovely, or at least an interesting opening scene. A good designer can, of course, create attractive settings for almost any play. But if the script calls for an untidy room or a dingy garret, a pleasing setting would be entirely out of keeping. The deck of a ship, a quaint picture-book cottage, an English railway carriage with swaying motion and far-off train whistle are all interesting settings for the first act of a play.

Variety in scenes is desirable, too. According to children who are accustomed to the many changes of scene in motion pictures, the more sets there are, the better. And since the number of settings in a play must be very limited, there is the more need of freshness and variety.

PRACTICAL CONSIDERATIONS

If it were not for practical considerations, a child's play might have eight or ten settings and it would please the audience accordingly. But costs, space, amount of work to build and run the show, as well as the important time element, limit the play reader in choice.

The size of the stage and auditorium has a direct bearing on the choice of material, elaborate plays with large casts being impossible on the small stage, intimate plays depending on dialogue being a poor choice for a large auditorium.

The amount and type of equipment, too, limit the kind of plays which can be used. *Peter Pan,* with its four heavy sets (excluding the island scene), its large cast, and its very difficult flying mechanism; and *The Blue Bird* with its elaborate and difficult scenery and lighting effects, are two of the plays which should never be chosen until a children's theatre has a large and finely equipped stage and a highly efficient production department.

Costumes, too, are a major item in the choice of plays, especially if there must be a large number of elaborate ones. Will the production suffer if cheap materials are used? Can the costumes be made of inexpensive cloth and painted or dyed? If so, are there artists available who will supervise the work?

ROYALTIES

A very important consideration in choosing a play is the royalty. Almost every really good play written by a modern author requires the payment of a certain royalty for its use. This is a just requirement and every organization should expect to pay it. The royalty is practically all that any playwright makes out of his plays, and he cannot be expected to write them without the hope of recompense for the time and effort he puts into them. If you think this an unnecessary expense, try writing one yourself!

Hard as it is for some organizations to get the money for royalty, it is very short-sighted to use only non-royalty plays. It is wiser to give no plays at all than poor ones. Since plenty of good children's plays are now available for ten or fifteen dollars (short ones, two to ten dollars), it should be possible for every group producing for a pay audience to afford a good play even though the admission is only ten cents. The publisher usually grants permission to use the play and collects the royalties, so that he is the one to consult unless the play is in manuscript, in which case the author is addressed. When more than one performance is given, the royalty is usually reduced for the additional performances.

It is both unsafe and unethical to use a play without permission. Fine and imprisonment are the punishments prescribed by United States statutes for infringements of the royalty requirement. Even if it were possible to elude the law, it would still be a wrong to the author and to the integrity of the organization presenting the play.

THE SEASON'S PROGRAM

Realizing that no two communities have the same problems, the following season's programs for children's theatres are suggested more to illustrate the principles of choosing and combining plays than to recommend actual material.

Since theatres vary in number of productions from one play (with perhaps many performances) to a weekly program with many different productions, it may be practical to strike a medium of four plays in a season.

The choice is based on the following points:

1. Variety in type of play. A keen anticipation and enjoyment of each play is best accomplished by variety. It is possible to have an idea behind the year's program if this idea admits of enough variety; as, for instance, a better understanding of other races, successive periods in history, plays characteristic of seasons, and the like.

The realistic and the fanciful play should each have its place on the year's program which might include fairy-tale, adventure story, modern realistic play.

2. Variety in cost of production. Beautiful and elaborate productions should be alternated with simpler, less expensive ones on the year's program.

3. Appeal to girls and boys. It is a matter of fact that girls will come to boys' plays more readily than boys will attend girls'. Therefore, a boys' play to open the season has certain advantages, especially if season tickets are sold. Plays with heroes, however, should not greatly overbalance those with heroines.

4. Appeal to various ages. If it is not possible to have two series of plays, one must consider the appeal to children from six to fourteen. Plays with a very wide appeal are most highly desirable, others being chosen for one definite age level or another.

5. A combination of favorite plays with those less popular. If a children's theatre is to continue year after year, it would be very unwise to fill the program of the first year or two entirely with the finest plays. Three lists might be made:

the *A* list, including the favorite stories or the best-selling titles; the *B* list, containing those a shade less well known or less popular; and a *C* list, good plays still, though perhaps very simple and not at all known. After five or six years a play may be repeated, since a new generation of play-goers will have come on. And the children who attend year after year never object to a revival if the production was excellent the first time they saw it.

6. Widest appeal in the first play. Whether or not season tickets are sold, the most important choice is the first play. If children attend the opening play and enjoy it very much, they are likely to be on hand for the rest of the season. The director or play chairman, therefore, saves the plays with the greatest drawing power for the opening of each season.

A SUGGESTED PROGRAM FOR A GENERAL AUDIENCE
(*Publishers will be found in the Play List*)

NOVEMBER.—*Jack and the Beanstalk*. By Charlotte Chorpenning.
JANUARY.—*Mr. Dooley, Jr.* By Franken and Lewin.
FEBRUARY.—*Aladdin*. By Theodora Du Bois.
MARCH.—*The Scotch Twins*. By Eleanor Ellis Perkins.

Jack and the Beanstalk is a title which can be counted on to fill the theatre, and Mrs. Chorpenning's dramatization is an unusually charming one. It has been widely used and has proved tremendously popular. It has the two disadvantages of being difficult to produce because of the beanstalk, and being sure to attract many tiny children who will be afraid of the Giant. In spite of this, it is an excellent choice for the opening of a season.

Mr. Dooley, Jr., a modern comedy, is especially popular because of its dog hero. It is equally entertaining to boys and girls, having most appeal to children from six to ten. Not difficult nor expensive.

To the realism of the previous play, the Arabian Nights' tale of *Aladdin* will prove a delightful contrast. Here is a play of wide appeal, rich in beauty and adventure. Though it belongs in the imaginative period, it is one of those plays which never lose their charm, and many of the older boys and girls will enjoy especially the lovely settings and costumes and the interesting magic effects, even if they consider the story too young for them.

Last in the season comes one of the ever popular "Twins" series which children ask for again and again. *The Scotch Twins* will have an especially strong appeal to the older boys and girls, for the children are their own age, and they have some very exciting as well as amusing adventures. The Scotch dialect and one of the settings make this play rather difficult, but it is thoroughly worth doing. Here are several other combinations. What are the probable reasons for their choice?

GENERAL

Robin Hood
The Little Princess
Darby and Joan
Youth's Highway
The Slippers of Cinderella
The Emperor's New Clothes

Tom Sawyer
The Christmas Nightingale
Hans Brinker
The Secret Garden

FOR CHILDREN FROM SIX TO NINE

Snow White and the Seven Dwarfs
Snickerty Nick
The Silver Thread
Pinocchio

Heidi
Little Black Sambo
Racketty-Packetty House
Peter, Peter, Pumpkin Eater

The Prince and the Pauper	*Treasure Island*
The Indian Captive	*Katrinka*
The Ballet of Ali Baba	*The Merchant Gentleman*
Little Women	*Radio Rescue*

When children are the players, far more short plays should be used. The difficulty in choosing one-acts is that the good ones are being constantly used in the schools, the supply being unfortunately limited to start with.

An occasional operetta, marionette show, magician or original type of dramatic entertainment will offer delightful variety in a season, though if they are given a voice in choosing the year's program, the children will ever shout, "The PLAY'S the thing!"

CHAPTER VII

THE STORY COMES ALIVE

FROM the pages of a book to the stage of a children's theatre come a host of story-book characters: Long John Silver, Sara Crewe, Friar Tuck, Tyltyl and Mytyl, Morgiana, and a thousand others. In the imagination of many children they have always been real people, but when a children's theatre director breathes life into the story and brings it actually before them, it becomes infinitely more vivid, more compelling. Boys and girls who have had hazy images or none at all will see the story as a new thing; those who have lived with it for years will take added pleasure in seeing it through the medium of drama.

When the audience has a preconceived idea about the story and its characters, the director as well as the playwright has an obligation to keep the play true to the author's conception. Instead of feeling any sense of disappointment in the dramatization of a novel, the children who see it should be able to say, "It's just exactly as it ought to be, only better!" Flesh and blood players enacting the story before their very eyes sharpen images and arouse emotions in such a way as to heighten rather than lessen their delight in what was already dear to them.

The playwright has a large share of responsibility for the degree of satisfaction experienced by boys and girls in a play that is based on a favorite tale. So have the designer, the technical director, the players. But when all is said and done, it is the director of the play who is most largely responsible. If she is a sensitive, understanding person, with a knowledge of children and their literature, with deep interest in all that a children's theatre should mean to boys and girls, in addition to real skill in directing, she will produce plays that the children will flock to see because they know she will not disappoint them.

THE RESPONSIBILITY OF THE DIRECTOR

Though some children's theatre organizations have a policy of hiring a different director for each production, or even managing with no trained director at all, those which hope to reach a high degree of excellence will find that the only way to do so is to have a first-rate director, a permanent one if at all possible. It is rather insulting, is it not, to the children who come to the theatre with faith in those who are doing the play, to give them shoddy performances directed by the trial and error method? It is like setting out a feast prepared by inexperienced cooks who perhaps have not even taken the trouble to glance at the recipes! What wonder if the children do not come to the second "feast"? The pathetic thing about it is that often they do come because they are so hungry for "shows" that they accept even poor ones, and knowing no better, their taste is formed by the poor director who does not know how to direct.

Such a situation may prove the strongest kind of an incentive to the director to get expert training. If children come to plays which she well knows are poorly done (in spite of the fact that people tell her that they are "wonderful!"), how thrilled they would be if they could have really good ones!

When expert training is impossible, she can do much in teaching herself if she is intelligent and imaginative. By reading the best texts on directing and applying their principles, she will steadily grow in skill, and, though the process may be slower than if she were trained in a good school, she can make of herself in time a really good director.

A PERMANENT DIRECTOR

The advantages of having a permanent director are many. Aside from the fact that she will undoubtedly be a trained person, she will expect to devote her time and thought to the theatre as no one else can do. As she grows in understanding of the organization, the audiences, the town, and as the children discover that her plays are always good, she will become the most vital person in the organization.

If a different person directs each play, the standard is almost certain to be so uneven that the audience has no assurance of the quality of the next play even though this one is good, nor does it know whether all the productions of the theatre will be poor because the season gets off to a bad start.

A permanent director looks not at a single production nor even a whole season, but at a succession of seasons. She takes care to distribute the surest successes over several years rather than to concentrate them in one season. She plans revivals at the right length of time after the first productions of the plays. She feels great responsibility in maintaining a high standard in the choice of plays and their production.

A general chairman of a producing group may conceivably give to a children's theatre many of the same values which a permanent director contributes. She may maintain a uniformly high standard in the productions, in the policies and practices of the management. The chances are against her, however, for she is probably an untrained person with many other interests and duties. It is next to impossible for her to know the theatre inside and out as a director knows it.

THE QUALIFICATIONS OF A DIRECTOR

Only the person who can see the world through the eyes of a child should try to direct plays for youthful audiences. The late Lucy Fitch Perkins, whose "Twins" books are so loved by boys and girls, kept around her a little group of neighborhood children whom she called the "poison squad." Whenever she had finished a story, she read it to them before it was sent to the publisher in order to get their view of it. Devastating as their criticism might be, she welcomed it heartily, for through them she retained the ability to look at things as children do. Her reward for the delightful simplicity with which, as a result, she was able to write, was the devotion of boys and girls the country over.

An understanding of children, then, is a first consideration in a children's theatre director. Respect grows with understanding, and deep interest in their happiness and their welfare follows respect. Children's spiritual nature is in the making, their artistic standards are forming, and though the theatre should bring them what they often designate as "swell shows," the director sees to it that the plays have quality as well as fun.

In order to understand her audiences, a director needs to have a knowledge of child psychology which comes partially from reading and study, partially from experience with children; an insight into the philosophy and the methods of modern pedagogy, made concrete by at least a small amount of teaching experience; an acquaintance with the art work done by children and that which they appreciate; and a sympathetic understanding of the point of view of parents and of schools.

An excellent background of children's literature other than plays is indispensable for children's theatre work, as well as a knowledge of the field of drama. Judgment and taste in the choice of material and good sense in the director's attitude toward it will insure the production of worthy plays without sentimentality or sophistication. With high standards in life and in art, and a conviction that only the best is good enough for children, a director will grow with each production.

The more technical knowledge she has in the field of design and construction of scenery, stage lighting, costuming, make-up, and the actual running of the show, the better her productions will be. Most directors begin with not a single trained person on their staff, and therefore have to train their own crews. It is thus imperative that they have enough technical knowledge and experience to teach others.

A knowledge of the business and publicity end of theatre work, too, is necessary, for even if capable people are available, the director must guide the publicizing of the plays, and work with the business manager in making and keeping within a budget.

Skill in the arts other than drama is undoubtedly an asset to a director of children's plays. Music, dancing, color harmony, design, and many other arts have a part in the theatre, and the director who knows how to use them to best advantage can bring beauty in large measure to the children who see her plays.

A genuine person who is far too devoted to the cause to exploit children in any way, whose enthusiasm makes play out of work, whose patience fits her to work with children, whose sense of humor keeps her well-balanced—such a person in the rôle of children's theatre director will be respected by young and old alike.

THE DUTIES OF A DIRECTOR

Let us suppose that we have a permanent, paid director, giving a large share of her time to a children's theatre. What will she be expected to do?

1. She will be a member of the executive committee of the board, and in most cases the guide, for she must know everything that is going on inside the theatre.

2. As she is the person best fitted to choose material, she will plan each season with reference to the programs of all the seasons which have gone before and those which are to follow. She will give the theatre a balanced diet of new plays, dramatizations of novels, and revivals, with perhaps one or two professional plays and entertainments. This program she will submit to the board for approval, justifying her choice and welcoming suggestions made for its improvement.

3. The duties of a *régisseur* will be hers, for she will bring together and harmonize all phases of the productions. By frequent conferences with technician, costume head, electrician, property manager, and others, she will keep in touch with everything that is being done.

4. She will choose the casts (with or without the assistance of a committee) and direct the plays.

5. She will be the final authority concerning every question that arises during the production. No person may question her command once it is under way, or chaos will result. Consequently, it is she who is responsible for the success or failure of the play.

DIRECTING ADULTS IN CHILDREN'S PLAYS

What are the differences in a director's technique when directing for a child audience rather than for adults? Much has been written and taught on the directing of plays for adult audiences,[1] and many people who have had training and experience in this kind of directing are called upon to direct plays for, and perhaps with, children. If the actors are adults, is the same technique used?

By studying child audiences at play after play, a director learns that though technique in general is the same, the approach is different. In place of a complex, sophisticated world, here is freshness and simplicity. Instead of subtlety and restraint, here is a clean-cut straightforwardness and freedom. Such a difference in the mood and outlook of children's plays means that of necessity the directing must be changed. Certain points, too, need more emphasis.

1. Careful enunciation and projection of voice are more important for an audience in which there are young children. Lack of experience makes it much more difficult for them to get the meaning of a sentence if they miss two or three words. An adult audience is much better at guessing!

2. For the same reason, lines should be pointed or stressed with exceptional care for young children.

3. The story should be told in action as well as in words, for children object to static scenes even if the dialogue is dramatic.

4. Comedy in business is far more effective than comedy in lines. The big laughs are always caused by what the characters do, not by what they say. The washing of the dwarfs'

[1] Since a general discussion of the technique of directing requires far more space than can be given it here, some of the best books on the subject are recommended in the Bibliography at the end of this volume.

faces by Quee, in *Snow White and the Seven Dwarfs,* is much funnier to children than the very amusing lines in which the dwarfs solemnly rebuke Quee for stealing, and in the next breath give him directions about what he is to steal the next night.

5. Broad comedy is understood and enjoyed by children far more than is subtle comedy. The director must, therefore, paint with rather bold splashes and bright colors. It may be said, however, that this practice can very easily go too far and insult the intelligence of the audience.

6. Emotional tension should be of shorter duration than for grown-ups. Though children enjoy suspense, the play is so real to them that they become over-excited unless they have frequent relief. Robin Hood's sudden encounters with Guy of Gisbourne, and Jim's hairbreadth escapes in *Treasure Island,* need the quieter scenes which alternate with them for relief.

7. If there is a romantic scene in the play, the director is wise to make as little of it as possible, shortening it, perhaps, and avoiding, as a rule, embraces and kisses. The Princess and the Woodcutter scene in Milne's *Make-Believe* often brings forth a disgusted "Aw—" from children who think the love scene unbelievably silly.

8. Children thoroughly enjoy fights on the stage because they are so exciting, and although the director may take less pleasure in staging them, she will not be wise to cut them. After all, to most children, heroism is entirely physical, and the clash represents the victory of the good forces over the evil.

If it is a duel with swords, an expert should by all means be called in to coach the players. Since the few weeks of rehearsal are far too short a period in which to learn to fence,

TREASURE ISLAND

Junior League, Denver, Colorado.

a few positions rehearsed many, many times are advisable, variety being attained by using them in different areas of the stage.

9. When using dialect, great care must be exerted to make the speeches intelligible to the audience. Lack of experience, again, makes it more difficult for children to interpret when they fail to understand several words. It may be said here, however, that children enjoy dialect, and if especial care is taken with the first few speeches, they will become accustomed to the unfamiliar manner of speaking and follow it more easily.

10. Players should be warned to be ready to allow time for laughs, though until the first performance no one can be sure where they will come. If the dialogue continues before the laugh ends, those who are eager to hear will try to "S-sh" the others, with the result that the players will be forced to stop after they have gone past the laugh lines.

11. Occasionally even a children's play contains something which may offend parents who attend. Most likely to be offensive are drinking scenes such as are found in *Rip Van Winkle* and *Robin Hood*. Unless the director feels that the drinking of ale is too remote in time and place to be objectionable, she may feel that she must cut it.

12. Sentimentality in a play can be corrected by a director, sometimes by cutting lines, as in Beth's dying speech in *Little Women,* and in Lottie's comforting speech to Sara in *The Little Princess* just after the news has come of her father's death; and sometimes by merely securing a sensible, vigorous reading of the lines.

13. If the climax of each scene, and especially the climax of the play, does not come at the end, the director may need to cut the lines, for after the tension is relieved, there comes

a movement of physical relaxation and a general lessening of interest.

14. Much care should be taken with the final speech of each act, especially in the last act of the play. Indefinite or weak endings leave children with an unsatisfied feeling, as if the play were not quite complete. In Walter de la Mare's *Crossings,* a child audience feels puzzled or baffled by several of the scene-endings. If a director finds that no manner of saying such lines will make them acceptable, she may think it necessary to change them.

DIRECTING CHILD PLAYERS

The process in directing plays for young audiences differs from that used for adult audiences far more when the players are children than when they are grown-ups. The form which the play is to take is the same; the objectives are the same. The manner of achieving them is somewhat different because the director is now working with immature personalities.

CHOOSING THE CAST

One children's theatre in opening its season let it be known that any child who wished to try out for the first play might do so. The day for the tryouts came and with it no fewer than eight hundred children! By eliminating all who were impossible as to size and type the number was reduced to two hundred and fifty. Thereafter the theatre management was careful to announce the sizes, types, and ages of the children who would be accepted for tryouts!

Some policy must, of course, be adopted in regard to those who may apply for parts in order to save disappointment for the children and time for the director or casting committee.

Policies adopted by various children's theatres in this regard
include:

1. General tryouts for all children who wish to try.

2. Tryouts for children who have done superior work in
dramatic classes in public or private schools.

3. Tryouts open to boys and girls whose parents are members
of a community theatre.

4. Tryouts open to all children who have paid a membership
fee in a children's theatre with a guarantee of playing
in at least one production.

THE AGE OF CHILD PLAYERS

Until children have reached the age of ten or eleven, they
are better off in creative dramatic classes, where they gain
experience in characterizing and where they are in no danger
of acting superficially or imitating a director.

The responsibility of carrying an important part in an
ambitious production is difficult for a young child, and if he
does it successfully he is likely to be made self-conscious by
praise. It is perhaps too much to expect that he keep a level
head in the face of the applause and the commendation which
always follow a successful performance. For walk-ons or very
small parts, little children are often necessary, but all of the
important rôles should be played by children who are eleven
or older. These children, if wisely chosen, will sustain their
parts more effectively than younger boys and girls, and they
will also be more sensible in the way they respond to praise.

A child of eleven or twelve who is small for his age is a
far wiser choice for such a part as Jack, in *Jack and the Beanstalk*, for instance, than a nine-year-old, no matter how appealing the younger boy might be. The same might be said
of *Heidi, The Japanese Twins,* and the children in *Mr.*

Dooley, Jr. By taking care to choose for the adult characters people who are enough taller to make a sufficient contrast, the pictorial effect is practically the same as if the younger children had been cast in the parts.

THE PROCESS OF CASTING

When a director or casting chairman is trying out a large number of children, the process is shortened and made easier if her assistant passes out cards or slips of paper to all children as they enter. On these cards each child writes his name, address, telephone number, age, and grade. As he tries out, then, the director jots down points which will help in her estimate of his ability or type. "Imagination," "no projection," "curly red hair," "very tall," and like notations will help to keep these points in her memory after the children have read.

It is desirable, when a whole cast is needed, to meet fifteen or twenty children at a time. When their cards are handed in with the necessary information, they may be given seats according to size, sex, and type, and then the director explains what they need to know about the play, the occasion, the dates, and the rehearsal schedule. Before going further, then, she may ask whether all in the group would be able and willing to meet the conditions if they should be chosen for the cast. Children who have paper routes, music or dancing lessons, ball practice, or other activities interfering with rehearsals are asked not to take the time to try out. If such interference comes but once a week and can be omitted the week of dress rehearsals, it need not make them ineligible, particularly if they do not play the leading rôle.

It is highly important that the director at this time make a point of the fact that she will expect each player to be present at all rehearsals in which his character appears, that this will involve sacrifices; and that she wants only those to try out who will so enjoy being in the play that they not only will give up other things for it but they will give them up gladly.

The result will be that the play will take on so much importance that it becomes the most highly desirable thing they can do. Then and there they sometimes determine to give up things they haven't mentioned to the director. She never knows about the family conferences which are held at home that night concerning outside lessons, dental appointments, and what not. Long after the child has been given a part she may hear of other activities which were postponed in order that he might have the experience of playing in the children's theatre.

The director, having aroused enthusiasm for the play, now proceeds to tell the children the story of the plot if it is not a book they have read. Reading choice bits, telling briefly but interestingly about the characters, she gives them enough to enable them to try out intelligently.

Now her assistant, whether a child or an adult, gives copies of the play (whole copies, not "sides") to several children whose names are called from the cards, and they take their places where the director can study them carefully. If the opening scene of the play contains characters which should be among the first to be cast, she may ask them to start at the beginning. If not, she will have chosen a scene which is a real test of ability. Each child will read only a few speeches, and as he reads, she may write on his card, "Voice fine for this part," or "Too sophisticated," and so on. Cards belonging to the most likely aspirants may perhaps be inconspicuously spread on the "hopeful" side of the table, the others placed in a pile on the other side.

All children will be given a chance to try once before anyone is given a second trial. An exception may be made when parts are shifted within a group which is reading if it is seen that one or more of the group would fit better into a part being read by some one else. The director, during the first reading, should note appearance, voice, enunciation, and evidences of imagination. She will work fast in order that there may be no loss of interest.

After all have taken part in the reading of one or another of the scenes (which the director had previously chosen and listed with page numbers) she is ready to try likely combinations of children. From her cards she calls several boys and girls who seemed most promising. This time she tries to see them as a family, as settlement children, as a king, queen, and court, or whatever the script calls for. She listens to their voices and judges whether they afford pleasing contrasts. This time she may call back children to read again with groups into which they might fit better. Continuing to listen to the children interpret various characters by reading until she has eliminated a number of children, and testing them, too, on voice projection by listening to their reading from a distance and noting how well their voices carry, she now turns, perhaps, to a different method.

PANTOMIME FOR TRYOUTS

Choosing a bit of business which can effectively be done without properties, she asks the children to lay aside their books and play in pantomime. Or, she may ask them to play creatively a scene which had been read several times. Using their own words, they enact the scene as best they can, and in the doing of it show their imagination, ingenuity, and grasp of the character.

The casting may be done in one tryout, but is likely to require two or three. If there is an unusual or difficult character, no child may seem to be at all adequate. In such cases other material is sought, and at the same time the most promising of those who have already tried out are given further chance to study the part. Sometimes a search will reveal just the right person; too often the director will have to use a child who seems inadequate and devote much time to helping him understand and interpret the character.

Before announcing the cast, it is wise to consult parents and especially teachers concerning the children who will have to give a great deal of time to the play. This is sometimes done before the second tryout, especially if the director is doubtful as to whether certain children can spare the time, whether their attitude is right, and whether parents will be coöperative.

If there are children whose scholarship is low or whose attitude is doubtful, it is often wiser to drop them at once. Sometimes, however, that child happens to be superior in a difficult rôle, and the director wants very much to use him. In such a case a consultation is sometimes held with his teacher and principal, his parents, and the child himself, in the effort to estimate what would be the probable effect of giving him the part. If all are satisfied that it may prove an incentive to him to improve in other respects, he may be allowed to have it.

REHEARSALS

The first rehearsal after the cast is complete is devoted to reading the whole play. This is the time to watch pronunciation and enunciation as well as the understanding of character. When a child reads a line as if he did not fully understand it, the director will do well to clear up the difficulty before a wrong meaning has become fixed in his mind.

Each child is encouraged to think out the interpretation of his own character, that it may come from within rather than be imposed by the director. Children who have had experience in creative dramatics will be quite capable of discovering for themselves just what their characters are like, for they are accustomed to the study and interpretation of various types of people. Others may need guidance in finding out the author's idea about the character, and the director will need to call their attention to what the author says about them, what the other characters say to them or about them, what they themselves say and do.

At this reading rehearsal the players will get a better idea of the play as a whole than they were able to get at the tryouts. Each one will begin to feel the reactions of his character to the rest of the cast, to understand the place his own character fills in the whole plot, to feel the story beginning to come alive.

When the play is difficult, a preliminary study of it over a period of weeks is of inestimable value. Interpretation is much mellower if the cast has lived with it for a long time. These weeks of study are usually very hard to manage, however, in addition to the four or five weeks of rehearsals, and many good plays are not so difficult as to require it.

BUSINESS

The first rehearsal with action or business should be held on the stage where the play is to be given. Even if the rehearsing must ordinarily be done in some other place, it is important that this rehearsal which will give the children the pattern of the first act be held on the stage. First impressions are strong, and if the players get the feeling of the scenes in relation to the stage, they will have no adjustments to make when they come to the period of dress rehearsals. In case a stage is not available until the final rehearsals, the next best plan is to secure a room large enough so that the acting space will be the same.

In this first rehearsal with business, nothing will be said about characterization, for the players will have enough to think about if they learn their general positions on the stage. Some directors, after indicating the exact stage arrangements and the properties, prefer to let the players move about as naturally as they may before giving any directions. By so doing they believe the pattern of the play will be largely determined by what feels right to the actors, and the director's part will be to guide subtly rather than to direct arbitrarily. Such a policy is more likely to be successful with skilled actors than with amateurs, though it is possible to use it successfully with either. Certain it is that regardless of what method the director uses, she should have worked out a pattern for herself even though she does not adhere to it exactly.

No small business will be indicated at this rehearsal, since the players are holding their scripts, but if the director believes in giving absolute positions, thus working out her own pattern, she will be very definite in order that the players may associate their lines with the business which accompanies them. If she sees that her plans are not working out well, she should change them before the next rehearsal and not again, for constant changes in directions are most unsettling to a player. Details will be added as the cast is ready for them, but the general pattern should be set early.

LATER REHEARSALS

In a three-act play, a director concentrates on the first act for several rehearsals after the cast has read the play. As business becomes fixed, she turns her attention again to character, watching that each develops naturally. If a player does not grow as he should she tries to stir his imagination to a better conception. When he cheapens the character she tries to show him how much finer this person really is. If the play is a dramatization of a novel, it is often wise to read to casts or individual players excerpts which will refine and make truer their ideas of the story and the people in it. This reading will serve to refresh in their minds what should be familiar to the whole cast before rehearsals began.

If the play is based on a popular novel a few of the children will have read it so many times that they will be very critical of the general interpretation. In one production of *Heidi* the little girl who played the title rôle, having read the book twenty-three times, was an authority on any question that arose concerning the episodes! If the play is in three or four acts, not more than three rehearsals should be devoted to the first act before the second one is blocked. After about two rehearsals of act two, both may be rehearsed together. By the seventh or eighth rehearsal, the director concentrates on the last act. After this all acts must be kept fresh and growing. Sometimes consecutive scenes are not rehearsed on the same day because it saves time to work with certain groups who appear together in various scenes throughout the play.

PROJECTION

As soon as the players are familiar with their lines, the director gives special attention to the projection of voice and character. If a person can be heard and understood at the back of the auditorium, and if the personality of this character comes over well, he is said to have good projection. By the third rehearsal of any scene the players should be free from their scripts, and after they have had time to become a bit sure of themselves the director should move back in the house to see how well the scene reaches her.

All that is necessary for sufficient voice projection in most cases is for the players to see where the director is sitting. If she has been careful to cast only children with sufficiently strong voices to be heard in the auditorium, they will enlarge their characterizations and their voices almost without effort. A few may be hard to understand because of rapid speaking and faults of enunciation, and she will have to insist that they speak more slowly and carefully. Sometimes a private lesson must be given a child in which he is required to go over all his lines like a moving picture shown in slow time. This has a tendency to make him careful in enunciating distinctly.

If such faults are the result of tense throat muscles, it will be impossible to correct them in a few weeks. This is something that should have been discovered in the tryouts, and it means that the director has made a mistake in casting. For any child who cannot speak distinctly in tryouts is too great a risk to cast, since the correction of bad faults is a long process.

Because of the need for careful attention to projection when directing a play with a child cast, it is dangerous to do much of the rehearsing in a small room. Experienced actors can adapt themselves to different conditions, but children will often seem quite lost in an auditorium if they have been rehearsing in a room which is much smaller. It is therefore important that at least some of the early rehearsals be held in the auditorium where the play will be presented.

THE NUMBER OF REHEARSALS

A long play done by child actors requires a period of four or five weeks for rehearsals after the cast is complete. Twenty rehearsals are as few as any such play will need, and extra rehearsals are often needed for individuals or small groups. A double cast, of course, means more rehearsals, though both casts may work simultaneously if the director has a capable assistant. Children of eleven and above can rehearse easily for an hour and a half or two hours if they are not constantly on the stage. Though they are not fresh after school hours, they will work with enthusiasm if they are keenly interested. Much can be accomplished in a long Saturday morning rehearsal, so that it is strongly advisable to plan one for every week.

A director who never fails to begin her rehearsals promptly (and children often arrive ahead of the scheduled hour), who wastes no time, yet has a large store of patience for those who do, gets things done without friction. A lively good humor goes far in keeping a rehearsal moving with zest, and coupled with a professional spirit which tolerates no slovenly work, it keeps players alert and doing their best.

FINAL REHEARSALS

As time draws near for the first dress rehearsal, the director must cease to work with details. She has been stopping the players in the midst of scenes to smooth out rough places and then to bridge them over by beginning a speech or two before the break and continuing to a point beyond it where all was well. Now she waits until the end of the scene before she makes a suggestion or criticism, for she knows that if the players are to give a smooth performance, they must have much practice in rehearsing without interruption.

Tempo is speeded up in the last two weeks, that there may be no chance of the deadly kind of performance which too often characterizes the amateur. Indeed, the director has given much attention to this throughout, knowing that a play that is rehearsed too slowly day after day is very difficult to act in faster tempo. Having become more sure of themselves by this time, however, the cast is able to cut minutes off the playing time by a crisper, more finished performance. The rhythm of the play is now more evident, though the children, of course, are unaware of it as such.[2] Each individual rhythm is blended into the rhythmical pattern of the whole in such a way as to give it beauty and meaning.

DRESS REHEARSALS

For a long costume play which is to be given an ambitious public performance, at least three dress rehearsals are necessary. Because of many adjustments to scenery, properties, and costumes, the first dress rehearsal is greatly slowed down. It is, therefore, strongly advisable to rehearse only part of the play. With an adult cast and a long rehearsal period, it is both possible and advisable to do the whole play at each rehearsal, but it is too wearing on youthful players. Consequently, the play should be divided for the first two rehearsals, the third being saved for a complete run-through, with scenes in correct order. The first two, then, are divided according to settings, the fewest changes meaning the greatest saving of time.

[2] See discussion of rhythm in *General Principles of Play Directing* by Gilmor Brown (French, 1937).

By rehearsing only one or two scenes in a day, the director is able to make the interruptions necessary because of the first use of scenery, lighting, and costumes, yet have time also to run through it without pause at least once. Though she should already have rehearsed such things as eating, sewing, and exchanging clothes (as in *The Prince and the Pauper*) there will be plenty of business which was impossible to do exactly without the setting, and she needs to try it again and again. She may have used the right amount of floor space in rehearsing, yet find that some of her groupings do not look well, so that she will be glad for time in which to improve them.

THE FINAL DRESS REHEARSAL

The final dress rehearsal should be as much like a regular performance as it is possible to make it. Lights, curtain, make-up, and sound effects should by this time be exact and dependable. The Prologue should make his announcements before the scenes, and both cast and crew should play their rôles in a professional manner. No interruption should mar the play, but the director, costume head, and technician, sitting in the darkened auditorium, will take note of any points which need changing. Many technical directors and electricians have telephone arrangements through which they can speak softly to the person at the switchboard, giving him direction for making changes in the lights. Others simply watch the scenes and make note of what should be different.

While scenes are being shifted during all dress rehearsals, the director may meet the children for a few minutes, giving them her criticism of the scene. If costumes are to be changed for another scene she may prefer to delay the criticisms, typing those for each individual and giving them to the cast later that they may be fresh in mind as they are to be used. Such a method has the effect of making them seem more important. Each child, reading his own suggestions individually, will be much more likely to put them into practice than if they were given verbally in a group. When a scene is to be rehearsed twice the same day, however, the children should have the criticisms in time to use them at once.

THE DIRECTOR'S TALK TO THE CHILDREN

At one of these last rehearsals, the director will need to prepare the children for any emergency that may arise. Sitting quietly in a corner where they will not be distracted, she may ask them what they are going to do if anything unexpected should happen such as a wrong cue, misplaced property, a sound effect that doesn't come on time. Inevitably, they will answer in a chorus, "Go on!" "Right," the director answers, and then she may tell them of an instance in which players showed splendid presence of mind when something went wrong. She leads them to think of it as sort of an adventure, and if they happen to have had creative dramatic experience, they are not in the least appalled. In fact, more than one group of children has asked a director after a performance if she noticed that they made up some lines to fill a gap when a player failed to make a change of costume quickly enough, or neatly cut out a telephone scene when they discovered that some green property man had removed the telephone! Had she noticed!

It should not be necessary to tell children that no player is to look at the audience, but it is wise to warn them even if they seem to have no tendency to do so. Some little child who has never been in a play before occasionally does such a thing, the director tells them, but no good player does for he is living in the story.

Following this talk the director may give careful instructions concerning the hour they are to arrive on the day of the performance, exactly where they will go for costume and make-up, where they are to stay when they are not on the stage. She will remind them that before each scene they are to go to the head of properties to get anything which they are supposed to carry in, and after the scene they will return anything they carry off the stage. She repeats the instruction to leave the stage immediately after their scene ends and go to the dressing-room, *never* to the auditorium, even when their part in the play is over. After they have taken off costumes and make-up, it is sometimes permissible, though never desirable, for them to sit in the back of the house. She warns them to remember to address whatever questions are really necessary to the proper person on the staff. The one who dresses them, for instance, will answer all questions about costumes; the person assigned to the giving out of personal properties is the only one who can tell them about such things. Excitement will cause some children to ask questions of every one, and a word of caution quietly given to all in advance will help to make them think before they bother anyone. When the rehearsal is over she sends them home with encouraging words that they may look forward with confidence to the opening of the play.

A second complete dress rehearsal is often given as a performance for a school or an orphanage, if this happens to be a play which is to be given for grown-ups. The idea is an excellent one, insuring more smoothness and finish than does an ordinary dress rehearsal. A children's theatre production obviously cannot do this, unless some underprivileged children who otherwise could not see the play are invited.

PERFORMANCES

In a well-organized children's theatre the director's duties are over with the dress rehearsals, and the performance could very easily go on without her. Now the assistant director takes general charge of the cast, the stage manager notifies them when they are to come on stage, the costume crew dresses them, another group of people makes them up. If a large number of children are appearing in certain acts, extra adults will be needed to entertain them while they wait for their scenes.

Though the director should have no duties at performances, she will keep a watchful eye on all that goes on, making decisions concerning the advisability of holding the curtain if there is a line in the foyer waiting to get tickets, or the amount of make-up on some of the characters, or regarding the plight of the little boy who came to this performance after missing the one for which he had a ticket.

Most of all, though, she can help create an atmosphere which is free from tension. If she is cheerful and confident, the children are likely to think there is nothing to worry about. Greetings to players and crew, with encouraging words to any who may need them, are the director's final contribution to the play before she takes her seat in the auditorium, eager to note the response of the child audience to this play she has directed with such care.

This organization may seem complex to some theatres and schools. Indeed, the less ambitious productions, with small casts and little change of scenery, will not need so large a staff. Every large production, however, involves the help of a considerable number of adults. If duties are not divided, every one, including the director, is worried and harassed, and things seldom move smoothly backstage. With careful organization such as has been described, the staff is calm and efficient, the child players are not greatly excited, and because the director is free to supervise instead of trying to manage everything herself, the performance from the opening curtain to the close is marked by spirit and by professional smoothness.

CHAPTER VIII

CALL THE PLAYERS!

TO BE an actor in a theatre for children is a new and responsible specialty. Small children must be given great art. Those who are not masters of great art cannot work in the Theatre for Children—it is on the basis of this conviction that our theatre has grown up." So wrote Natalia Satz, director of the Moscow Theatre for Children—a professional theatre famous throughout the world.

Artistic merit, an objective of most children's theatres, is to be attained only by considering the audience of supreme importance. Respect for the children who will see the performances, and a deep interest in presenting good plays, skilled players, and beautifully complete productions, should supersede all other considerations.

This means that the theatre does not exist to give people a chance to act. No person is cast in a play because the experience will be good for him. Most certainly he will not be cast because his mother is chairman of the board. If he can play the part better than any other available person, it is given to him, and the director is happy if he happens to be the one who will gain most from the experience.

The policy to be followed in casting plays should be determined by a children's theatre at the outset. Is the theatre to be an outlet for the desire to act on the part of either children or grown-ups? Or are the casts to be chosen because they will give the very best illusion to the audience, because they will make the story come alive? A theatre should not compromise in this matter. If it expects to win a following in the community, it must adopt the policy of casting plays with the people who can most capably act the parts.

The reason for this point of view is obvious. The audience pays to see a good entertainment. It has a right to see the best we can give. Is it fair to lower our standard for the sake of a few individuals who would profit by playing parts which could be done more effectively by others? A school of acting may accomplish the double purpose of training young people and giving a good show at the same time. Such situations are rare, however, and do not alter the statement that the audience should be of first consideration.

The idea that children are not good enough judges to know the difference would be beside the point even if it were true. Boys and girls are not always able to analyze what is wrong, but they are convinced by good characterizations and unmoved by poor ones. Motion pictures, too, have had a strong influence, and children constantly grow more discriminating. Quite aside from this, however, we have a grave responsibility when we are molding young ideas and tastes, and we should hold always to the belief that nothing short of our best is good enough to bring to them.

CREATIVE DRAMATICS

The place for experience, in the case of children, is in creative dramatic classes. Here is where personality unfolds and blossoms in the most natural way. From the child's standpoint, the creating of plays from stories or experiences, with original characterization and dialogue, is worth infinitely more than taking part in formal plays. A non-exhibitional experience such as this gives them a much better idea of characterization, to say nothing of the various other benefits, so that children make more intelligent players when they finally have a chance in a formal production. As this is not the place to discuss the remarkable development of the child which may result from this type of self-expression, the reader is referred to the book *Creative Dramatics*.[1]

School plays, to which parents and children are *invited*, are an entirely different matter from children's theatre plays. Though standards should be high, the entertainment value need not be so strong a consideration. The play takes on something of the nature of a demonstration of school work, and the audience sees it from that point of view. Children who could never play in the children's theatre may take part on such occasions with a sufficient degree of success to make it a satisfactory and educationally valuable experience. The same may be said of the plays given at camps, playgrounds, and clubs, where dramatic work is taken less seriously, and the playlets and sketches are often in the nature of stunts.

CHILD OR ADULT PLAYERS?

Existing children's theatres differ in their policies concerning the type of players in their productions. Professional companies and adult organizations use mature players almost exclusively. Private studios, public schools, and some civic theatres cast children in all parts; while theatres sponsored jointly by elementary schools and colleges or universities oftenest use young adults in the older parts, with children from about ten to fourteen years in the children's rôles.

[1] Ward, *Creative Dramatics* (D. Appleton-Century Co., 1930).

If skill alone is considered, an entirely adult cast is most desirable. Only grown-up players can give the illusion of the older characters either in appearance or in maturity of conception. It would be a mistake to cast *The Merchant Gentleman* with players younger than high-school age, and even they cannot give a perfect illusion. *Rip Van Winkle, Little Women, Make-Believe,* and many other children's theatre plays are much more effective with grown-ups in the adult parts.

In child rôles, however, adults are often unconvincing. Size, shape, voice, and, even more important, outlook on life, belie them. Lacking freshness and naïveté, they often overact in trying to seem youthful. Many slender young adults are exceptions to this rule, creating as perfect an illusion as children themselves. Even when adults are too large or too sophisticated for children's parts, young audiences often accept them as a matter of course just as they accept women in men's rôles.

A perfect illusion is impossible to achieve with an entire child cast, regardless of how beautifully the children may act. Size alone would prevent them from playing adult rôles convincingly; but shape, voice, immaturity, and lack of experience are even greater handicaps. It is hard to imagine such characters as Miles Hendon and John Canty in *The Prince and the Pauper,* the old toymaker in *The Toymaker of Nuremberg,* the doctor in *The Poor Little Rich Girl,* or Uncle Tom in *Uncle Tom's Cabin* being played satisfactorily by children. Youthful audiences will accept a child cast, however, supplying with their imaginations what is lacking in the illusion, and gaining at least a part of their enjoyment by fancying themselves in the shoes of the players.

As far as appearance is concerned, a cast of combined chil-

RIP VAN WINKLE

Goodman Theatre, Chicago.

dren and adults is most satisfying. More than one children's theatre which has experimented with all three methods of casting has found this custom to be the most pleasing to its audiences. If a play has only adult characters, no children act; but grown-ups never play child rôles, such parts being filled by pupils from the creative dramatic classes of the public schools, from private studios, or from the town in general.

WHEN ADULTS ACT FOR CHILDREN

In James M. Barrie's directions to the actor who plays Nana in *Peter Pan,* he writes, "All the characters, whether grown-up or babes, must wear a child's outlook on life as their only adornment. If they cannot help being funny they are begged to go away. A good motto for all would be 'The little less, and how much it is.'"

A text for a sermon to grown-ups who play for children is this warning of Barrie's. It should be read and taken to heart by every one of them. There would be less of over-playing, less insult to the children's intelligence if they could get Barrie's point of view. Instead of condescending to children, they would recognize the very genuine quality of their audience and consider it worth their highest efforts.

True, the experienced player will find that acting must be broader and more obvious for a youthful audience. Subtleties in acting are often appreciated by children; but less likely to be understood are subtleties in the manner of speaking lines. An adult player often gets much enjoyment in the children's theatre from "cutting loose" and acting with less restraint than for audiences of adults. The characters in children's plays are conducive to this type of overplaying; but there is a tendency on the part of some adults to burlesque what should be played seriously.

Playing to the gallery in this way will get laughs from children just as it does from adults, and there will be fewer discriminating spectators to grieve. Actors who thumb their noses at their audiences, however, by resorting to slapstick have no place in a children's theatre. Let them keep to the adult stage where the audience is past saving. We want players in our theatres for young people who are genuine, who have respect for children. When they are funny, let them be sincerely funny. When they play parts which are eccentric or evil, let them build real characters, not absurdities.

Artistic standards are in the making in child audiences. Whether the actor realizes it or not, he is helping to set those standards. If he insults children's intelligence, he leads them to think that this is what one may expect from the stage. If he believes that only the finest acting is good enough for a child audience, and that he has a responsibility in the development of taste, he will never be guilty of ridiculing a character that he plays, nor of feeling superior to an audience of young people.

WHEN CHILDREN ARE THE PLAYERS

" ... and please, God, help me to get the part of a Lost Boy!" How many such prayers go up when children are trying out for a children's theatre play no one will ever know. But now and then one of them reaches the ears of a director and she has the chance of her life to play the part of God!

The delight in playing to many hundreds of children and grown-ups in a children's theatre production is entirely natural, and so appealing is it that a director or casting committee usually passes around the privilege even though it would be easier to use the same children over again. This, in a way, is a compromise, for skill comes only through experience. There are usually enough children with ability, however, so that the only duplication that need occur is the casting of a child in a leading rôle after he has proved himself in a small one.

DOUBLE-CASTING

A two-fold purpose is served in double-casting children's rôles. More children may take part, each cast playing half the performances; and the production is safeguarded in case of illness. Contagious diseases have a way of appearing overnight, and if a second child is ready to step into a part, a director feels sure of avoiding either a postponement of the play or the hurried coaching of another person. A double cast involves far more work on the part of the director, who needs two assistants instead of one if the two casts are rehearsed separately—these people to alternate in watching the director and rehearsing the other cast. The director introduces all new business to both casts, her assistants helping them to fix it in mind. When no capable assistants are available, it is wiser to double-cast only the leading parts and rehearse all players together.

Every person that rehearses in a play should have the chance of taking part in at least one performance. Paid understudies are necessary in professional productions, and it is conceivable that a student of acting might consider it worth while to understudy a leading rôle without having a chance to play it. But amateur players, whether children or adults, have not the same incentive, and should play at least a minor character even if they are understudying a major part.

When one person is very superior to all others in a particular rôle, it is naturally not desirable to double-cast this part. In that case, it is wise in preparing for a big production to use some capable child in a minor part for an understudy, rehearsing him rather frequently in the more important rôle, so that he would be ready to step in at a few hours' notice. There is no disappointment connected with this plan, for the second child easily becomes acquainted with the lines— most children being able to say the speeches of every other character by the time the play is given, anyhow—and he has all the fun of being in the production even if he has only a minor part.

THE EFFECT ON CHILDREN

If a children's theatre is an important institution in the community, it is a big experience to play an important part in one of its productions. Some children are not level-headed enough to stand the publicity, praise, and applause which accompany such an experience without feeling over-important. For this reason a director needs to consult parents and teachers before giving children parts in any big production. Are the children in the best of health so that they can stand without ill effects the four or five weeks of daily rehearsals? Are they steady as to nerves? Are they having any difficulty in school subjects? Do they have a fine attitude? Are they dependable? Do they have sensible parents? These questions answered to the director's satisfaction, she feels safe in casting a child, remembering that her own attitude can do much to keep him steady and unspoiled.

Throughout the rehearsals, she sees to it that a fine, work-manlike spirit prevails in the cast; that the children are absorbed in the play itself and are possessed with a great desire to do it well; she avoids individual publicity; and she keeps the children sane and happy. Acting with adults prevents them from becoming over-confident, for they realize that the grown-ups are far more experienced than they, and if the older members of the cast are warned never to let the boys and girls feel that grown-ups consider them "cute," there is usually a delightfully friendly feeling between children and adults.

A child's whole attitude is sometimes changed for the better by the experience of playing successfully in a children's theatre. Perhaps he hasn't had a great deal of self-respect; his schoolmates have not thought highly of him, his teacher may have been doubtful about the wisdom of allowing him to take a part. Because he seems so promising for a particular character, he is permitted to do so. He is treated with respect by the director, does a fine piece of work. He rises in the estimation of the other children in the cast, and then wins praise from the audience. From then on the child seems to be on a different level. He has grown appreciably from the ex-perience, and there is a chance, at least, that the influence will be lasting.

Though the director is responsible for the general attitude in a cast, one or two members may influence the morale so greatly as to make the rehearsals either a joy to every one or merely a necessary preparation for a performance. Until an actor has had the experience of directing, he cannot realize how important is the attitude of each individual, no matter how small his part.

Every experienced director knows what it means to the morale of a cast when one player, especially a generally liked person, has unflagging enthusiasm throughout the rehearsals, eagerness to understand and improve his character, willingness to rehearse long and hard in order that the play may go exceptionally well. Sometimes one player gives a spiritual lift to the whole cast, so that every rehearsal is an exciting and happy experience in which the play grows appreciably, never seeming to pause on a plateau.

So vital is this matter of attitude that when a director knows personally the people who are trying out for a play, she never willingly casts a person who is undependable or habitually late, who wanders out of the room and has to be called when his cue is given, who talks constantly when he is backstage, who frowns at an announcement of an extra meeting, who asks how long he must stay to-day, or if he may be excused to-morrow. Knowing how important such matters really are, she prefers to work with an individual whose loyalty and fine spirit can always be counted on, even though he may have less ability in acting than the other. In the long run, it was the tortoise who won over the hare. During the rehearsals for a play the talented but indifferent actor is outstripped again and again by players who start at a disadvantage but, equipped with a capacity for steadiness and hard work, with a warm glow of enthusiasm and loy- alty, arrive at performance with a quality in their acting which convinces by its sincerity and by mellowness which can only be achieved by long study and rehearsal. Dramatic ability is indeed necessary, but every director discovers that the people who can best act the parts in a play are not always those who appear to greatest advantage in the tryouts.

CHAPTER IX

DRESSING UP FOR THE OCCASION

GOLDEN-HAIRED Amy March, running lightly down the stairs to meet Laurie, is a vision in white ruffles and pink rosebuds and curls. The audience suddenly and audibly catches its breath, so charming does she look in her billowy party frock. It is one of those things which can happen only in a children's theatre, this utterly natural and spontaneous expression of admiration.

Such a charmingly naïve response as that in the *Little Women* audience is one of innumerable instances showing the part that costume plays in children's productions. Indeed, the fun of dressing up is enjoyed by boys and girls for itself alone, and it is a common sight to see little girls parading down the street dressed as "movie stars," or boys as "cow punchers," even though the dramatic show goes no further than the parade.

Delighted as children are with costumes, however, they are seldom discriminating concerning those which they see or wear in plays, for they do not know what is correct. The heroine might appear in a fifteenth century head-dress, an Empire gown, an Elizabethan ruff, and modern high-heeled slippers, and the audience would find no fault with the ensemble! For this very reason, the costume manager has much responsibility in costuming plays for children. Here is the place to set standards in style and color combinations. Here is the chance to illustrate historic periods. From moving pictures which are usually accurate as to period costuming, children are gradually absorbing a knowledge which will make them more critical in the future. The children's theatre should make an important contribution to this knowledge.

The appearance of a character the first time a child has met him, either in a picture book or on stage or screen, is likely to be the image which persists in his mind. If he has first seen Heidi in motion pictures he expects the children's theatre heroine to appear like the little actress who played the part there, regardless of what the author has said about her. Any child who has seen the Tenniel illustrations of *Alice in Wonderland* is disappointed if the children's theatre does not dress the characters in the same manner. Those who have seen the original Birch drawings of Sara Crewe could never be satisfied with a "little princess" who did not resemble her. Because of many differing editions of the traditional tales, most story-book characters are not nearly so fixed in appearance, but the costumière would do well to be guided by some popular edition of the story.

At present children are far more impressed by color than by style, and they respond especially to materials that shine. Rayon silk and satin have proved a boon to costumières, for these materials have the sheen which is such a delight to children yet are cheap enough for limited budgets. Gold and silver cloth, too, are very popular. Painted patterns add to the color and richness of the costumes, heightening their interest in the eyes of young audiences. Striking color combinations are enjoyed by most children, though the minority appreciate more subtle effects. Most of their comments are general rather than specific, such as:

"I like the spring colors in *The Secret Garden*."

KAI KHOSRU, PRINCE OF PERSIA

Children's Theatre, Charleston, West Virginia.

"The costumes in *The Silver Thread* were gay and cheerful."

"I liked the knights' costumes the best although I was not for the knights."

Detail is of little use on the stage, and children see it less than do adults. The successful costume designer will take care that silhouettes are right and that colors are as cheerful as the mood and period of the play will permit.

LARGE PROPORTION OF COSTUME PLAYS

Plays for children present far more of a costume problem than do those for adults, since so few of them are modern. Why this should be so is explained by the fact that a much larger proportion of plays liked by children are dramatizations of literature. Even the children who have passed the fairy-tale age enjoy plays of pioneers and legendary heroes, and because stories of far-off times furnish such rich material, the best plays have almost invariably meant costume productions.

Casts are usually larger, too, in children's plays, a small number of characters being relatively unusual. Crowds of peasants, neighbors, pirates, or vagabonds are common, so that a costume manager welcomes with a sigh of thanksgiving the occasional play with the small cast. Costumes, labor, and time spent in dressing large casts of children's plays are all to be taken into consideration when planning a production.

QUALIFICATIONS OF A COSTUME MANAGER

The qualifications of a costume head include a thorough knowledge of materials and period costumes; skill in designing, in cutting patterns, and in sewing; and an ability so to organize her work that costumes are completed for the first dress rehearsal, and the crew and assistants are carefully informed as to the running of the show.

In addition to her knowledge of the historic periods in which plays are set, she needs to know all the best sources of information concerning style, ornament, color, and accessories.[1] She does not depend on costume books for a children's play so much as on a beautifully illustrated edition of the story, and before designing her costumes she investigates all the resources of the public library. With the director and the scene designer she plans the costumes to harmonize with the backgrounds and to suit the personalities of the characters, both in color and design. Indeed, the same person may design both settings and costumes, thus assuring more perfect harmony than if done by two people.

Many children's plays may be set in one of several periods. The fairy-tales are most often mediæval, though in which century is entirely optional. Indeed, they are sometimes set in the fifteenth, sixteenth, seventeenth, or eighteenth centuries, so that a designer has a fairly wide range of periods from which to choose her fashions! Fairy tales and other fanciful plays may be costumed in a fashion which combines characteristics of the whole mediæval period (Figures 2 and 3) or according to no period at all. No matter how imaginative a designer may be, however, she usually bases her style on one or two periods, using her imagination for many original touches.

MATERIALS

Materials are constantly changing with new fabrics available each season, and a good costume manager is always on the alert

[1] See costume references in the Bibliography.

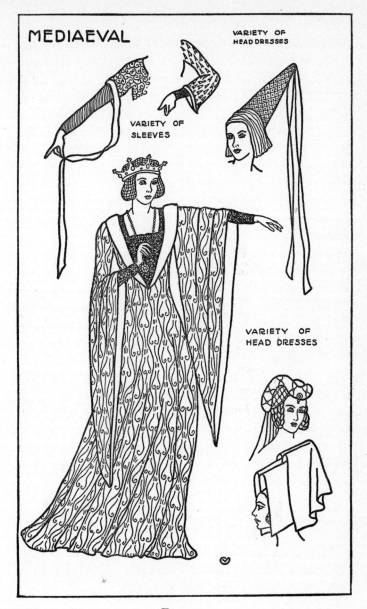

MEDIAEVAL

VARIETY OF
HEAD DRESSES

VARIETY OF
SLEEVES

VARIETY OF
HEAD DRESSES

FIGURE 2

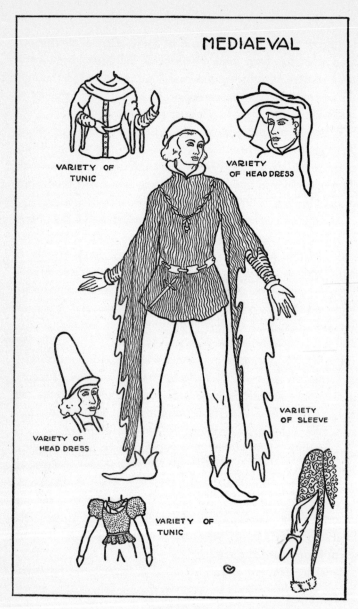

MEDIAEVAL

VARIETY OF
TUNIC

VARIETY
OF HEAD DRESS

VARIETY OF
HEAD DRESS

VARIETY
OF SLEEVE

VARIETY OF
TUNIC

FIGURE 3

to discover materials which will be more effective or cheaper than what has been used. She secures the latest sample-card from dealers in theatrical materials, and she wanders through the basement bargain sections and the drapery departments to find whatever will best fit her purposes.

When she can get so useful and inexpensive a fabric as cotton duvetyn from theatrical houses, she discards canton flannel and other materials which she has been using to simulate wool. This material is so like fine broadcloth in appearance that it can be used for practically any garment supposed to be woolen.

An efficient buyer of materials finds, too, that it does not pay to make costumes from cambric or cheese-cloth. Other materials look much better and wear longer, and if she expects to build up a wardrobe which can be used in varying combinations for many plays, she knows that it pays to buy better materials. She therefore depends upon percale and gingham for most cotton costumes, for they look well, launder nicely, and can be bought in many attractive colors.

For dyeing, muslin in a coarse grade is found most satisfactory, though she must dye it before cutting out the garments as it shrinks greatly. She uses a finer grade when patterns are to be painted on it, though she discovers that percale and gingham take such patterns even better than muslin.

A costume manager finds much use for crinoline petticoats in children's plays, for they hold out the peasant skirts and are lighter to wear than muslin. Buckram, being much stiffer, is in use steadily in her work-room for crowns, hats, and all manner of head-dresses. By sewing picture wire around the edges she holds them firm, and in addition is able to bend them to any desired shape.

It is in silks, satins, and velvets that the greatest improvements have been made in recent years. No longer is it necessary to use sateen to give the illusion of silk, for rayon satin and taffeta are far more lustrous and rich in appearance. Cheaper than the best grade of sateen, they may also be had in practically every shade one could desire. Corduroy is used often for children's theatre costumes, for it is the least expensive substitute for velvet. Long capes, king's robes, and many other garments have the appearance of velvet if made from corduroy. Velveteen is not so cheap, but as some colors are better in that fabric than in corduroy, an occasional costume is made of it.

Drapery departments supply the leatherette which makes the sleeveless leather jackets for Robin Hood and his men. They can furnish, too, materials which give the illusion of brocade, but these are rather expensive at best, and the costume manager is glad to find that the firms dealing in theatrical materials are making a growing variety of good substitutes for brocade, which may be used for such plays as *The Merchant Gentleman* and *Master Skylark*. Metal cloth, gold braid, jewels, and sequins come from theatrical houses, also, as well as artificial fur and other materials which are hard to find elsewhere.

DYES

Children's plays with large casts seldom can be costumed without dyeing some of the materials and tights. The person in charge of costumes thus needs to add a knowledge of this process to all her other accomplishments. For aside from the fact that in smaller cities and towns a very narrow selection of material is obtainable, a set of costumes can be made very handsome by the careful and artistic dyeing of cheap materials.

Pastel shades can be obtained by merely dipping white material in any dye. Deeper shades require boiling. Loosely woven fabrics usually dye most successfully. Tights, often bought in white from a theatrical house or costumer, must always be boiled if they are to be dyed. The same is true for long hose or underwear which are often substituted for tights when children are the players.

Best for painting borders on garments are aniline dyes which come in powder form by the pound. As only a tea-spoonful is required for ten quarts of water, the costume manager is likely to buy a small amount from a local dyer. Since aniline is a transparent dye, it cannot be painted on a deep shade without showing the color underneath. For this reason it is advisable to paint on a white background, cut out the pattern and appliqué it on to the garment. Shellac, mixed with the dry color, makes the border more durable.

STOCK COSTUMES

Children's theatres which have been in existence for some years, as well as schools which have been building up a ward-robe, have found that a certain few types of costumes are required over and over again for children's plays. Many garments will be made which have to wait several years before they are used again, while these others may be needed several times in one season. It behooves the person in charge of costumes, therefore, to build up a stock of those which are most often used, taking care that they are of good wearing quality, that many of them are inconspicuous, that they may be worn in many different combinations.

A queen's robe, thus, may be assembled from the collection of semi-fitted gowns worn by mediæval court ladies, with one of the long circular capes to which a handsome upstanding collar has been attached. A metal girdle and crown complete the costume. It may be seen that instead of one queen's gown, the wardrobe will thus be able to supply several, so that the many queens and empresses who appear in children's plays may have distinctive costumes. Kings are more difficult to outfit because they ordinarily wear long robes unlike those of the nobles. Occasionally, if the king is young he wears a short tunic and tights with his long robe or cape.

Pages, usually in pairs, appear even more often than kings or queens, and almost invariably wear tunics and tights. Both pages and heralds are seen often in tabards (Figure 4) with the coat of arms of a king or noble emblazoned on the front. Several sets of such costumes with small round caps to match should be in every children's theatre wardrobe.

Tunics and tights, it can be seen, are needed more often than any other type of costume, for they are worn in various styles and degrees of richness for nobles, peasants, and pages during the whole mediæval and Renaissance periods. Because even cotton tights are expensive, many school theatres manage with long hose or old-fashioned underwear. Tights are much more satisfactory, however, as they fit better and do not require short trousers. If the costume assistants launder them after each wearing, they will last for many shows. With the tights plain house slippers are generally worn, since they resemble the type of footwear worn much in the mediæval and Renaissance periods. Long pointed shoes of the soft variety worn especially in the fourteenth and fifteenth centuries may be simulated by the use of men's socks stitched to a point and rolled at the top. These wear out quickly but are quite satisfactory for one production. Tights, of course, should never be worn without shoes of some sort.

PAGES

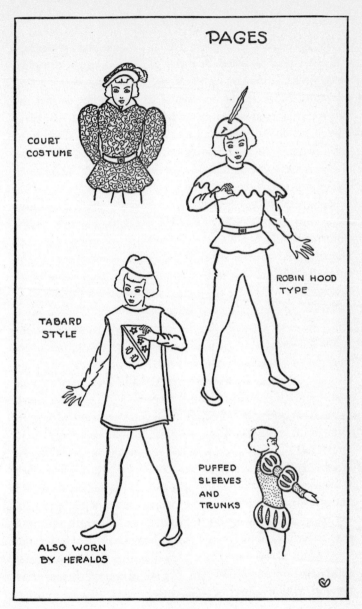

COURT
COSTUME

ROBIN HOOD
TYPE

TABARD
STYLE

PUFFED
SLEEVES
AND
TRUNKS

ALSO WORN
BY HERALDS

FIGURE 4

A most interesting variety in styles and color combinations for tunics may be found in costume books and illustrated novels. There is the plain tunic with long tight sleeves and high collar, the same style with over-sleeves which are flared and scalloped, the latter type with only a remnant of the outer sleeve in the form of a band and a hanging strip of material, and many, many other styles. The tunics of nobles are made, if possible, of velvet, brocade, or wool, while peasants wear plain ones made of coarse materials resembling homespun. In length they vary, the usual type for children's plays reaching about half way from hip to knee. Belts are worn for all except the tabard style worn by heralds and pages.

Mediæval ladies' costumes are needed in rather large numbers because of the many casts which include court ladies. If early mediæval costumes are to be used, the best style is the long, semi-fitted dress in one piece, often with a slight sweep, long tight sleeves with flaring outer sleeves, sometimes with scalloped edge. The one illustrated in Figure 2 represents no one century but can be used for any mediæval play.

The veil (preferably of chiffon, possibly of voile) will often be used, either draped over the head-dress or with a fillet. This head-band should be worn rather low across the forehead rather than above it. When a wimple and gorget are worn the hair is not seen, but when only the veil is used the hair is often in two long braids over the shoulders.

Ladies' costumes belonging definitely in the fifteenth century should be high-waisted with neck low-pointed in front, long tight sleeves, full skirt, sweeping in back. The head-dress will be of the more extreme kind, such as the pointed hennin with a veil, the heart or horn head-dress, or one of

PEASANT WOMAN

GAY SHAWL OFFERS VARIETY

TYPE OF HAT

KERCHIEF WORN LOOSE OR TIED UNDER CHIN

VARIETY OF HEAD DRESS

VARIETY OF HEADDRESS

COLORFUL OVER SLEEVE

BASIC COSTUME

BRIGHT EMBROIDERED BODICE

VARIETY OF HEADDRESS

APRONS OF EVERY DESIGN AND COLOR

FIGURE 5

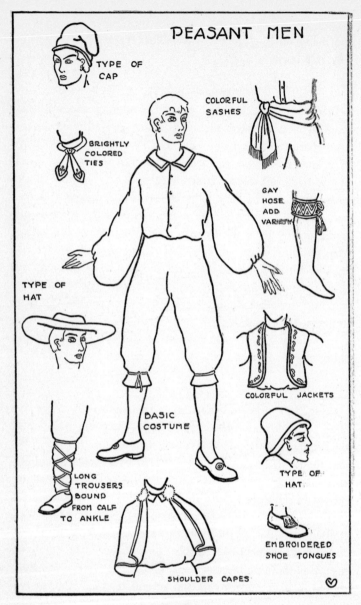

PEASANT MEN

TYPE OF CAP

COLORFUL SASHES

BRIGHTLY COLORED TIES

GAY HOSE ADD VARIETY

TYPE OF HAT

COLORFUL JACKETS

BASIC COSTUME

TYPE OF HAT

LONG TROUSERS BOUND FROM CALF TO ANKLE

SHOULDER CAPES

EMBROIDERED SHOE TONGUES

FIGURE 6

the many other elaborate styles. Shoes in every case will be soft and heelless.

PEASANT COSTUME

Play after play requires peasant costumes, the mediæval women wearing very plain variations of ladies' costumes, with characteristic caps or kerchiefs. Peasant women in plays of a later date wear the typical full skirt, decorative apron, blouse with full sleeves either long or short, and one of the many styles of bodices. (Figure 5.) To represent different nationalities a distinctive head-dress is used, the Russian differing greatly from the French, the German from the Italian. Men peasants to go with the full-skirted peasant women are usually dressed in knee-breeches, and blouses with long, full sleeves. (Figure 6.) Some nationalities add a gay sash or a belt, and the headgear is always distinctive. To dress peasants in gay holiday attire, unless for a festive occasion, is, of course, a mistake, but a certain amount of liberty is forgivable in children's productions in order that they may be colorful.

PIRATES

Long, full trousers gathered at the ankles are used very often in children's plays. (Figure 7.) They can be adapted for pirates, for the costumes used in *Aladdin* and *Ali Baba,* and for Dutchmen. With loose tunics, wide, soft girdles, kerchiefs around their heads, rings in their ears, some of the pirates in *Treasure Island* may be garbed very picturesquely. With square-cut jackets, mufflers, and Dutch caps, these trousers will do for the boys in *Hans Brinker.*

Another garment which has many uses in a children's theatre is the long circular cape. (Figure 8.) Every wardrobe should include a black one and several in color. One or two may have striking linings, though they are less noticeable when repeated if they are lined in a self color. Plays in almost any period can make use of them both for men and women, so that they fully pay for the cost and time of making them.

These then are the costumes which will be needed most often for children's plays: kings, queens, pages, mediæval lords and ladies, men and women peasants, and the long capes which have so many uses. In addition, school wardrobes need Colonial costumes both for Puritan and Cavalier. Men's Colonial costumes, especially, are rather widely used for seventeenth and eighteenth century European plays as well as for American. Costumes of many countries will sooner or later find their way into the theatre wardrobe as plays are produced which require Egyptian, Scotch, Spanish, Chinese, and dress of other peoples. Indian garments will be needed for Colonial plays and historical pageants. Animal costumes are much used in plays for the younger children.

WIGS

Wigs are to be avoided whenever possible, especially for child players. Even the best of them have an artificial look, and children's small faces are overshadowed by wigs which are unnaturally thick and heavy for them. Even though real hair may not answer to the description of the character given by the author, it has the advantage of looking natural.

This is not to say that wigs should never be used, for they are often necessary when the character is much older than the player. The short modern hair-cut of a boy or a man cannot be made to look in the least like the hair of men in former periods, and for plays set at a time when long hair

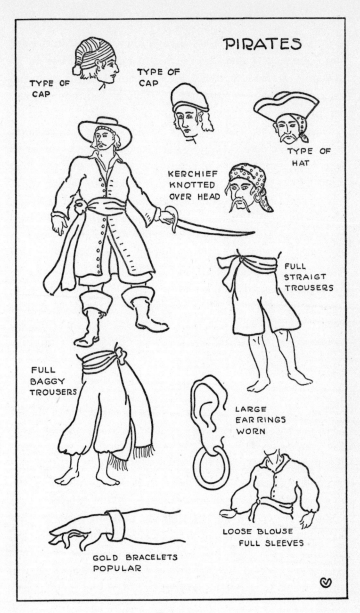

PIRATES

TYPE OF CAP

TYPE OF CAP

TYPE OF HAT

KERCHIEF KNOTTED OVER HEAD

FULL STRAIGT TROUSERS

FULL BAGGY TROUSERS

LARGE EARRINGS WORN

LOOSE BLOUSE FULL SLEEVES

GOLD BRACELETS POPULAR

FIGURE 7

CAPES

WORN ON BACK OF SHOULDERS

SAME CAPE WORN DIAGONALLY

DESIGN AND PIN BROOCH CAN CHANGE THE PERIOD

CLASP BROOCH AND BORDER AID CHANGE

HIGH COLLAR FOR ROYALTY

DAGGING ADDED TO HEM FOR CHANGE

LOW COLLAR AND SHORT CAPE ADDED

DESIGNS MAY BE APPLIQUED ON CAPES FOR CHANGE

FIGURE 8

was commonly worn, wigs must be used. A young girl playing the part of an elderly woman may need to disguise her
looks thus in order to create the right illusion. The powdered
wigs of Colonial days and the periwigs which men wore in
the days of Louis XIV have no substitute, of course, and
are always worn for plays of those periods. One should always consult costume books, however, concerning the class
of society that wore wigs and the occasions on which they
were worn.

Most schools and theatres rent whatever wigs they use, as
they are expensive to buy and have to be specially dressed
for every production. Long braids and curls, obtainable at
dime stores, are a boon for youthful characters who wear caps
or ribbons to which they can be attached. A large cast of
boys who played in an operetta set in the Civil War period
were made up to look like charming girls by curling their
hair (which had been allowed to grow for some weeks) and
adding curls fastened to the ribbons tied around their heads.

FANCIFUL COSTUMES

It is the fanciful costumes which have least permanent use.
Such characters as Sugar, Bread, Fire, and many others in
The Blue Bird require a kind of dress which probably can
never be used again. This is the time to economize in fabrics,
substituting clever designs and striking color combinations
for good materials, and creating costumes which will be highly
effective for the moment.

After a few years of collecting stock costumes, a school or
children's theatre will find costuming becoming an easier part
of the production. Plays will not now have to be costumed
throughout, for the wardrobe will be so large that it can

outfit complete productions. Very few new things need be made during an entire season, and these can be done with especial care for important characters, the crowds of villagers, vagabonds, pirates, and what not, being garbed from the wardrobe. We shall need the costume manager, though, for there is much to be done in choosing and adapting costumes, as well as in running the show. Some dresses must be taken in at the waist and lengthened in the skirt. Others need new painted borders. Certain hats are out of shape, and several more are needed—enough work to keep a crew busy for several evenings without a single costume to make. Then we must think of combinations which will make them seem new. If a costumière has chosen her colors carefully, she can make so many harmonious combinations that the costumes will always be lovely. By changing collars, sashes, trimmings, and combining different tunics and tights, the children who have seen every play for the last four years will fail to recognize them.

ORGANIZATION FOR PERFORMANCES

A costume manager who has had four or five assistants in making the costumes has ordinarily the same people to work during performances. This is, of course, an advantage, for no other crew will know so well as they how the costumes should go on. If mothers have made the costumes for a child cast, they will be the best assistants during the performance.

Each costume as it is finished is tagged with the name of the character who is to wear it, and hung with the others ready for the dress rehearsals. If they can be taken from the sewing-room in high enough boxes so that they can be hung rather than folded, they will reach the theatre in much better condition. All costumes are carefully pressed before each performance.

Whether the actors are adults or children, each is assigned to some one particular assistant to be dressed. He receives his costume from her, is instructed as to the manner of getting into it, and reports back to her for inspection and adjustments. If he wears a wig she always puts it on for him, and if he must make a quick change during a scene, she is on the stage with his costume ready to help him.

During the dress rehearsals the costume manager inspects the costumes from the auditorium and makes note of every change which must be made before the performances. Sometimes she sees that skirts are too long or too short or that they do not hang well; often she sees that the color scheme would be better if some of the minor characters exchanged costumes; or she may find that certain accessories are missing.

At the end of each rehearsal and after every performance all costumes are brought back to the crew-members responsible for them and are checked to make sure they are complete before being hung back in their places. If any mending is necessary, these assistants attend to it. If tights are worn they see that they are rinsed out after each performance that they may keep their shape as well as be more lasting. When the production is ended the costumes are all cleaned or laundered before being returned to their boxes in the costume room. The expense incurred by keeping costumes always fresh is considerable, but it is necessary both for preserving the garments and for sanitary purposes.

Thus it is seen that in a smoothly running children's theatre production a capable and well-organized costume crew is an important part. A person who can coöperate with director and technician in plans and their execution, and in the emergencies which are sure to arise, who can provide lovely and suitable costumes and so organize her work as to have them ready on time, who can train a crew in the dressing of the cast and the care of the garments, who is, withal, a real person with a live and human interest in all that the theatre is trying to achieve, such a person at the head of costumes is one of the most valuable assets a children's theatre can have.

CHAPTER X

THE CURTAINS PART

AS THE LIGHTS in the theatre slowly dim for the opening of the curtains, there is a moment fraught with such joyous expectancy that a youthful audience feels an impulse to burst into a shout of joy. Whether or not the outburst is restrained, the tendency is inevitably felt throughout the auditorium. It is the child's spontaneous expression of eagerness to see what is on the other side of the curtains.

How satisfying will be the picture he sees as the curtains part depends largely on the designer and the technician of the production. If they (or he, for one person often executes his own designs) are not only artists, but artists who understand children, the setting is likely to be simple but full of color. Whether it happens to be the forest depths, a picturebook house, an underground cave, or the jungles of Africa, it will stir the imagination of every child in the house. If there are mechanical effects such as the sound and motion of an English railway train in *The Secret Garden,* or the flying in *Peter Pan,* the technician will have spent endless thought and time working them out, knowing as he does what a delight such effects always prove to children.

Letters which boys and girls write to directors are full of such comments as the following:

"I enjoyed *Peter Pan* the most. The way they could fly was like magic on the stage."

"The silver-gray mountains were very enchanting."

"At sunset the sky was a beautiful orange with the mountains getting gray."

"The olive-green crocodile was evil and sly."

From an older child: "In *Radio Rescue* the lighting effects and the storm were good, but I think the smell of frying fish did the trick. It made me forget that it was a play. I seemed to be going through the experience with them."

WHAT CHILDREN EXPECT

What children expect in settings is influenced by illustrations in books, by the crude backgrounds of school plays they have seen, and by moving pictures. The result is such a diversity of standards that they expect almost anything in the way of scenery until they have found out what the children's theatre has to offer. Certain it is that they prefer many different settings, following one another with lightning-like rapidity. Moving pictures have led them to expect frequent changes, and though they know these are impossible on the stage, they are nevertheless highly pleased to see the curtains open each time on a different setting.

Because children's plays so often call for four or five scene shifts, the technical director has a problem on his hands in devising settings which can be changed quickly. Without a revolving or wagon stage, he must plan carefully, sacrificing detail to speed, selecting those features which will mean most to children. By the use of color changes in the lighting, and by using hinged screens or permanent settings, he can achieve a great variety with few changes.

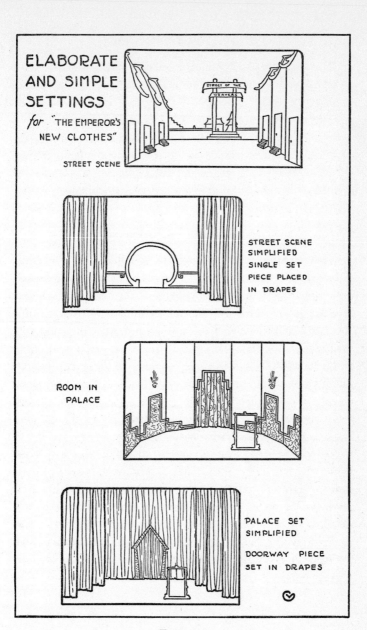

ELABORATE AND SIMPLE SETTINGS

for "THE EMPEROR'S NEW CLOTHES"

STREET SCENE

STREET SCENE SIMPLIFIED SINGLE SET PIECE PLACED IN DRAPES

ROOM IN PALACE

PALACE SET SIMPLIFIED

DOORWAY PIECE SET IN DRAPES

FIGURE 9

A THEATRE WITH A SMALL BUDGET

Theatres which can afford only very inexpensive scenery have practically as much chance to please the children as do those which stage their plays elaborately. Success depends not on costly productions but on whether the designer knows what appeals to boys and girls. The plans for *The Emperor's New Clothes* (Figure 9) illustrate what can be done to simplify stage settings if it is desired to use curtains instead of scenery. With one set piece placed between curtains, the first and third acts could be played very satisfactorily, especially if it were gaily painted in Oriental design. The second act would be effective done with only a door-frame in which had been hung curtains contrasting with the stage draperies.

With very limited facilities and small funds, it is possible for a designer to achieve remarkably interesting effects. If the stage is already equipped with draperies, a few set pieces such as arches, windows, and levels, can be used in combination with them for many kinds of interiors. When this is done it is important that the pieces should be distinctive in line and design, setting the period, nationality, or style of production. A castle door with massive hinges, a Gothic arch, an Egyptian vulture design, a stained glass window, a massive column, a fantastic cave, easily stir the imagination to complete the picture. Banners and tapestries (Figure 10) can do much to transform a bare stage into a palace, and a few tree-trunks seen against a sky which is framed by curtains will with careful lighting suggest a forest. Such curtains are most effective in black velours, but may be gray-green, sand, gray, or blue rep.

Screens with irregular tops (which are cut from profile board and screwed to the screens) may be used for a palace,

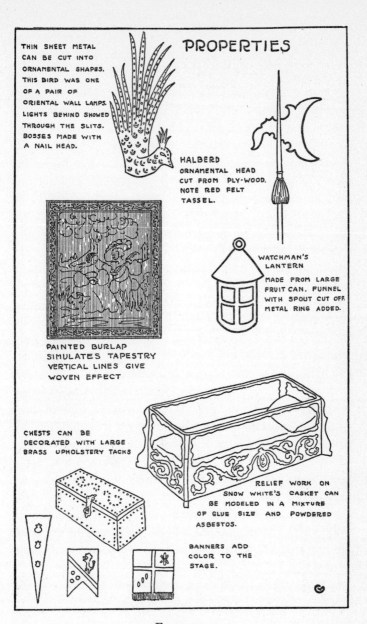

PROPERTIES

THIN SHEET METAL CAN BE CUT INTO ORNAMENTAL SHAPES. THIS BIRD WAS ONE OF A PAIR OF ORIENTAL WALL LAMPS. LIGHTS BEHIND SHOWED THROUGH THE SLITS. BOSSES MADE WITH A NAIL HEAD.

HALBERD ORNAMENTAL HEAD CUT FROM PLY-WOOD. NOTE RED FELT TASSEL.

WATCHMAN'S LANTERN MADE FROM LARGE FRUIT CAN. FUNNEL WITH SPOUT CUT OFF. METAL RING ADDED.

PAINTED BURLAP SIMULATES TAPESTRY VERTICAL LINES GIVE WOVEN EFFECT

CHESTS CAN BE DECORATED WITH LARGE BRASS UPHOLSTERY TACKS

RELIEF WORK ON SNOW WHITE'S CASKET CAN BE MODELED IN A MIXTURE OF GLUE SIZE AND POWDERED ASBESTOS.

BANNERS ADD COLOR TO THE STAGE.

FIGURE 10

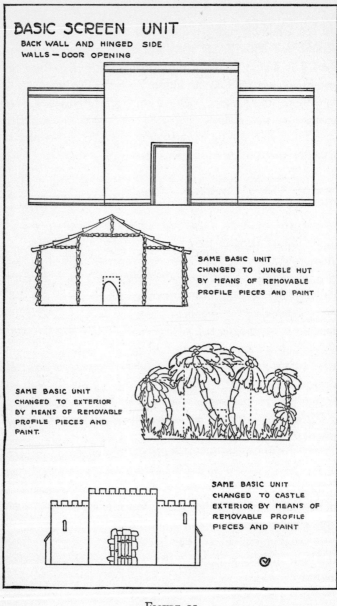

BASIC SCREEN UNIT
BACK WALL AND HINGED SIDE
WALLS — DOOR OPENING

SAME BASIC UNIT
CHANGED TO JUNGLE HUT
BY MEANS OF REMOVABLE
PROFILE PIECES AND PAINT

SAME BASIC UNIT
CHANGED TO EXTERIOR
BY MEANS OF REMOVABLE
PROFILE PIECES AND
PAINT.

SAME BASIC UNIT
CHANGED TO CASTLE
EXTERIOR BY MEANS OF
REMOVABLE PROFILE
PIECES AND PAINT

FIGURE II

a street, a humble cottage. The many scenes in *Ali Baba* and *Aladdin* are effective set with screens which have Oriental lines. The quaint house of the *Seven Dwarfs* may show the roof in silhouette. Note the hinged screens (Figure 11) with suggestions for changing them to suit various purposes. Such settings are not realistic, but they are practical and often beautiful. If they can be set in front of a sky-drop, they always make strikingly picturesque settings.

UNUSUAL STAGE-EFFECTS

New and unusual stage-effects should be used in a children's theatre because they are interesting in themselves in addition to affording opportunities to educate the artistic taste of young people. A designer with imagination may do much with a plastic set, devising all manner of variations; he may use a stereopticon or moving-picture machine to project the clouds and mountains needed for *Heidi,* or the magic palace of Aladdin; he may so design settings and lighting as to use several stage areas in succession (a device needed in the pantomime of *Ali Baba*), blocking out by lighting all but the one on which the scene is being played. With marionettes and animated cartoons he may achieve most amazing illusions.

Beauty there should be in children's theatre settings, beauty which transcends the realistic and reaches for the ideal. Just as the plots of the plays have poetic justice in their outcomes, so may the settings be idealized. Inner loveliness is usually represented in children's stories by outward beauty; and children, drinking in lovely stage pictures, become more sensitive both to beauty which is seen and that which is symbolized.

THE TECHNICAL DIRECTOR

Though superior settings can never make up for poor directing and acting, they add immeasurably to the success of any production. The contribution of the technician, therefore, is one of the determining factors in the success of any children's theatre. In order to simplify the discussion concerning qualifications and duties, he will be referred to henceforth as 'the person who both designs and constructs (or supervises the construction of) the settings. He is responsible also for the lighting plans, whether or not he operates the lights.

A technician who builds from his own designs has a great advantage over the one who carries out the designs of another. An artist who can construct usually turns out more delightful settings than does the prosaic builder. If a line or a color effect is a bit disappointing when the scenery comes on the stage, he is free to change it without calling back the designer. In professional theatres such a combination of work is impossible, but amateur groups are fortunate if they can find a man who can do both. At all events, the artist should supervise the execution of his drawings, for the unimaginative builder can ruin an inspired design.

Since the technical director necessarily handles scenery both in construction and in the running of the show, it is an advantage to have a man in this position. It is conceivable that a technician might supervise entirely, employing others to do all the heavy work, but this is so seldom the case that we shall consider him as a man who designs and executes the scenery, moves it, and runs the performances.

The qualifications of a technical director are varied, and they include both artistic and practical abilities. If he were

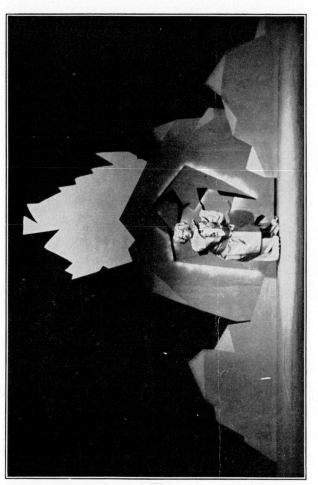

ALI BABA AND THE FORTY THIEVES

Children's Theatre, Evanston, Illinois.

a fine artist without a knowledge of the theatre, he would have to learn that settings must be something more than pictures. In the integrated process of production, every element must take its proper place in the whole. Recognizing the fact that the play itself is of cardinal importance, the artist should so design the settings as to strengthen the mood of the play rather than to smother the story and its characters by scenery which shouts, "Look at me!" His appreciation of dramatic values then is as valuable as his ability to design.

The fundamentals of electricity as applied to stage lighting are necessarily a part of the technician's training. Even if he has an electrician on his staff, he needs to understand thoroughly the lighting equipment of the stages on which he works. In most children's theatres he must supervise the lighting of the plays, and usually he has to train the crew members who work the lights. Electricity is a fascinating subject to many boys, and in almost every theatre are several boys of high-school age or older who become faithful and valuable members of the lighting staff.

A technical director who has real interest in children's theatre work is usually more successful than one who has merely the desire to use the children's theatre as a stepping-stone to adult theatre work. If his heart is young, if he thoroughly enjoys children and gets real pleasure in their response to the plays, he will find great satisfaction in producing for them.

Because he heads the crews who must work day after day for long hours without the glory which the cast enjoys, he needs to be a person who is respected and thoroughly liked. If he himself works hard side by side with the crew, they are ashamed to do less than their best. If he is patient with their mistakes, they will try hard to please him; and if he gets a deal of fun out of seeing the sets grow, the crew, too, will enjoy them. The feeling around a workshop when a director is cheery, optimistic, and appreciative of good work, always makes for a high morale among the crew.

Ability to organize is very necessary also, since careful estimates must be made of the time required to build the scenery that it may be completely ready for the first dress rehearsal. The building of a children's theatre show requires many evenings, and the technician should avoid the mad rush which comes at the last if he has not allowed plenty of time. When the crew is so organized that each member has a definite piece of work to carry through, time will not be wasted in explanations at the beginning of every work period.

Economy in ordering material and in rebuilding and re-painting old settings and properties is a valuable asset in a production manager. Lumber, hardware, cloth, and paints are large items of expense, and he can save the theatre a great deal of money if he is economical.

Before the technician makes his designs for the settings of a play, he meets with the director and the costume designer to decide upon the style of production. Some plays can be nothing but frankly realistic, while others might be stylized or given fantastic settings and costumes to intensify the unreal mood of the play. Agreement on period is necessary unless the story is outside of any period, in which case harmony of production will require even more care.

Many different nationalities are represented in children's plays, and the technician may have to do much research work to find pictures of Russian stoves such as Katrinka used as a bed or French goldsmith shops for *The Boy Knight of Reims*.

Vitally important to the play's success is harmony between

director and technician, and if their tastes are not in accord, they would do well to separate at once. Only by working as one person can the staff attain that unity of production which is achieved by the European *régisseur*. If the technical director has the ability to catch the spirit of the play and reflect it in his settings and if he sees his work in its true relationship to that of the director, the costume manager, and the electrician, then, indeed, is he a valued member of the children's theatre staff.

THE STAGE-MANAGER

Until the period of dress rehearsals the director and the technician have been working apart from each other, one in rehearsal rooms, the other in the shop. When the two forces which make up the production combine on the stage they seldom fit together perfectly. Many adjustments are necessary. Each phase must come to understand the requirements of the other. To save time and frustration in this, the most nervous period of the production, the job of stage-manager is introduced. He (or she) has divided his time between the crew and the cast, thereby familiarizing himself with such details as the size and shape of a stool which is being built and also the placement of it on the stage for the business of the actor.

The stage-manager then is logically the person to be responsible during rehearsal and performance for all cuing of curtains, of lighting-effects, of sound-effects. He coördinates the mechanical elements produced by the technician with the intricacies of the business worked out by the director.

During a scene change each crew head reports to the stage-manager when his particular phase is ready, whether it is the setting, the lights, the properties. When all phases are ready and he has checked each of them, especially the properties, from the actor's standpoint, the stage-manager gets the act under way.

ELECTRICIANS

Several weeks before the first performance the electrician confers with the director, the technician, and the costume manager, and makes general plans for the lighting of the play, that it may harmonize with the other phases of the production. He receives a light-plot from the director with all cues and light-effects required, and at the technical rehearsal he and his assistants set and adjust the lights in accordance with the advice of the stage-manager. At this rehearsal duties are divided, making one person responsible for the house lights, another for the switchboard, another, perhaps, for changes of spot-lights.

At each dress rehearsal changes will have to be made until the best effects possible have been ascertained. If new lamps, cable, connectors, or other equipment are found to be necessary, the matter is reported to the technical director before the first dress rehearsal, and if the budget permits, he issues requisitions for the needed materials.

The electrician and his assistants care for the equipment between rehearsals if the stage is used by others, and see to it that any resetting of lights necessary is done before the following rehearsal. After the final performance of the play, all equipment which is to be stored is neatly put away and note taken of reconditioning which should be done before the next production.

THE PROPERTY-MANAGER AND CREW

The head of properties, having, of course, read the play, lists the properties and consults with the director to ascertain whether she has certain wishes concerning any of them and whether changes are to be made in the number and kind of properties. "A jewel-case" might mean anything from a small wooden box to an exquisite gold casket. "A pile of satin cushions" may need to be inconspicuous or gay. In order to harmonize with scenery and costumes, and to suit the personality of the character who uses them, the property-manager must work close to both director and designer.

After making separate lists of properties which are to be built, borrowed, and rented, he begins, with a group of assistants, to build and collect them at the time the construction of settings is begun. Authors of children's plays stop at nothing in the properties they require. It is not unusual to ask for a whole pet shop with live animals, a cave full of jewels, magic smoke, fish to be fried and eaten on the stage. The property crew, therefore, needs to be resourceful and ingenious in building, indefatigable in its search for exactly the right properties, and thoroughly dependable in the cues for sound-effects required in the play. So complicated are these effects for some plays that a special sound crew is appointed. In such a play as *Radio Rescue,* where all kinds of sounds must come exactly on cue, a crew for this work is imperative.

MAKE-UP CREW

Experienced actors make up themselves for plays, but many amateurs require some one to do it for them. For this reason several people with some experience are needed to make up

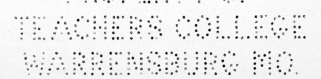

amateur casts, the number varying in proportion to the cast and the number of difficult make-ups. The head of the make-up keeps the make-up box supplied, sees to it that a table is in readiness if there are no regular stands, supervises all the make-ups, sees that they are removed after performances, and keeps the box in order.

Aside from knowing the play thoroughly, the make-up crew should observe one or more rehearsals before dress rehearsals. They are also guided by the director's list of the characters with description of the make-up for each, and they must often do some research to find out the shape of beards, hair-arrangements, and other points of period and racial make-up. Unless these people are skillful, it is wise to experiment, making up the cast for each of two or three dress rehearsals.

This, then, is the crew which the technical director organizes for backstage work in a children's theatre. In size it varies from eight to twenty or twenty-five members. Fewer skilled workers are obviously to be preferred to many inexperienced crew members, unless it is important that new people be constantly in training. Good management on the part of the technical director, with careful organization and thorough rehearsing, will insure smooth performances even though the production is handicapped by an unskilled crew. Several permanent heads, such as electrician, property, and make-up managers, will make his work much simpler, however, and help greatly in the assimilation of new and untried workers.

CHAPTER XI

ADVERTISING OURSELVES

IN THESE DAYS of garish billboards, extensive newspaper and magazine advertisements, persistent radio announcements concerning the virtues of toothpastes, baby foods, automobiles, and so on, the world is well acquainted with all manner of publicity. Indeed, so blatant has advertising become that one could wish to dispense with much that already exists rather than to add to the volume. But the fact remains that unless such an institution as a theatre is given much publicity, a surprisingly large number of people in a community will remain unbelievably ignorant of its existence for years.

To know just what kinds of publicity will bring children to a theatre, and to make use of them, solves the attendance problem, granted, of course, that the productions are well done. The methods are different in several respects from adult advertising, and they should be studied and tested thoroughly.

In the first place, the publicity manager will determine whether it is more important to convince children or their parents that the plays are worth seeing. It is the parents who must give permission and money and sometimes accompany the children, but after all, the children will bring pressure on their parents if they really want to see the play.

Parents are best reached through newspapers, parent-teacher associations, and other club meetings. Children are reached through information given out in schools, in school papers, handbills, posters, and in little previews of the play. Many other methods of advertising there are, such as broadcasting a scene over a local radio station, advertising at the moving-picture house if the managers are willing to coöperate, distributing stickers for cars, and in novel ways suited to individual plays or communities.

Most experienced children's theatre people will agree that publicity must interest both parents and children. The parents must be made to realize that the plays will be a delightful and suitable form of recreation for their children, offering a partial solution for the problem of leisure time and a substitution for adult moving pictures. Vicariously, too, many parents will be able through their children to satisfy their own hunger for the make-believe world which was denied them in their youth.

As for the children themselves, offer them a good show, and if it sounds better than anything else they might do on that day, and if the money is forthcoming, they will be there. The publicity must make the play sound very attractive and interesting, and must continue to remind them of it up to the very day of performance; for children are easily distracted from the enthusiasm of the moment, and unless they actually have their tickets, they may decide at the last minute to go tobogganing or skating or to the movies instead of to the play.

HOW TO BEGIN THE PUBLICITY

If a children's theatre is new in a community, a process of education for both adults and children must go on for a long period of time. Suppose there was much newspaper publicity at the time the theatre was organized in the spring and that the opening play was announced for November. At the parent-teacher meetings in September a children's theatre worker should be present to explain what it hopes to do for the children of the community, to tell of its plans for the season, and to enlist the interest of parents and teachers.

These first talks can do great things for the children's theatre if they are given by a dynamic person who convinces by her sane reasons and at the same time fires to enthusiasm the members of the organization. It is strategic to induce the program chairman to make this person the chief speaker, thus increasing her prestige and giving her far more time for her message than if she merely made an announcement. If this is impossible at the first meeting, she may plan for her few minutes' talk so carefully and make it so provocative of interest that she may be given more time at a later meeting.

There are other groups of mothers in clubs and churches who are worth the time and effort of a speaker, and the various men's organizations might very conceivably be interested by a live talk, preferably by a man. All adult groups concerned either with child interests or with the drama should lend their help and encouragement, particularly if they have faith in those sponsoring the theatre.

NEWSPAPER PUBLICITY

Concurrent with these talks should be one or more newspaper articles concerning the new project. An intelligent feature-writer of the paper itself is preferable to the publicity manager of the theatre for such articles, which may be in the form of interviews with the director or general chairman. It is of very great value to interest newspaper people so that they believe personally in the work of the theatre.

Whether or not the children's theatre is a new institution,

it is well to inform the public about plans for the whole year shortly before the season tickets go on sale. The schedule should be ready early enough so that the announcement can be complete. If for some reason this is impossible, the list from which the uncertain plays will be chosen may be published. This article should make the season's program sound so attractive that parents will feel that it is an opportunity that they cannot afford to have their children miss.

For about three weeks there should be continual newspaper publicity. How often stories will appear depends upon the policy of the papers. In a city paper the Sunday edition is sometimes the only one which will accept a story. At this time, however, a long, interesting article with an attractive caption, accompanied by a large picture, will have more publicity value than a whole series of short articles. Such a story is usually written by a feature-writer from notes given him by the theatre, and the picture is taken by a staff photographer of the newspaper.

Of all newspaper advertising, pictures give the greatest amount of publicity. No one who looks over the paper misses a picture, and even when it is poor it seems to count for more than does a good story. A striking picture three or four columns wide with only the bare facts underneath is of so much publicity value that it is worth the extra work of bringing some of the scenery for a background before time to move it to the stage for dress rehearsals, getting several characters into costume and make-up, and perhaps even renting wigs. For if the picture turns out to be especially striking, it is likely to appear in a large size in so prominent a place in the paper that it will be noticed by children and adults alike. The accompanying story will be all-inclusive, telling something, perhaps, about the children's theatre, the author, the plot of the play, the cast, the scenery, the production staff, besides the actual facts concerning the time and place of performances.

Newspapers in smaller cities and towns are often glad to print three or four stories as a matter of news. When the players are townspeople, the paper is usually generous in giving publicity. Some newspapers accept contributed articles if written to conform to their accepted style, though others prefer to write their own stories.

In sending material to more than one newspaper in a town, the publicity manager must be absolutely impartial in releasing announcements of plays and casts to all at the same time. If one paper is a daily, another a weekly, the former depends upon the freshness of its news and will not publish anything which has appeared in the weekly. Since the latter reviews the whole week, it must necessarily print news which has already come out in the daily. This material should vary enough, however, so that the opening part, at least, has freshness when a reader sees it in a second paper. Minor details and often whole feature articles should differ for various papers.

THE FIRST STORY

Let us suppose that this is the second season of a children's theatre which was successful in its initial year. We are about to write a first story designed to interest parents in buying season tickets, the sale of which will open a week hence. Shall we stress the first play, or distribute the interest evenly over the whole season? How detailed a story do we need? Are dates important? What can we say which will make parents want their children to come?

Suppose we analyze the following story which might appear in a local newspaper.

CHILDREN'S THEATRE TO OPEN SEASON WITH "TOM SAWYER"

By popular request of the children, Mark Twain's classic, *The Adventures of Tom Sawyer,* is to open the second season of the Children's Theatre of Blankton. Miss Marylee Smith announced to-day that the first performances will be at Lincoln school on November 14, at 10 in the morning and 2:30 in the afternoon, with the two final performances at Central school on November 21 at the same hours.

In all American literature there is perhaps no more popular boy's hero than the adventurous, fun-loving Tom, and it is not to be wondered at that at the end of last season, Children's Theatre audiences gave the play a unanimous vote for this year's program.

Four productions are scheduled for the Children's Theatre season, the January play being a dramatization by Eleanor Perkins of the popular Haskell novel, *Katrinka.* The story of the little Russian girl who danced her way into the Czar's favor and won a pardon for her exiled parents is to have its première production in the Children's Theatre of Blankton. A ballet from the Martin School of the Dance is to be a feature of the play, the girls acting as the pupils in the Imperial Ballet School at St. Petersburg.

An Arabian Nights' adventure is to be the third offering of the season. Theodora DuBois' *Aladdin,* with all the color and magic of the Orient, will be presented late in February.

Climaxing the season in March is Charlotte Chorpenning's *Radio Rescue,* a modern melodrama based on a true story. All sorts of thrills await the children who see this play. A two-way radio set which Sparky and Jill are forced to hide in an old mill brings a message which enables them to save a train from plunging over an embankment. Radio and train effects, a searching party, a storm, a washed-out trestle, make the play exciting, though at the same time it is far more human and convincing than the old type of melodrama.

Reserved season tickets for the four plays go on sale at all grade schools next Wednesday, following a short preview of the play which is to be taken on a tour of the schools on Monday and Tuesday. On Friday of next week, reserved tickets for the first play as well as for the season will be put on sale at the Harris Book Store.

The Children's Theatre, which is sponsored by (names of organizations), last season established beyond a doubt that such an institution was needed in this city. So great was the response to its first play that four instead of two performances were scheduled thereafter, with an increasing number of children at every production. This season's plays, chosen for quality as well as popular appeal, will be staged more elaborately than heretofore because of the additional equipment made possible by last year's patronage.

Notation of the following points in connection with this article may perhaps help the inexperienced person who must write publicity for a children's play.

1. Caption. It is of no use to try to think of a clever title for your story, for the newspaper will not use it. Captions are supplied by a member of the newspaper staff.

2. Since it is desirable that the paper use the title of the play and the name of the theatre in the caption, it may be well not to begin your story with either of them. Needless to say, however, both will be mentioned in the first paragraph.

3. An attention-catching phrase at the opening of the article is better, naturally, than a prosaic one. Instead of writing, "The opening play of the Children's Theatre season will be *Tom Sawyer*," the phrase, "By popular request of the children" is more likely to gain interest. "The immortal Mark Twain story, *The Adventures of Tom Sawyer*," would be quite as good. Even though this is not a feature story, it may be allowed a striking or picturesque opening phrase, especially since it is a children's play that is being publicized.

4. A rule of any such article is that it must tell what, when, where, and by whom either in the first sentence or at least in the opening paragraph. Newspapers always summarize the facts and then enlarge upon them.

5. Write in the third person. School papers are often more informal, with many articles in the second person, but town newspapers use the third person.

6. The facts about season tickets were put late in the story because they required so much space that they would have pushed the accounts of the three other plays too far down in the article.

7. The story should sound like news rather than advertising, and as if it were written by a reporter rather than a publicity manager. Note that "tickets go on sale Wednesday" rather than "get your tickets Wednesday."

8. Newspapers do not allow prices to be quoted, for this would turn the story into advertising. They will write of "a small sum" or "a nominal price," but not mention the amount. If a theatre can afford advertising space, prices can appear there. In a city such advertising is often so expensive that it is really prohibitive for such an institution as a children's theatre.

9. A play not generally known needs more of description in order to awaken interest. Thus, *Katrinka* and *Radio Rescue* have more space than the two better-known plays.

10. All interest in this first article is centered on the play itself rather than on casts, scenery or costumes. It is often advisable, however, to say, "The play is cast from the members of such and such an organization," or "from the public schools." The cast itself is saved for an issue of the paper near the day of the play.

11. Exact dates of only the first play are necessary, mention of the months being sufficient for the others.

12. Articles should always state very clearly when and where all immediate performances are to be given and where tickets may be obtained. A reader is inconvenienced if impor-

tant facts are omitted and he must find them out in some other way.

13. The sponsors should by all means be mentioned in the story. They serve to give stability and prestige to the theatre. According to their reputation, the probable standard of production will be judged.

14. Newspapers are conventional in their choice of words, and will usually modify original phrasings. To make a story interesting and a bit distinctive is difficult under these circumstances. It may be said, however, that they will usually accept more unconventional writing for a children's play than for many other events.

15. The length of this first article should be four or five hundred words. Succeeding ones will be shorter, averaging from two to four hundred. Paragraphs should be brief.

After the first play of the season, only one will be publicized at a time. The first story in that case will tell more about the plot, taking care, however, to stop short of telling too much of it. The author will always be mentioned, with a comment on his other plays or stories. If this play has been successfully produced in other cities, that point would be stressed.

FEATURE STORIES

About a week after the general news article, a feature story should appear in the newspapers. Such a story enlarges upon some aspect of the play, the author, the cast, or the production. The subject of this article may be one of many interesting features concerning this production, such as the locale of the story; the historical events concerned in the plot; customs of foreign peoples such as are characters in the play; the author; the producing organization; special music or dancing required in the play, with the names of groups or individuals who will present it; the cast; the costumes; the sound-effects which are sometimes so elaborate as to require a special crew; period costumes or properties loaned for the play; interesting incidents connected with rehearsals or preview or cast; the ticket sale; and many other things according to the production which is being given. Obviously, the choice of the feature and the tone of the story should show good taste, convincing the parents that this is a play they would be glad to have their children see. Some features will not be sufficient for a whole story, so that two or three related ones may be used. In advertising *The Indian Captive,* for instance, one story might tell of the customs and the dress of the Seneca Indians, going on to speak of their characteristic music and dancing, and mentioning the people who are making costumes and working out the movements of the dance.

The following are points to remember in connection with feature articles:

1. Do not take for granted that your readers have seen previous articles. Each story must carry the time and place at the beginning. The brief story of the plot will not be repeated, however.

2. Choose for your features those aspects of the production which will make the strongest appeal to adults, for they are the ones who read the newspaper. The most commonly used features are the cast, the scenery, costumes, staff, and the demand for tickets.

3. Take much care with your opening sentence, so that it may catch the interest of the readers. Here are a few from actual newspapers:

"The production of *Uncle Tom's Cabin,* which is opening Saturday afternoon at the Children's Theatre, is taking on the scope of a community affair with a cast drawn from the town, the Negro Little Theatre, the university and the public schools."

"Stone angels that lean out of their niches and speak to the boy Jean in the dark shadows of Reims cathedral will be unique characters in the Children's Theatre play, *The Boy Knight of Reims*, which opens Saturday morning at Washington school."

"At a novel tryout for *Mr. Dooley, Jr.*, Children's Theatre play opening on January 19, dogs instead of persons contested for the title rôle."

" 'If people of quality wear the pattern upside down,' exclaims Jourdain in the Children's Theatre play, 'then I will have my coat that way.' And to the distress of the costume crew for *The Merchant Gentleman*, which will open at the Children's Theatre Saturday, one of the beautiful Louis XIV coats had to be made with the flowers wrong end up.

4. Greater informality is allowed in feature stories than in general news articles. Here is an opening sentence which appeared in the Sunday edition of a large city paper:

"The somnolent folk of old Riverboro will be rubbing startled eyes again, for adventurous Rebecca Rowena Randall of the pink parasol and the agile imagination is returning from Temperance to the Brick House and crotchety Aunt Miranda and gentle Aunt Jane."

This, too:

"Like polite Chinese visitors who remove their slippers on the doorstep before crossing the threshold, grown-up folk will leave the sophisticated years outside next Saturday on entering the auditorium of Blank school to join the audience of boys and girls assembled to see a revival of *Snow White and the Seven Dwarfs*."

5. Exaggerated claims for the play and its production are most unwise. To enlarge upon the wonderful magic effects which will be seen in *Aladdin,* the spectacular, broken-down trestle and approach of the train in *Radio Rescue,* or the aërial party in *Mary Poppins* would be to invite criticism if the scene did not live up to the claim. Since it is impossible to know just how effective these things are going to be, it is wise to refrain from over-enthusiasm about any phase of the production.

6. The cast is usually featured a week or ten days before the first performance. The leading characters, naturally, are made prominent, though if they happen to be children, it is far better for their own sake to feature a group rather than an individual. Often there are two or more leading characters, as in *The Slippers of Cinderella* or *The Scotch Twins* or *The Blue Bird,* and in many cases these parts are double-cast. To feature a group of children seems to have a much less personal effect than to allow one child's name to appear in a headline.

In the case of adults, the leading character is given special prominence, and point is made of former rôles in which he has appeared. Minor people are often grouped, their own names being given but not the names of their characters in the play.

A day or two before the first performance, a picture of several members of the cast in a scene from the play should appear. No story will be run on this day, only the bare facts of the name of the play, author, names of the people in the picture, the scene which is shown, the organization, the director, the place, date, and time.

OTHER KINDS OF PUBLICITY

Early in the school year there should be some advance publicity in the public and private schools so that the season-ticket sale may not find the children unprepared either as to money or enthusiasm. This publicity may come through stories and pictures in the school paper, clever advertising skits at assemblies or public entertainments, or any other effective type of announcement. If the theatre has a children's board, the members will find ways of advertising suited to their respective schools.

POSTERS

Just before the season-ticket campaign, about three weeks previous to the first play, the posters should be ready. For the remaining plays of the season, ten days ahead is sufficient time. This type of advertising reaches many people who do not see any other publicity. Posters in school halls are especially useful to keep children reminded of the plays, and placed in shop windows, libraries, Y.M.C.A.'s, and any other place where children go, they are a good, though not the best, kind of publicity.

Results from poster advertising are relative not only to good placing but especially to appearance. Large posters, striking in color combination and design, attract attention wherever they are placed, whereas ordinary white ones cluttered with too much information are nearly useless for children. All the printing really needed on such posters is the name of the play, the place, dates, hours, and "Children's Theatre." A very simple picture suggestive of the story is an asset. The card may be of one color, the printing and picture in one, two, or three contrasting colors.

Gaily colored original posters made by children are used

by many theatres, a poster competition having been found to serve the double purpose of arousing interest in the play and procuring a supply of attractive posters.

Probably the handsomest type of poster, however, is that made by the silk screen, illustrated in this chapter. As it is a patented process, it cannot be described so that one could reproduce it, but an address where such a machine can be obtained is listed in the appendix of this book. Since these posters require time and effort, a limited number, carefully placed to the best advantage in school and store windows, may be all that will be used. Much of their effectiveness depends upon a bold design and a small amount of printing, so that not more than one play should be publicized by each poster. Smaller season announcements, therefore, may be printed for bulletin boards, class rooms, libraries, and for mailing to schools and libraries in neighboring towns. These may be printed on a good quality of paper which may be folded for mailing.

THE PREVIEW

Of all types of publicity, by far the most effective for children is the preview. This is a short scene, usually about five minutes in length, which is taken on a tour of the schools just before the season-ticket sale. Because children remember better what they see than what they hear, and because when well chosen it can arouse a desire to see the whole play, this little scene is extremely valuable for advertising purposes.

Arrangements for such a tour require time and patience. If the theatre is a school project, or if the schools coöperate, the preview will be allowed, but the consent of every principal must be secured for the time of the showing in each school. To conserve the time of all who go on the tour, the publicity

POSTERS

Children's Theatre, Evanston, Illinois.

manager should make an exact schedule according to the shortest route from school to school, and telephone to the principal ten days or two weeks in advance. If only one school is unable to have the showing on the scheduled day, it may be necessary to change the time for the whole tour in order that that particular school may not be missed.

It is really a concession for the superintendent to allow this tour, for it means that all the pupils (above the first or second grade, perhaps) must be brought together, often at the most inopportune time, for about ten minutes of advertising. To ask that all the schools disrupt their programs for this purpose is expecting a great favor, and for this reason it is advisable to ascertain whether or not the general preference is for afternoon hours. If so, one, two, or three afternoons may be used rather than whole days. Needless to say, this preview should be undertaken only for the first play of the season unless it can be shown in certain big schools at their regular assembly periods.

The choice of the scene used for the preview is, of course, highly important. It should be one of the most dramatic or humorous bits in the entire play, and should not be so dependent on the rest of the story as to require a long introduction. Though costumes should be used, very little in the way of background or properties can be set up hastily, so that a scene which will be least handicapped by their absence is advisable. Because a definite beginning, with action rising to some sort of climax is necessary, this scene may require some revamping.

Illustrations of several scenes which have worked especially well for the purpose are the following:

1. *Uncle Tom's Cabin.* The deliciously funny scene in which Miss Ophelia makes Topsy's acquaintance, including Topsy's

classic answer to the prim New Englander's question, "Do you know who made you?" "Nobody as I knows on. I spect I jes' growed."

2. *Peter Pan.* The medicine scene in the Darling home, when father "misses" taking his medicine as Michael gulps it down.

3. *Jack and the Beanstalk.* The giant counts his money bags, while his wife manœuvers to keep him from missing the one she has given to Jack. The scene is both exciting and humorous.

The question of whether it is taking the freshness off the children's enjoyment of the play to show them one of the best scenes in advance would seem to be a pertinent one. Experience has proved, however, that this method heightens rather than diminishes their enjoyment. They like to see good things over and over; and when a scene they have enjoyed in a preview appears in the play, they get additional pleasure in recognizing it in the midst of the action with all the interest of setting and context.

When children are included in a cast which makes publicity tours, the theatre faces the problem of taking them out of school. Teachers and principals are coöperative, however, because of their pride in the players, and if there is a double cast, each may act the preview in the district in which it is to play.

HANDBILLS

When each particular school has assembled, the publicity manager, director, or some good speaker may tell the children about the season of plays and stir enthusiasm for the approaching ticket sale. Then he or she will announce the little sample of the play which is to follow, giving briefly any necessary exposition. The curtains will then open on the scene, or if there are no curtains, the actors will enter and begin to play. Because some schools may not have a stage, it is always an advantage to choose a scene which allows the players to enter and exit in character.

This ends the preview except for gay handbills which may be given by the teachers to all the pupils as they leave the school. These handbills, announcing the entire season, with place, dates, price, and time of season-ticket sale, are intended for the parents, since the younger children especially seldom remember the information correctly. It may be said here that unless the season's plays have been chosen to appeal to very young children, they probably should not be summoned to the auditorium nor given handbills to take home.

Thus the season may be advertised. It is no small business this, and much time, thought, and energy will be spent on it. Little money is necessary if home-made posters are used, and the cheap handbills probably pay for themselves many times over by interesting the parents. But an intelligent, enterprising, and dynamic business manager, who believes in the theatre, can by unflagging zeal contribute more than any amount of money could accomplish. And when a successful season is ended, a generous measure of appreciation should go to the enterprising and indefatigable person who has made the children's theatre known to the community.

CHAPTER XII

WE PAY THE BILLS

IF YOU are looking for a money-making scheme, choose something besides a children's theatre as a project. If, on the other hand, you are considering whether your organization dare take the risk of financing one, you need not be afraid, providing you have people who are capable and willing to work. The time is not far past when the chief reason for giving amateur plays was to raise money for school papers, football uniforms, class gifts, charities. Even yet, a club of women occasionally proposes to finance some pet service project by giving a children's play, thinking it an easy way to earn money.

ITEMS OF EXPENSE

Quite apart from the fact that a children's theatre is a worthy end in itself, it is not a good means of making money. In the place of financing some other cause, it more often needs subsidies itself. It can be made to pay its own expenses; indeed, it can make money for its promoters. The point is that it *should* not earn any considerable amount. The reasons follow:

I. Children's plays are expensive if well chosen and well staged.

To begin with, there is the royalty which ranges from ten to twenty-five dollars a performance. This is less than for

most adult plays, but a considerable item if several performances are to be given in a small auditorium.

Then there is the rental of the theatre if the sponsors do
not have one of their own. This is so likely to be prohibitive
that any group of people interested in a children's theatre
will do well to secure as one of the sponsors a school or
other institution which does have an auditorium with an
adequate stage.

The scenery and costumes for children's plays are usually
costly. Instead of the one or two easy interiors which are
characteristic of so many adult plays, they are likely to require three or four, ranging, perhaps, from a raft on the
river (*Huckleberry Finn*) to a scene in the mouth of
a fish (*Pinocchio*)! Though scenery can be simplified, imagine
Treasure Island without a stockade, *Jack and the Beanstalk*
without a gigantic beanstalk, and *Aladdin* without a cave full
of gold and jewels!

If any responsibility is felt for the development of children's
appreciation of beauty, to say nothing of the pure joy young
people get from the visual appeal of a production, those who
present plays for them will see to it that the staging is as
beautiful as means will permit. This requires that as rapidly
as receipts rise above expenditures they should be used to
build up equipment. Such a procedure constantly improves
the quality of production and helps to make every children's
theatre play a really fine occasion. One would not wish to
compete with motion pictures in elaborateness of setting;
but no one can deny that they have their influence on what
children expect in their entertainment.

There is no possibility of estimating a budget for a children's theatre in dollars and cents, for no two institutions are
in the same situation. A theatre in a small town might

happen to have a playwright of its own who could not only write good plays but direct them as well. An art teacher might be interested in designing settings, and workers from the organization could make all the costumes. Under such circumstances, an enthusiastic group of people might conceivably produce plays with practically no cost at all. Another group would have to pay for all of these things. Naturally, too, prices differ widely for labor and materials, productions costing all the way from nothing to a thousand dollars.

Though no figures can be given, the items of expense, being more or less the same in all situations, may be helpful.

1. The royalty or fee for the use of the play. Very few first-rate plays for children's theatres can be produced without this fee. It is a just requirement and should be one of the first considerations when choosing a play. Royalties on children's plays are low, and can be met by any organization which charges admission to its plays.

2. The rental of the auditorium if one is not donated, and sometimes rental of rehearsal space.

3. The books or manuscripts for the players. Do not give your players "sides" (merely their own lines and cues) if you wish an intelligent understanding of their part in the play.

4. The tickets, both season and single.

5. The posters and pictures for publicity, unless the former are hand-made, and the latter taken by the newspapers.

6. The programs, if they are used.

7. The electrical supplies, which amount to a good deal even after the first investment.

8. The scenery and properties. After two sets of scenery have been acquired, they can often be repainted and adapted to other productions, so that the paint is the only additional cost.

9. The costumes, which are one of the largest items of expense, since casts are large and children's plays usually require period or fanciful dress. If but one children's play is to be given in a season, the honor of taking part may be so great that the cast is glad to pay for its own costumes. This plan is extremely short-sighted, however, for aside from the fact that it is undemocratic to limit casts to people who can easily afford their own costumes (some characters needing two or three), the theatre should be building up a stock of costumes for future plays. Indeed, the accumulation of costumes begins soon to reduce the cost of production, since costumes, like scenery, can be remodeled and adapted again and again.

10. The cleaning of costumes is no small item in a theatre which produces several plays with large casts every year. Every piece of a costume which has gone through several dress rehearsals and performances is so soiled that for sanitary reasons alone it must be sent to the cleaner's or the laundry. With a few exceptions of robes and capes which do not come in contact with make-up and which are not worn next to the body, everything should be cleaned before being returned to costume-boxes or wardrobes.

11. The make-up box needs extra supplies for each play after the original investment.

12. Trucking may not be an expense if scenery is built in the same building in which the productions are given. So many theatres tour to several buildings or towns, however, that this expense is quite general.

13. The janitor should be paid for extra work unless this is included in rental. If performances are given in a school where rent is not paid, they cause a considerable amount of work for the janitor for which he receives no extra salary.

It is not only right that the theatre should give him a regular fee, but it will be money well spent in gaining his respect and his willingness to work for the interests of the theatre. If the city regulations require that a fire marshal be present at every large gathering, it may be necessary to pay him also.

14. Music. Even when a theatre does not use *entr'acte* music, it often needs special music for the play. A skilled harpist, an oboe player, a trumpeter, may be necessary for certain off-stage effects, and unless such a person has a definite interest in the theatre, he should not be asked to give as many hours as are required for rehearsals and performances without remuneration. The same thing is true of dancing or fencing teachers.

15. Incidental costs, such as books of plays for consideration, stationery, stamps, 'phone bills, occasional taxi bills, and other minor obligations.

Such a list of expenses takes no account of salaries aside from the smaller fees. Many services which begin as voluntary help are likely to become paid offices if the theatre grows into an established institution. Though it is quite possible to continue through the years with volunteers doing all the directing, staging, publicity, and business management, the organization is strong indeed if it can keep indefinitely an efficient volunteer staff with enough leisure time to do it successfully.

A paid director is the most necessary expense, for he (or she) needs to be a specially trained person who must give a large amount of time to the theatre. The production manager or technical director is often a salaried member of the staff, especially if the productions are at all ambitious. The business and publicity manager's job is a big one, especially if one person fills both offices. Since it is a responsible and exacting position which requires a great deal of time, it usually pays in actual dollars and cents to hire a person of business ability and have the work well done. By taking care of the money which comes in, checking carefully on everything which goes out, and publicizing the productions in a way to bring large audiences, an active and responsible person in this position can earn for the theatre much more than the salary he is paid.

When public or professional schools are sponsors of a children's theatre, all of this work may be a part of the regular duty of faculty members. If they supervise their students in producing or managing the theatre, the problem of salaries is solved.

II. The admission should be small. It is unfortunate that every child who wishes to see a children's theatre production cannot do so. But the plays can be put within reach of most of them if the tickets are cheap; and far better than discriminating between rich and poor by charging a dollar for tickets and then giving special free performances for poor children, is a reasonably small charge to all. What the price shall be will differ with the community. In many towns it must be as small as ten cents, in others twenty-five or thirty-five cents, with a reduction for season tickets.

It can thus be seen why a children's theatre, far from being a money-making venture, should be an altruistic undertaking, paying modest salaries to the most necessary people on its staff, but devoting much of its income to the building of something beautiful for the children of the community. If a theatre for children does not offer good enough plays to attract a large number of boys and girls at a low admission, it is not worth subsidizing; but if it is able to achieve both quality and popular appeal, it should be sponsored by adults whose support will open its doors to hundreds, perhaps thousands, of children who could not otherwise afford to see the plays.

THE BUSINESS MANAGER'S DUTIES

The business manager, the director, and the production manager or technician often constitute the financial committee of a children's theatre. Together they estimate the expenses for the year and make up a budget, if the theatre operates under this system. When theatres are new it is very difficult to know just what expenses to expect, but after one season the budget can be based upon the preceding year.

Some organizations have both a treasurer and a business manager, and when this is the case, the treasurer signs all checks. More commonly, the business manager acts in both capacities, being the only person in the organization who can receive and disburse money. All checks are turned over to him, for he alone can sign or endorse them. He banks the money for the performances, checks over the monthly statements, and makes reports after each play and at the end of the season.

The selling of tickets and paying of bills are obviously the chief duties of a business manager. But linked with these two are many related duties, all of which require that he continually look out for the financial interests of the theatre.

Discovery by careful investigation of the best firm to do the printing of tickets and other advertising is one of his first jobs. Prices and quality of work should be compared before the order is given, and when a printer proves satisfactory in the first year's work, he is likely to become official printer for the children's theatre, understanding its needs and taking a personal interest and pride in working for it.

Season as well as single admission tickets are used in many children's theatres, the former being of distinct advantage to the management because they determine a definite income and concentrate the selling campaign into a few weeks. In theatres with a ten-cent admission fee, season tickets would not pay, but they offer every advantage when the season price is as much as a dollar. It is highly advisable that they indicate reserved seats, for a strong selling-point is that a ticket bought early in the sale will assure a good seat for every play of the year.

Such a ticket may be a coupon book with a perforated ticket to be taken out for each performance, a sheet of attached, perforated tickets, or a single ticket bearing the dates and hours of the various performances, together with the seat number. The last is far cheaper than the others and quite satisfactory. The one disadvantage of season tickets is the children's tendency to lose them. To safeguard this danger, the ticket may indicate that the owner's name and address will be found on the back. To make doubly sure, the name of every person buying a ticket may be registered and in case of loss a duplicate ticket may be issued.

SELLING SEASON TICKETS

How to make reserved season tickets easily obtainable to the children in all parts of town is a problem in cities of more than a few thousand inhabitants. One central ticket office is inadvisable, principally because it will not be accessible to all children. To sell unreserved tickets and then require that reservations be made at a central box-office is no better arrangement.

Since the boys and girls who will make up the audience

are in school, the best solution to the problem is to apportion the tickets to the various schools according to their enrollment. This is taking for granted, of course, either that the school is one of the children's theatre sponsors or that the superintendent has been convinced of the worth of the theatre and is willing to coöperate in every way. He is most likely to do this if the theatre is a community institution, for he must withhold permission when the purpose is any private gain. If the board of education is coöperating in the children's theatre, and tickets may be sold in the schools, the selling dates are advertised in advance, and a fair proportion of tickets is taken to each school. After this preliminary sale, which may be conducted by one or two ticket-sellers in each school, the tickets which are left may be put on sale at a central box-office convenient for adults. No single tickets need be sold in this campaign, the idea being that buyers of season tickets may have the choice of seats. A few of these tickets given to the principal of each school will find their way into the possession of children who are especially deserving of the joy of attending the plays but cannot afford to buy tickets.

THE BUSINESS MANAGER'S ASSISTANTS

Organization of a staff to assist in selling tickets is one of the duties of a business manager. This is no small task if they are to be sold in many places on the same day. When a preview of the play is taken on a tour of schools, the ticket sale should begin on the following day to get the best results. But regardless of the matter of a preview, the greatest amount of satisfaction results from giving each school an equal opportunity to get good tickets.

Coöperation with the principal of each building in the mat-

ter of time may mean selling-hours which are inconvenient for
the sellers but which are sure to result in the best sale. Just
before school and at noon are considered best in many grade
schools. Occasionally a principal prefers to manage the tickets
himself, and in such cases the sale is likely to be especially
good because of his efficiency and the backing of his teachers.
It is never fair to request him to do this, but such a fine help
may well be appreciated if he offers it.

The most careful information should be given to each person who goes to a school to sell tickets. Every conceivable question should be anticipated and the answer given to the seller
not only verbally but also on a mimeographed sheet to be
taken along. The plays to be produced, dates of season and
single tickets, the policy concerning the exchange of tickets if
illness prevents attendance on the scheduled date, the knowledge of seating arrangement so that first buyers will get the
best seats, as well as other information will help to make the
ticket-sellers efficient and satisfactory.

Standing in a gaily decorated booth topped perhaps by a
banner emblazoned with a children's theatre emblem, the
ticket-seller has no need to ask any child to buy a ticket. If
the sale has been well-heralded, a long line of children is likely
to form down the hall, each eager to exchange his money for
a precious ticket. In order to keep the line moving rapidly, the
ticket-seller must work fast, keeping his best tickets ready for
each successive child, then passing each buyer on to a second
person to have his ticket registered.

An exact record of tickets taken by each seller, with a report-
blank to be filled out concerning tickets sold, money collected,
and probable need for the following day, is necessary for the
business manager's accounts. And if this daily record is kept for
each school it will be very valuable in apportioning tickets for

the following season as well as for noting which schools need more thorough campaigns.

Because many children forget or are unable to bring their money on the first day, it is advisable to conduct the sale on the two following days, and after that to put the tickets on sale at a central box-office. Single as well as season tickets will be sold there, a certain number of seats being reserved to be used for single admissions rather than being sold as season tickets.

Many more tickets, both season and single, will be sold at the door at first performances, so that unless the line at the ticket-booth moves very fast, the curtain will have to be held or the audience is disturbed by those who had to wait in line. It is the business manager's job to see that all ticket-selling is done efficiently, and that accurate reports are made after ticket stubs have been checked with the cash.

PAYING THE BILLS

"Who bought this fifteen yards of muslin that is charged to us by the Morgan store? Was it used for scenery, properties, or costumes? And didn't we pay for that lumber several months ago?" Familiar questions in a children's theatre which has no requisition system or files for records.

Occasional plays do not require the complete business system so necessary to a children's theatre which produces several plays a season. But authority for all expenditures should be required and a complete record kept or else bills for materials which no one remembers buying will come in long after the play is over.

A requisition book in triplicate form and three colors is a very good method of assuring correct accounts when plays

are given regularly. Two of the pages are perforated, the first
to be given to the firm where the purchase is made, the second
to the business manager who clips it to the bill and files them
together after it has been paid. The third remains in the book
as a final check on the expenditure. Carbons are used, of
course, in writing the order. The three pages have the same
number printed in the corner. A convenient form follows:

REQUISITION ORDER

DATE ————————————

No. ————————————

PLAY ACCT. ————————————

FIRM ————————————————

ORDERED BY ————————————————
(*The name must be that of Jane Jones or John Smith*)

Payment guaranteed by the Children's Theatre of
Blank only upon presentation of this official order
properly signed.
[Space for order]

A loose-leafed ledger is used for the accounts so that it may
go on serving its purpose indefinitely. One section is used for
receipts, one for the general expenditures of the season (as the
stock of paints, lumber, tickets, etc.), and a double page for
the expenses of each individual production. A simple form
for this account is to head the page with the name of the
play, listing down the page the numbers of the checks and
the names of the persons or the firms to whom they are written.
The amounts are then entered under the department where
they belong, these headings (as Royalties and Books, Scenery
and Properties, Wigs and Make-up, Service, etc.) having been

written across the top of the two pages. The columns are added across the two pages and then down, the lower right hand corner showing the total expense of the production.

All bills, with attached requisitions, are filed alphabetically, the year's canceled checks in numerical order, together with the stubs and bank statements, being kept in the file for reference. In this way, the management can tell at any time just how it stands financially and how its expenditures and receipts compare with those of former years.

If a budget has been determined upon for each production, the business manager watches expenditures carefully, giving warning if expenses threaten to exceed it. Since he enters all items in the ledger and writes all checks, he is in a position to guard against mistakes in bills sent to the theatre. By insisting on the use of requisitions for everything charged, and for the petty cash paid out for purchases made at stores where the theatre has no account, he may save both time and money.

Other duties he has, many of them, including the renting of an auditorium when necessary, application for the exemption from government taxes on tickets since this is a non-profit organization, the insuring of the building if the theatre is lucky enough to possess one, or of valuable properties on the rare occasions when these are necessary, the sending of complimentary tickets to newspapers and to others when requested by the director, and, in general, taking charge of all financial transactions of the theatre.

It is thus easy to see that the office of business manager is an important one. Absolute honesty and dependability, a fine business sense, a coöperative spirit in working with other organizations, and a deep interest in the welfare of the theatre—all these are indispensable in the person to whom the business side of the children's theatre is intrusted.

CHAPTER XIII

WE GO TO PLAYGROUNDS, CAMPS,
CLUBS, AND AUDITORIUMS

OUTSIDE the children's theatre is a whole world of drama for children. Far greater than the audiences reached inside the organized children's theatre are those in playgrounds, camps, clubs, and assemblies. In the platoon schools over the country, where an hour daily is spent in the school theatre at the auditorium period, great numbers of boys and girls are engaged in presenting as well as seeing plays.[1]

Most of the dramatic work done in such places is in smaller units than in children's theatres. Less pretentious than in theatres where plays must have a strong popular appeal to their audiences, the drama of playgrounds, camps, clubs, and schools has a different reason for being. The interests and needs of the players rather than the tastes of the audiences are the first considerations here, the objectives of such work being educational or recreative.

When no admission is charged there is less obligation to stress the amusement quality of a play. The director, therefore, is free to choose material which will contribute most to the development of his players, regardless of whether it will have strong entertainment value to an audience. The plays he chooses are chiefly short ones, so that responsibility is divided among the players much more equally than in long ones.

[1] Material for these uses will be found in the Play List.

In casting he may use children who long for and need the experience of taking part even though they have little talent. He must be careful, however, to cast several better actors to carry the play. He spends less time and money on the staging than if the plays were for children's theatre, and the costumes are either taken from a school wardrobe or brought from home.

PUBLIC PLAYGROUNDS

Attendance at the clubs and classes operated by municipal recreation bureaus or departments has grown by leaps and bounds during the past few years. It is not unusual for the population of a public playground to double from one year to the next. Such wholesale increase in the number of children and adults often makes necessary so many teachers and supervisors that it is an acute problem for cities to handle. The amount of leisure time is accountable in large measure for the tremendous new interest in recreation. Though municipal departments for such work are still relatively young in the smaller cities, at least, people are rapidly becoming educated as to the opportunities they offer. More and more free hours each week must be filled by the general public with something or other, and it is gratifying to realize what great numbers of people are using their leisure constructively.

Children in the country or in little towns have always had space in which to play. Without interfering with the rights of others they can have ball games, races, and all manner of fun. It is a different matter if they live in the city. Crowded together without space to play, children get into the juvenile court for pranks that would go unnoticed in the country.

Thus it is that the playground, far from being a luxury, is indeed a necessity if cities are to safeguard their children by giving them a wholesome and satisfying way of using their energy. Athletics, dancing, handicrafts, dramatics, and other activities provide for boys and girls, men and women, a physical, social, and artistic outlet which contributes much to their health and enjoyment.

The dramatic activity in recreation centers is found in both classes and clubs. Children are often divided as to sexes, principally when boys consider that to be in classes with girls is "sissy." There is every advantage, however, in having boys and girls in the same groups, and when such a custom is established and the clubs or classes have won general respect, it is finally taken for granted.

CREATIVE DRAMATICS

For the children's dramatic classes and clubs, the type of work to carry on is creative dramatics.[2] This is the informal, original kind of drama in which little plays are developed from stories, rhythms, or purely from the imagination. The dramatization is a coöperative process, the class planning and playing it together, building it to completion through suggestions, criticisms, and replaying again and again.

Since no lines are memorized, and the children play first one part, then another, they are afforded far more delightful experiences than if they were rehearsing one part for a play. The irregular attendance on the playground makes creative dramatics desirable for another reason also, for since the children play the parts turn about, the absence of several boys and girls will not materially interfere with the work of the class.

Aside from the fact that children enjoy creating their own plays more than rehearsing formal drama, the values to be

[2] The technique of teaching this work is given in the author's book *Creative Dramatics* (D. Appleton-Century Co., 1930).

gained from it are greater. Imagination is stirred by such stories as Kipling's *How the Camel Got His Hump,* Isaacs' *The Rabbi and the Diadem,* Stockton's *Old Pipes and the Dryad,* and innumerable others, and it is used to good purpose in turning them into plays. The most careful thinking is required to make a logical sequence of scenes leading to a climax, and to make criticisms and suggestions for the improvement of the playing. The children who participate get much practice in the oral expression of ideas, and since the dialogue is extemporaneous, they must learn to think quickly and speak fluently.

In such work as this, the emphasis is put on the creating of the play rather than on the finished production for an audience. If any incentive is needed, the dramatization may be presented at last for another club or class, or for the parents. Children as a rule do not need this incentive, for dramatization is intrinsically interesting to them.

THE CLIMAX OF THE SUMMER

Many playgrounds end their season with a festival or pageant in which every group has some part. Dances, songs, and playlets are often woven together in such a way as to form some picturesque entertainment to which the public is invited. It may represent the history of the community; or Nottingham Fair, with a story made from Robin Hood ballads; [3] or perhaps it is just a varied program showing what the playgrounds have been doing during the summer.

Play contests are often used as an incentive to sustained work, each playground contributing a short play or dramatization. On a given day the spectators may gather on bleachers

[3] See Nina B. Lamkin's *Good Times for All Times* (French, 1929).

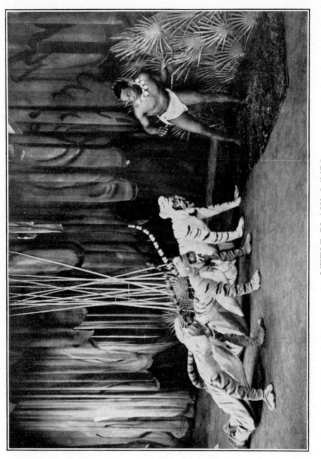

LITTLE BLACK SAMBO

Federal Theatre Project, Chicago.

erected for the purpose, as all of the plays are presented in an open space without a stage.

The material used at such times is often formalized dramatizations made by the children, since royalties make most good plays prohibitive for such purposes. If an expert judge can meet the players afterward in a group and explain their merits and faults, such a contest has definite value. At any rate, the better pieces of work help to raise general standards, directors profiting more, perhaps, than the children. The non-royalty plays listed at the end of this book may prove useful for playground use.

CAMPS

In holiday mood, the boys and girls of every camp delight in some form of dramatic activity. Far away from the moving-picture house, they consider it great fun to supply their own theatrical entertainment, with the result that all over the country plays and original dramatizations fill many summer evenings, with pageants, water festivals, or outdoor plays for the more ambitious programs.

The dramatic counselor who takes his work seriously finds plenty of problems along with the advantages of camp dramatics. With all the freshness and zest of the children, the lack of strain, and the fun of developing resourcefulness in the staging of plays, he likewise discovers that it is very difficult to maintain high standards in dramatic work.

The many activities which occupy the time in both boys' and girls' camps make it necessary for him to present his plays with very few rehearsals. The audience is not usually critical at these performances, and because they are satisfied with so little, there is real danger of setting low standards both for himself and the children. Costumes and properties, too, are a problem. Perhaps there is an old trunk with a collection of faded and wrinkled parts of costumes which have accumulated from year to year. Often, too, the children bring masquerade finery or costumes they have worn in a school play. But there are seldom enough which can be used together to suffice for even one production. There are few properties to borrow in a camp, materials for making them are hard to find, and days are so full that it is difficult to get help in building them.

It must be remembered, however, that camp is the place to stress outdoor activities; that costly facilities for swimming, canoeing, hiking, and riding have been provided, and they are the reason for the camp's existence. Because dramatics is essentially an indoor activity, even though rehearsals and plays may be held out-of-doors, it cannot take first place. This being true, the dramatic counselor must think how to make the best of a difficult situation; how to plan his program so that drama shall make a real contribution to camp life without requiring a great deal of time. For this reason he needs imagination and resourcefulness in greater measure than for other kinds of directing. A high premium is put on originality, for some of the programs will be stunts rather than plays. Because they concern happenings of camp life, they cannot be anticipated. True, they are usually created by the campers themselves, but much guidance is needed, and ideas must be forthcoming to make the stunt or playlet dramatically effective.

In one boys' camp which ends its season with an elaborate minstrel show, the seniors work out many of their sketches when they go on over-night hikes. Around the camp-fire, miles from the boys who will make up their audience, they collaborate on the masterpieces which are to be woven together for the great evening of the summer!

A girls' camp which wrote and produced an Egyptian operetta based the plot on *Aïda*. Using the music of familiar songs, one of the girls wrote a complete libretto, and with improvised Egyptian costumes and little more than a suggestion of scenery, they presented the six scenes of their "opera" before the diminished audience left after the large cast had been subtracted.

Such original productions are exceedingly popular with both players and audience, and they have unquestioned value from an educational standpoint. The incentive which they furnish for originality, for creating something fresh—and if possible, clever!—for extemporizing and coöperating, is remarkably strong, and will challenge the best efforts.

Creative dramatics or improvisations are ideal for camps, since they fit in with both the spirit of camp life and its full schedule. Freedom from the routine of memorizing lines and of giving finished performances means more joy in the activity itself, and the premium which such work places on originality and resourcefulness makes it a valuable asset in the type of education which goes on in camps.

One camp director says that she urges her dramatic counselors to keep their ears to the ground in order to discover what special interests of the campers can be used in a dramatic way. If the interest in archery is strong, the mood is set for Robin Hood plays; if sailing is a favorite sport, dramatizations of sea-stories are desirable; and at all times plays and pageants which make use of horses are popular.

For Sunday afternoon vespers, rather lovely outdoor dramatizations of such stories as Oscar Wilde's *The Young King, The Happy Prince,* and *The Selfish Giant,* Van Dyke's *The*

Other Wise Man, and scenes from Bible history can be made very impressive. With a narrator who tells or reads the parts of the stories which are not enacted, such presentations can be well done with very few rehearsals.

PLAYS

When choosing plays for camps, it is advisable to look for short ones which will suffer least from curtailed rehearsal. Those with outdoor settings are particularly desirable. If it is customary to present an ambitious final entertainment it may be either a pageant or a festival made up of music, dancing, and short plays or dramatizations. All should be unified, of course, with a central idea to which the various parts of the program have some relationship.[4] Such a program might be an Indian Festival, showing by story-telling and pantomime customs of some tribe of American Indians.[5] Or it can be a water festival suggested by the *Ring of the Nibelungs,* or based on a Greek myth or an Hawaiian folk tale.[6]

DRAMATIC CLUBS

As extra-curricular school activities, in playground, settlement, Y. M. C. A., or Scout organizations, dramatic clubs have long been popular. Sometimes conducted as classes, oftener as recreational activities, these groups vary in quality of work as widely as they do in type.

When they serve as interest groups of large organizations, they meet once a week, perhaps, for the good time which may be afforded by dramatics. With a capable, trained leader they

---

[4] See Lamkin's *Good Times for All Times* and *Camp Dramatics* (French).
[5] Such a one is described in *Camp Dramatics.*
[6] *Ibid.*

will get more than amusement from these meetings. Pantomimes, improvised scenes assigned by the leader, the reading and discussion of plays, the study and experience of characterizing, discussion of moving pictures or children's plays attended, with an occasional formal play (rehearsed largely outside of meetings and presented for parents) may make up the year's activities. Such a program might mean pleasurable recreation for the members of the club with an increased understanding of what makes good drama.

When such clubs have little interest in doing actual work, they might better be purely social organizations, for nothing worth while can be done without work, and taste is cheapened by half-hearted attempts. The enthusiasm of a teacher or leader may be so contagious, however, that the members will work as hard as for a class, and even though no pressure is brought to bear on them, they will be unwilling to miss a single meeting of the club.

If formal plays are given, many rehearsals outside of the regular meetings will be necessary. Indeed, unless all of the club members have parts in the production, rehearsals may be outside entirely, for it is impossible to interest children if they are not included.

Plays used for this purpose should have some real value, both for the players and for the audience. If people are asked to buy tickets, the responsibility is greater, even if they are the friends or relatives of the club members. Boys' clubs often inflict programs of farces, burlesques, and cheap melodramas on audiences in the name of recreation. The result is that instead of improving taste, the leaders have lowered it, and so have missed the opportunity to be of real value to their members. Entertaining and popular the plays should be, but they should also be worth the time spent on them. It is not easy to find good material for this purpose, especially since the plays must usually be non-royalty. Whoever can write them will be real benefactors. One is inclined to believe that unless better material is soon forthcoming, it would be advisable for children's clubs stressing recreation to turn their interests elsewhere than drama.

Clubs with a more serious purpose can have an equally good time but in quite a different way. Perhaps their meetings will be used for creative dramatics which is of unquestioned educational value. If they occasionally wish to present a program it may be in the nature of an interesting demonstration of their regular work, done without costumes or scenery. Or it may be a formal dramatization which has been written down and thus set as to dialogue, done with simple scenery and costumes. If it is a formal play, it will be something good like *Kings in Nomania, Youth's Highway, The Knave of Hearts, The Slippers of Cinderella,* or one of the interesting little pieces in *Plays of the American Colonies.* It will be thoroughly rehearsed, too, so that it can be presented with real finish.

ASSEMBLIES AND AUDITORIUMS

Compared with the dramatics of playground, camp, and club, the quality of plays produced in schools at the regular assembly or auditorium period should rank high. Presented, and usually rehearsed, in school hours, they have every chance of success, and, indeed, they usually are much more carefully done than the others.

The first advantage results from the attitude of players and audience. School is serious business, and though the assembly hour means a certain amount of relaxation, it is nevertheless a part of school, and therefore a dignified occasion. The players, knowing what is expected at such a time, regard the play and the rehearsals as something of importance.

Another great advantage is that rehearsals are not difficult to schedule. Whether or not they are held in school hours, as, of course, they should be, or immediately after school, the pupils are on hand. They do not have to come from the other side of town. There is space for them to rehearse, and there need be no delay in getting started.

THE CHOICE OF MATERIAL

A wide choice of plays is possible for the auditorium and assembly, since they need not be so entirely of the popular type. Episodes from history such as *A Rose for Captain Bacon, West o' the Alleghenies, Sojourners,* are appropriate and well-liked. Thoughtful plays such as *What Men Live By, Theories and Thumbs,* and *The Fifteenth Candle* can be used here to good advantage.

It is advisable in producing such school plays to stage them very simply, using curtains for a background, with perhaps the addition of window and door flats, and some levels if needed. Screens can be used in place of curtains, either painted or hung with rugs, banners, or "tapestries."

New costumes should never be required from the children, since the plays are not for the public, and it is better to build up a wardrobe of such costumes as are suggested in Chapter IX than to make new ones. Unless a school has a fund provided either in the budget (which is unlikely) or by the occasional presentation of programs for which a charge is made, it is imperative that such costumes be used as are already on hand.

In a platoon system, the daily auditorium hour is an intrinsic part of the plan. It is a meeting place for the activities of the whole school. Music appreciation, singing, visual education in the form of motion pictures, outside speakers, talks by the children on interesting material learned in various classes, dramatizations and plays; such programs as these make up a theatre which unifies the whole school and correlates all its departments.

The approach to the production of plays in such a situation is decidedly educational. They are to be studied and criticized by the audience as well as enjoyed, and so it behooves director and players to maintain a high standard of excellence. Here, as in the ordinary school assembly, the plays are staged simply, and little or no make-up is used.

In both situations, the pressure for programs celebrating certain holidays such as the birthdays of Columbus, Washington, and Lincoln, Armistice Day, Thanksgiving, and the rest, lead to the use of much inferior material. Unfortunately, few good plays are written for special occasions, so that a teacher often feels forced to present poor ones. It might be better in such cases to make up a program without a play, using suitable music, literature, and talks.

More difficult still are the days devoted to health, fire-prevention, better speech, and the like. Few plays of any merit have been written to make vivid the effects of carelessness and the rewards of vigilance! Most of them are effective neither as plays nor as warnings. It is far better to be direct about such matters than to try to implant the idea by a play. Slides and moving pictures, talks with charts about health, demonstrations by the fire marshal, often prove very effective. If there were more such scenes for Better Speech Week as that which takes place between the butler and the King's English in *The Poor Little Rich Girl,* they would be a boon to the speech teacher. Original plays can be developed, however, for this occasion and for Book Week by the boys and girls with the teacher's help, and though they may not be highly effective, they will have more educational value than a formal play.

For Christmas there is so much material of great beauty in song, story, and drama that no junior auditorium need ever resort to cheap Santa Claus "pieces" or plays. From the general favorite, *Why the Chimes Rang,* on through such satisfying plays as *The Christmas Guest, Good King Wenceslaus, The White Christmas, The First Noël,* and others of like merit, there is plenty of good material for any school; and, indeed, the Nativity plays created by teachers and pupils all over the land, heightened in their performance by lovely Christmas carols, can scarcely be surpassed by formal plays in the values which they hold for the authors, the players, and the audiences which gather to see them.

CHAPTER XIV

THE AUDIENCE IS HERE!

The spark that is ignited when we fling our play into
the auditorium is the central fact in the theatre, and ,
it requires for its consummation the rapport of people
gathered within the same four walls with the actors.[1]

THE MAGIC MOMENT has at last arrived! The play,
chosen so many weeks ago, has been rehearsed and publicized; the costumes have been made, the scenery built. Hopes
for success have been high, but now that the time to "fling" it
into the audience has come, the director's heart beats fast.
Will the hundreds of eager children sitting in the auditorium
be moved as one person by what happens on the stage? Will
the miracle really happen?

Moments when a whole audience is lifted out of reality and
drawn close together in a bond of expectancy, laughter, or
sympathy are less rare in a children's theatre than in adult
productions. For children live in what is happening on the
stage; they suffer and rejoice with the people of the story;
and in the hush of suspense and the burst of spontaneous
laughter, the spark ignites, and those grown-ups who have
made the theatre possible feel a rich reward for all the trouble
it has cost.

Children are the most genuine audience in the world. They
may disappoint the director by failing to grasp delightful sub-

[1] Roy Mitchell, *Creative Theatre* (John Day Co., 1929).

tleties over which the players have chuckled throughout the rehearsals; they may laugh at a well-played romantic scene; and they may begin to put on their coats five minutes before the play is over. But these are proofs of their genuineness. Subtleties and symbolism are unchildlike, for children lack the experience necessary to interpret them; romance is silly to them, or if they are old enough to enjoy love scenes, they nevertheless feel embarrassed in seeing them; and they put on their coats because the play has made the mistake of going past the curtain. When they are satisfied as to the outcome of the story they make ready to leave. The discourtesy of such an action does not occur to them.

Children make no pretense of being interested if they do not care for a play. As soon as interest lags, there is a general restlessness on the part of the younger children, with whisperings and glances about the house. Because reaction is so natural, the playwright and the director can learn much by sitting in a child audience. In such a scene as that in *Radio Rescue,* where Jill is hiding in a barrel while Martha and the officer are searching the old mill, when the utter silence of suspense is broken by excited but cautious whispers from the audience warning Jill to "get down, get *down!,*" it is obvious that the scene is proving intensely real to the children. Or when they burst into applause to save Tinker Bell's life when Peter Pan cries, "Do you believe in fairies?"—such reactions as these, to say nothing of the delighted shouts of laughter when the children in *The Scotch Twins* play upon the superstition of the evil gamekeeper as he starts his climb to their cave, are the more obvious of innumerable responses indicative of a play's effect.

Conclusions resulting from such observations are most useful if the audience is of uniform age. One can then learn exactly what appeals and what leaves children cold and profit by the knowledge in writing, choosing, and directing plays. But when all ages are represented, the observer is likely to judge that the play is over the heads of the whole audience if he hears a stirring and whispering; or that children appreciate only slapstick comedy when that variety of humor is greeted by the biggest laughs. In other words, the most obvious response does not necessarily indicate the reaction of the majority. It may simply be the noisiest. Even the sensitive observer who learns most truly from a child audience cannot hope to satisfy all ages with one play. She finds that the best she can do for a general audience is to vary each season sufficiently to please every child at least part of the time.

THE ENTR'ACTES

When a play has been chosen, staged, and sold out—then surely the producers may sit back and enjoy it with the children, secure in the belief that their work is done. Ah, no, not in a children's theatre. One must think of the *entr'actes,* when many tense muscles relax and cry out to do some acting themselves. For though children are full of wonder and awe, perhaps, when the experience of seeing a play is strange, familiarity leads to more and more freedom until the problem of audience management between scenes is sometimes really acute. One has only to go to a Saturday movie and hear the shrieks and boos of the children at some exciting serial to find where their audience training comes from. This is, of course, license rather than real enjoyment, and it constitutes a problem for all other entertainments.

EFFECT OF RESERVED SEATS

"Afternoon performance at two-thirty." And a mob outside the door, faces pressed against the glass, at one! One little boy came so early that he brought his lunch. When the doors are opened, the crowd surges in, and a mad scramble for front seats starts the afternoon off in disorder. A group of girls seat themselves in the center section, then decide to change to the side in order to be nearer the stage. They call to two more to join them. A half-dozen boys hurry in noisily from a ball game. It is an audience which is hard to pull together into the mood of the play because of the commotion inevitable at the start.

Reserved seats, when possible, prevent this unfortunate beginning. There is no necessity for coming early, for seats will be waiting for their owners. The gang will separate at the door, for they are to sit far apart. There will be no changing of places, for each belongs to some one. As the ushers quietly show each child to his seat, there is no incentive for noise and disorder, and as a consequence, the opening of the play will have little difficulty in drawing the children into its mood.

The line at the box-office waiting to buy tickets for a popular play is always a minor problem. Even an expert cannot sell reserved tickets fast enough to finish by the time the performance should begin. Unless the curtain is held these people miss the beginning scene and disturb the audience when they do come in. If it is held, the children inside not only become restless, but more of them will come late to the next play. In this matter a compromise seems wisest. By holding the curtain five or ten minutes—never more—all who had allowed a reasonable time to get tickets will probably be in; and the others can be held at the back of the house until the end of the scene.

Those who have had experience in selling reserved tickets know that a box-office, or ticket-booth, is greatly to be preferred to a table. For plays given at schools, a gaily painted ticket-booth (which is no great task to make) not only looks jolly and inviting, but forces buyers into a single line which can be served much more efficiently than at a crowded table.

UNIFORMS

Attractive uniforms for the house manager and ushers contribute to the general festivity of the scene, besides marking the officials who can answer questions and look after the comfort of the audience. Because amateur plays seldom have the same ushers throughout the year, it is advisable to use costumes which do not fit closely. Russian blouses or distinctive smocks, with skirts in three lengths will fit almost any group of ushers. The colors may be varied, and if the theatre has an insignia, it may be worn on one sleeve.

Uniforms are much to be preferred to varied costumes reflecting the play. If the ushers were to be garbed in Dutch dress for *Hans Brinker* or as pirates for *Make-Believe,* they would make common the costumes on the stage. Uniforms, moreover, give style and dignity to the theatre staff.

PROCTORS

City theatres to which parents or nursemaids bring children for Saturday performances do not require proctors. Strange surroundings, the presence of many adults, and the fact that few of the children are acquainted keep boys and girls on their best behavior. But in a familiar scene, with many of their friends, the bubbling spirits of these same children need some one who represents authority to keep them from too unrestrained bubbling.

And so several proctors are asked to be on hand to see to it that the mob spirit does not lead the audience into misbehavior. Such proctors are most effective when they stand for authority in the eyes of the children. Teachers, whether men or women, often understand the management of children best, though many adults who are not teachers may serve as well. These proctors should not be more conspicuous than necessary, having seats on the aisles and merely seeing to it that no disturbance arises. On very rare occasions it may be necessary to take out a persistent offender and either give his money back and send him home, or talk to him outside, and if he seems penitent, allow him to see the play from some other part of the house. However difficult a group of children have been, when such an incident as this occurs they are so sobered that their conduct becomes nothing short of perfect.

Whether or not a child audience is difficult to manage, it is highly important that there be a friendly spirit at all times. Adults who put the best possible construction on children's actions, expecting them to conduct themselves well, sometimes asking their help with windows, doors, tiny children, etc., usually find that boys and girls respond with far more coöperation than if they were scolded.

WAITS BETWEEN SCENES

Many elements enter into the problem of handling a youthful audience. If waits between scenes are very short, there is seldom a problem at all. With only a few minutes to relax, there will be little restlessness and consequently no disturbance. This matter of waits between scenes is one which every children's theatre would do well to consider when designing its plays, for quick changes make audiences happier, probably, than elaborate scenes.

PROGRAMS OR PROLOGUE?

Printed programs, too, influence audience behavior. Taken for granted in an adult theatre, they are entirely unnecessary for children. In a community of any size, only a fraction of the audience is personally acquainted with the players, and the newspapers have already made public the names of the cast. The younger children care little about programs except as pieces of paper out of which several fascinating articles can be made, the favorite being an airplane to sail around during intermissions. Even when they are read, they often end in small bits on the floor.

All necessary information can better be given by a clever Prologue who may greet the audience, introduce the story, and set the mood of the play. Whether he is a child or an adult, it is important that he be a personality that boys and girls will like, that he speak very clearly, and that he give just enough exposition so that the audience will understand and anticipate with lively interest the play that is to come. He may or may not introduce each act. But he should make it clear how many scenes to expect. There is no reason for announcing the cast since we are concerned with illusion, not the exhibition of players. Indeed, it is far better to center all interest in the story itself and allow the play to introduce its characters naturally.

Prologues may be costumed as pages, as characters in the

period of the play, or in any other manner that seems appropriate. The play sometimes provides for them, as in Owen Davis' *Robin Hood,* when a minstrel appears before the curtain and speaks or sings a merry rhyme which creates the mood for the familiar story. Constance Mackay has written delightful little prologues for many of her plays. Eleanor Perkins devised a clever introduction to *The Japanese Twins* by having a little boy from the audience climb up on the stage and peer through the curtains, his horrified sister on the front row calling to him in a loud whisper to come down. Eventually, curiosity gets the better of discretion, however, and she, too, goes up and takes a look. Into their conversation is introduced certain necessary information about Japanese customs, especially about the Samurai. Thus, she builds the mood and the understanding for the charming play which ensues.

Occasionally a story-teller is a part of the play, notably in Louise Armstrong's pantomime of *Ali Baba and the Forty Thieves,* where each scene is preluded by her exposition. And though Charlotte Chorpenning's *The Emperor's New Clothes* does not so indicate, the Gong-Bearer may very impersonally introduce each act by the striking of his gong.

THE ORCHESTRA

A third factor in audience management is an orchestra which plays between acts. For and against this custom there is much that might be said. It makes the occasion more festive, contributes to the mood of the play if the numbers have been chosen to this end, furnishes school orchestras with the incentive of public appearances, gives children a larger part in the theatre, and when schools have really excellent child orchestras, it adds interest and enjoyment to the performance.

Granted that the music is good, however, the talking which is almost sure to go on during the playing is the more to be deplored. The custom so prevalent in adult theatres persists with children, and it is a question whether to afford the opportunity for discourtesy or try to train boys and girls in better manners.

Time for relaxation between scenes is necessary because intense concentration demands relief. Any break in the play should allow a few minutes for conversation and movement—not necessarily the leaving of places, but a change of position at least. If there is to be music, the orchestra should not make the mistake of beginning to play immediately after the fall of the curtain, but should wait until just before the following scene.

A clever idea for concentrating attention on the orchestra is that used for years in motion-picture theatres: the dimming of house lights and flooding the orchestra with light from spots as well as stand-lights. This has almost a magic effect in heightening the importance of the music. If in addition to good playing of well-chosen music, the orchestra leader occasionally introduces solos or ensembles, it is not difficult to hold the attention of the audience. At best, however, the pieces should be short, for not only do the children become impatient for the play, but the stage-manager is likely to wait until the scene change is almost completed before giving the music signal, and so the opening of the act may be delayed by several minutes.

ENTERTAINMENT BETWEEN SCENES

Many forms of entertainment have been used between scenes by children's theatres to amuse the audience during

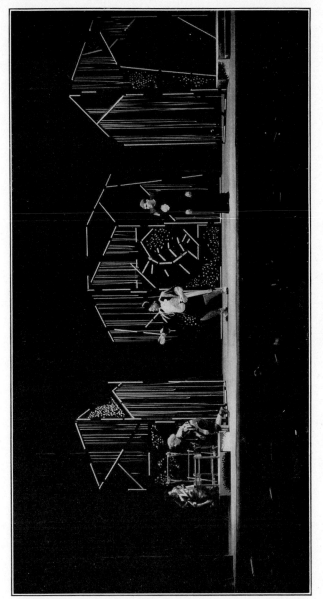

THE EMPEROR'S NEW CLOTHES

Federal Theatre Project, New York.

intermissions. Victrola music with loud speakers has been proved useless, for the audience merely raises its collective voice above the record. Rising and stretching, playing a calisthenics game or singing, is restful and amusing to little children, but considered babyish by older boys and girls. Interludes in the form of charades or story dramatizations may be of general interest, but they confuse the younger children who think they are part of the play. At best they cause an even greater break in the mood of the story than the intermission itself. Occasionally the director converses with the audience about various policies of the theatre such as the choice of plays, the kind of players (children or adult), suggestions for next season and the like. Sometimes she may discuss aspects of good plays and suggest what may be noted in the present production. Children are always ready to take a lively part in such discussions.

Foreign theatres often have one or two long intermissions when the children leave the auditorium and have a thoroughly delightful time in a nearby recreation room. Some are led in songs or games by an adult, others roam through rooms and look at pictures and stage-models. Sometimes a grown-up is stationed in a corner under a sign, "Ask me what you want to know about the play," and children crowd around asking all sorts of questions about the plot, the characters, and the mechanical effects.

If the grown-ups responsible for children's plays have a real interest in boys and girls, they will be concerned about the attitudes developed in their audiences—not only the many attitudes which have to do with the play and its production, but also those concerned with audience courtesy and good sportsmanship. They will not be satisfied in getting through performances without disturbances, but will consistently work toward greater discrimination and good taste in the children whom they serve.

To build pride in their theatre and coöperation in making it a thoroughly enjoyable place for every one is the ambition of all children's theatre directors. In order to do this, the children themselves need to have a hand in managing the organization. They may elect representatives to an advisory board, they may influence the choice of plays by suggestions given the director at the last production of each season. In some theatres children act as stage and house staff. But the coöperation of their teachers in. school can help more than anything else to build up a widespread interest and pride in the theatre. When principals and home-room teachers accompany their children to the plays and discuss them afterwards, the children's theatre can hope for more far-reaching effects than it can ever gain alone.

AFTER EFFECTS

If a play dies as the children troop out of the theatre it has been mere amusement, and no children's theatre sponsors can be satisfied with such an achievement. What it does to the boys and girls, what lasting effect, though ever so intangible, it makes on their lives, is the thing that really counts.

Propaganda or teaching is not necessary in order that a play may have a worthy influence. Ethical problems may possibly not even present themselves in some of the plays. But every production which is beautifully done should become a permanent possession in the lives of the children who see it. That they remember these plays with joy has been proved again and again in theatres which have existed for some years. Perhaps the sheer beauty of the colors, the lighting, and the music make one production a standard for appreciation in art. Another has shown the ugliness of jealousy, pettiness, dishonesty, selfishness, winning sympathy for characters with contrasting qualities. Still another has awakened their sense of justice in a matter of social unfairness. No preaching sent the lessons home; in fact, no comment at all was made. The ideas, made concrete in real people, were merely set out, and the audience judged for itself the deeds done and their reward or punishment.

THE MOSCOW CHILDREN'S THEATRE

Coöperation of parents, teachers, and theatre workers is needed if tangible evidence of the play's results is to be obtained. The scientific procedure of the Moscow Theatre for Children, which has discovered many interesting results concerning the effects of productions, may well be an example for such institutions in this country.

On the staff of the theatre are authors, psychologists, and child-specialists in addition to the artists. These people have for a long time made a study of the audiences, noting the reactions of various types of children not only at performances but, with the help of parents and teachers, for some days afterwards. Letters to the director, drawings of the scenes, stories the children tell, games they create, even chance remarks which seem to have been caused by the play are carefully studied.

Since many of their plays contain a large dose of Soviet propaganda, and others provoke thought on subjects of ethics, friendship, the nobility of labor, the struggle for knowledge, the senselessness of race prejudice, and many other questions, it can be seen that the chief purpose of the theatre is to educate through art. It may be said, however, that the plays do not make the mistake of overdosing. Each play is gay and highly entertaining, with plenty of action and plenty of fun, and it drives home its doctrine by sympathy for very real and very human heroes.

We in Amercia have not reached the place as yet where we take our theatre seriously. We congratulate ourselves if we give the children of our community a few Saturdays of charming entertainment. We are satisfied if we offer them plays in which they can escape for a brief moment from our matter-of-fact world into the fascinating adventures of the Never Land.

The strides we have made in our children's theatres have without doubt been rapid. From the nothing-at-all of a few years ago, we have progressed to many hundreds of productions a year throughout the country. We have brought joy to hundreds of thousands of children. This achievement is great and worthy. But we have still a long, long way to go.

We need better understanding of boys and girls. We should make a scientific and detailed study of our audiences and profit by it. This will involve producing our plays for definite age levels rather than for all children together. Adult productions may appeal to people from eighteen to seventy, but for children a three-year variation is often enough to change completely the appeal of a play. The coöperation of parents, teachers and theatre workers will be necessary in order to make this study thorough.

More care in the direction and production of our plays will preserve the illusion for our audiences and make the story live. Because we are working for children, we have no right to do shoddy production. The most skilled and sensitive direction, the most sincere acting, the most imaginative staging we can offer should be the standard of every children's theatre in the country.

If we do study our audiences carefully and produce our plays beautifully, we will stimulate the writing of better plays. For in our theatre we need finer and more significant plays, some of them full of thoughts and ideas which will help our children to interpret life more truly, to build a better society; others to enrich our communities by developing a greater appreciation for beauty, a discriminating taste in art; and all of them to bring great and lasting happiness to our boys and girls.

PLAY LIST

THE FOLLOWING LIST of children's plays is offered with the hope that it will make the search for good material a little less difficult for producers. That a title appears here means that the play carries a greater or less degree of this author's commendation. That it is not listed may not mean the opposite. Though hundreds of plays were discarded in our selection, it has been impossible to read all of them, so that many good ones, doubtless, have been overlooked.

When it was difficult to find good plays of any particular type, we have chosen the best we could find even though they might not measure up to the finest in the list.

In connection with each play we have indicated the source of production rights, but we have not attempted to quote royalty charges because they are subject not only to change but to negotiation in special circumstances. Permission must be sought for every play unless it is specifically noted as non-royalty.

ALADDIN. By Theodora DuBois. In *Ring Up the Curtain* by Montrose J. Moses. Little, Brown. For permission apply to Nannine Joseph, 200 W. 54th St., New York. 7 scenes (4 int., 3 street scenes). Many characters.

A very colorful and dramatic version of the *Arabian Nights* tale. Opportunity for beautiful and imaginative settings and costumes. Popular with child audiences. For a children's theatre.

ALADDIN. By Clare Tree Major. In *Playing Theatre*. French. Permission from author, 480 Lexington Avenue, New York.

8 scenes (4 sets). Indefinite number of characters. Settings not especially difficult, though production is rather elaborate.

The *Arabian Nights* tale, with scenes announced by a slave. Younger children may be used as gnomes. For children's theatre. May be done by a child cast.

ALIAS SANTA CLAUS. By Percival Wilde. Appleton-Century. One scene (int.). 10 boys, 3 girls.

A play for Christmas about a poor little rich boy and his friends from the streets. A good assembly play for 5th and 6th grades. The humor will especially appeal to boys.

ALI BABA AND THE FORTY THIEVES. By Louise Van Voorhis Armstrong, 536 Fourth St., Manistee, Mich. Pantomime in 5 scenes, 2 settings: a street showing the inside of two houses, and the outside of the cave. Indefinite number of characters may be used.

A clever version of the *Arabian Nights* tale told by an Arabian story-teller and acted in pantomime by the characters. Ballet music has been written for it by Maybelle Townsend. Can be done simply by children or elaborately by skilled dancers. For children's theatres and girls' camps.

ALICE IN WONDERLAND. By Charlotte Chorpenning. Ms. Junior Leagues, Inc., Waldorf-Astoria, New York. A part of this play is given in Chapter IV. An unusually appealing dramatization of the Lewis Carroll story.

ALICE IN WONDERLAND. By Alice Gerstenberg. French. Also in *A Treasury of Plays for Children*. Little, Brown. 3 acts, 8 scenes (4 int., 3 ext.). 21 characters, most of which can be played either by boys or girls.

A dramatization of Lewis Carroll's immortal story which has been very widely used in children's theatres.

ALICE IN WONDERLAND. By Mrs. Burton Harrison. Dramatic Publishing Co. 3 acts (2 ext., 1 int.). 4 boys, 5 girls, 12 men, 9 women, extras.

A short dramatization of Lewis Carroll's story including the scene with the Cheshire Cat, the Mad Tea Party, and the trial of the Knave of Hearts. Tableaux, songs, and dances are suggested. 5th or 6th grade.

ALICE IN WONDERLAND. By Eva Le Gallienne and Florida Friebus. French. A cast of 50 or more children and adults. Adapted for the stage from Lewis Carroll's *Alice in Wonderland* and *Through the Looking Glass*. A very elaborate dramatization of this story. For an experienced children's theatre with unusual equipment.

AND THEN WHAT HAPPENED? By Jean L. Latham. Dramatic Publishing Co. No royalty. 1 Act (int.). 4 boys, 3 girls.

A book-appreciation play in which bored children find interesting friends in a library. For Book Week. 5th and 6th grades.

AROUND THE BLUE WIGWAM. By Olive Price. In *Short Plays from American History and Literature,* Vol. 1. French. No royalty. 3 scenes (ext.). 10 men, 3 women, extras, Indians.

An Indian play based upon the incident of the saving of John Smith's life by the Indian princess Pocahontas. A good assembly play for 7th and 8th grades. Easily produced. Girls' camp.

THE ARROW-MAKER'S DAUGHTER. By Grace E. Smith and Gertrude Knevels. French. No royalty. 5 scenes (ext.). 1 hour. 13 characters, extras.

Adapted from Longfellow's poem *Hiawatha*. A good play for the final production of a girls' summer camp program. Suggestions for costuming, dances, and music are given.

AT THE SPANISH COURT. By Anna Jane Harnwell. In *Plays for Autumn and Winter Holidays,* ed. by Sanford. Dodd, Mead. For royalty apply to Mrs. F. W. Harnwell, Brunnermill, Frederick, Md. 1 scene (palace int.) 20 minutes. 6 men, 2 women, pages and extras.

A dignified and dramatic scene in which Queen Isabella pledges her jewels to aid Columbus. If costumed as described, the play would be too costly for its length, but if rich-looking costumes could be had from a school wardrobe, the play would be most effective for Columbus Day. 8th grade.

THE BABE AT THE INN. By Delle Oglesbee Ross. In *New Plays for Christmas,* ed. by Sanford, Dodd Mead. 1 act. (int.). 2 boys, 3 girls, 8 men, 3 women.

At the Inn in Bethlehem the great crowd learns of the birthday of the Christ Child and honors Him in celebration. A good play for Junior High School or a Sunday School group.

BABOUSKA SEES IT THROUGH. By Gertrude S. Buckland. In *Let's Give a Play*. Crowell. No royalty if no admission. 1 scene (int.). 5 boys, 3 men, 4 women, extras.

The little children in the schools of Soviet Russia have just learned that the government forbids any Christmas celebration. They cry bitterly until Babouska with the true spirit of Christmas "sees it through" and the children are happy. A short Christmas play for a school program or for an assembly. 7th or 8th grade.

THE BELLMAN OF MONS. By Dorothy Rose Googins. In *The Atlantic Book of Junior Plays*. Atlantic Monthly Press. 3 acts (1 ext., 1 int.). About 40 minutes. 1 boy, 1 girl, 6 men, 6 women.

The organ of Mons Cathedral, which was built with the money of a man who had robbed the poor, has been silent for 100 years. A peasant lad, by virtue of his unselfishness, is able to play the organ. A good assembly play for 8th grade.

THE BIRDCAGE-MAKER. By Louise Housman and Edward T. Koehler. In *Footlights up!* Harpers. No royalty. 3 short acts. Indefinite number of characters. Italian in setting.

An old folk tale of the young birdcage-maker who brings happiness to himself by bringing it to others. For 7th or 8th grades. Suggestions for costuming and setting are given.

THE BIRDS' CHRISTMAS CAROL. By Kate Douglas Wiggin and Helen Ingersoll. Houghton, Mifflin. 3 scenes (int.). 6 boys, 10 girls.

A good dramatization of this story, with a happy ending. Suitable for a Christmas play in a rural school, or wherever it is desired to use children of various ages.

THE BIRTH OF OLD GLORY. By Gertrude S. Buckland. In *Let's Give a Play*. Crowell. No royalty if no admission. 1 scene (int.). 1 girl, 3 men, 1 woman, extras.

General Washington and Betsy Ross decide on a flag for the country which symbolizes the courage, loyalty, and purity of the early colonists. A short play suitable for a Flag Day program. For 7th or 8th grade.

THE BIRTHDAY OF THE INFANTA. By Stuart Walker, 824 N. Whittier Dr., Beverly Hills, Cal. In *Portmanteau Plays*. Appleton-Century. Also in *Another Treasury*. Little, Brown. Permission from the author. 1 scene (int.). 2 boys, 1 girl, 3 men, 1 woman.

A little hunchback happily entertains the Princess, but dies of a broken heart when he finds that it is his disfigurement and not his art which has made her laugh. A difficult but excellent play which can be done by 8th grade children or older.

A BIT O' SHAMROCK. By Gertrude S. Buckland. In *Let's Give a Play*. Crowell. No royalty if no admission. 1 scene (ext.). 2 boys, 1 man, 1 woman, extras.

Through the efforts of St. Patrick, Ireland is freed from the serpents. A bit o' shamrock is given by an angel to the Irish settlers as a promise that the serpents shall never again return. A good assembly play for St. Patrick's Day. For 7th grade children.

THE BLACK KNIGHT. By James Gardner Hellmann. French. An elaborate mediæval play in 3 scenes (1 ext., 1 int.). Indefinite number of characters.

A beautiful story showing the evils of war and the way in which a wicked knight changed his mind about sacking a city because the children came to him with a plea that he let them have their Christmas. For adults and children to act for a children's theatre.

THE BLUE BIRD. By Maurice Maeterlinck. Dodd, Mead. 5 acts, 6 scenes. Elaborate and difficult settings, with effects which should be attempted only by well-equipped theatres with experienced director and technical staff.

Tyltyl and Mytyl, the woodcutter's children, guided by the Fairy Berylune, go out in search of the blue bird of happiness. After visiting the Palace of Night, the Land of Memory, and the Kingdom of the Future, the children return to find it in their own home. The forest and graveyard scenes are usually omitted. One of the most beautiful of all plays for a children's theatre.

THE BLUE PRINCE. By Alice C. D. Riley. In *Ten Minutes by the Clock and Other Plays*. Doubleday Doran. No royalty. 2 scenes, prologue and epilogue (int.). 2 boys, 7 girls.

Billy falls asleep after reading Hansel and Gretel and dreams that he is the Blue Prince who helps the princess to escape from the witch. Might be acted by children from 10 to 12 for an audience their own age or younger.

THE BOY WHO DISCOVERED EASTER. By Elizabeth McFadden. French. 40 minutes. Based on R. M. Alden's *The Boy who Discovered the Spring*. 2 short acts (1 int.). 1 boy, 1 man, 2 women.

The return of spring as illustrated by the Easter story. For children in the Easter season.

A BREWING OF BRAINS. By Constance Mackay. In *The Silver Thread*. Holt. 1 scene—a simple cottage interior. 3 characters.

A young man comes to the Wise Woman asking for brains, and wins the hand of a lovely girl in marriage as well as a recipe for brains. For children from 11 to 13. 7th and 8th grade assembly.

THE BUBBLE PEDDLER. By Alice C. D. Riley. In *Let's Pretend*. Baker. 3 very short scenes (1 int., 1 ext. which can be done before the curtain). Characters: Granny, Red Riding Hood, the Bubble Peddler.

A sequel to Red Riding Hood which is a gay little play about a balloon-peddler who cures Granny's rheumatism. For children's theatre, girls' club, or 6th grade.

BY CANDLELIGHT. By Rupert Sargent Holland. In *Plays of the American Colonies*. No royalty. 1 scene (int.). 12 men, 3 girls, extras.

Tyrannical in his rule, the Royal Governor of New England demands the charter from the Connecticut Colony. During the excitement the candles are blown out and the charter mysteriously disappears, saving Connecticut for the colonists. The historical interest with an exciting freshness and humor will appeal to 7th and 8th grades for whom it will make an excellent assembly program.

CABBAGES AND KINGS. By Rose Fyleman. In *Eight Little Plays for Children*. Doubleday Doran. 2 short scenes (1 ext., 1 int.). 11 characters.

An amusing little play in which Peter Simple grows a larger cabbage than either King Corum or King Dorum. For children of 3rd and 4th grades.

CAP O' RUSHES. By Louise Housman and Edward T. Koehler. In *Footlights Up!* Harpers. 3 acts (int.). 7 boys, 13 girls.

A play based on the English fairy story of the same name. Suitable for a school program. 5th and 6th grades.

A CHRISTMAS CAROL, arranged by Frank Shay from the Dickens' story. Appleton-Century. Prologue and 6 scenes. Many characters. A very fine arrangement of the story which is suitable for all ages.

THE CHRISTMAS GUEST. By Constance Mackay. French. 1 scene (int.). 1 man, 2 women, 2 boys, 3 girls.

A group of children in sixteenth-century England are beautifully rewarded for their generosity to a beggar by the vision of the Christmas angel. A very fine and dignified little play for church or school. For players from 9 to 13, 5th and 6th grade assembly.

THE CHRISTMAS NIGHTINGALE. By Phyllis Newman Groff. The Children's Theatre Press, Charleston, West Virginia. 3 acts, 5 scenes (2 int., 1 ext.). 4 boys, 3 girls, 7 men, 7 women, extras.

A little boy lost in the Poland woods is found by the Charcoal Burner on the eve of Christmas. His voice is as beautiful as that of a nightingale, and a year later he sings carols when the Charcoal Burner's children take their puppet show to the city. Through his singing he is reunited with his lonely mother and a happy Christmas ensues. A fine Christmas play for Junior High School.

CINDERELLA. By Charlotte Chorpenning. Ms. 1504 Oak Ave., Evanston, Ill. 3 acts (1 int., 1 ext.). 5 men, 5 women, 1 child.

One of the most charming dramatizations of this well-loved fairy-tale. For a children's theatre.

CINDERELLA. By Clare Tree Major. In *Playing Theatre*. French. Permission from author, 480 Lexington Ave., New York. 5 scenes (2 int.; 1 ext.). 8 men, 6 women.

This dramatization has a good deal of charm. For an adult or children's cast to act for a children's theatre.

CINDERELLA OF LORELAND. By Frances Homer. Dramatic Publishing Co. 3 acts (2 int.). 5 men, 12 girls, a cat.

A modern version of the beloved fairy-tale in which Ashes, a cat with a little boy's tongue, plays an important part in assisting the fairy godmother in her magic kindness to Cinderella. A delightful play for a children's theatre for younger audiences. The magic transformations present no production difficulties.

THE CRADLE. By Iris Vinton. In *New Plays for Christmas*, ed. by Sanford. Dodd, Mead. No royalty. 1 act (ext.). 9 boys, 4 girls, extras.

In early Brittany, Anatole, the little Vicomte, carves a beautiful crèche. In so doing he wins a place in the hearts of the little children who formerly despised him because of his father's stern rule. An unusual Christmas play. For a 5th and 6th grade assembly.

THE CROWSNEST. By William Ford Manley. Dramatists Play Service. 1 scene (the crowsnest of a ship). 5 men, 1 boy.

An exciting little play in which the Kid, at sea off the coast of South America, finds out that the ship, instead of being the tramp that he thought it was, is a gun-running smuggler. The play builds to a surprising climax. Popular at boys' camps and clubs, and of unusually good quality.

DANIEL BOONE BLAZED A TRAIL. By Phyllis Marschall. In *Plays of Story and Legend*, ed. by Sanford. Dodd, Mead.

An historical play showing several striking incidents in the life of Daniel Boone, the daring pioneer. For a boys' camp. For 7th grade assembly.

DARBY AND JOAN. By Rose Fyleman. In *Eight Little Plays for Children*. Doubleday Doran. 1 scene (ext.). 1 boys, 2 girls.

Darby and Joan, the little weather characters, cannot keep from quarreling when they are together, so they must be controlled by the weather until they can live at peace. The quaint little barometer house and the stiffness of the characters until the spell is broken will greatly appeal to younger children. A good curtain-raiser for a children's program. Players should be small but not younger than 10. Would make a good puppet show. 5th and 6th grades.

THE DAY WILL SHAKESPEARE WENT TO KENILWORTH. By Katharine Lord. In *The Little Playbook*. Dodd, Mead. Prologue. 4 episodes. Many characters.

Will Shakespeare, a little boy, goes to Kenilworth to see the celebration in honor of Queen Elizabeth, and while there meets Oberon and Titania. A pageant play which might be very elaborate and effective.

DICK WHITTINGTON. By Louise Housman and Edward T. Koehler. In *Footlights Up!* Harpers. No royalty. 3 short acts. 3 children, 13 men, 16 women.

The interesting adventures of Dick Whittington's boyhood provide much action for this play. For 6th grade.

DICK WHITTINGTON. By M. Jagendorf. In *Pantomimes for the Children's Theatre*. Brentano's. 6 scenes. 10 boys, 2 girls, extras.

The old English folk story arranged in pantomime form requiring approximately one hour for performance. Music and suggestions are included. Suitable for 6th grade.

DOLLS. By Louise Van Voorhis Armstrong. Longmans, Green. 3 scenes (1 int.). 1 hour. 3 boys, 8 girls.

A Christmas Eve fantasy in which a little girl's dolls come to life. The fashionable doll disdains Genevieve, the old doll, but it is Genevieve whom the little girl really loves. The dialogue is unusually clever and funny, the various dolls having very decided personalities. Can be played by children from 10 up, a girl cast being effective in this play. Its only difficulty is the fact that the players in the second scene must be dressed exactly like the dolls of the first scene.

THE DYSPEPTIC OGRE. By Percival Wilde. French. 1 act (int.). Characters: an Ogre, an Irish cook, a Jester, who acts as master of ceremonies, a little girl, some Boy Scouts, and others.

A lovable ogre eats children only because he thinks he cannot digest any other kind of food. Frances and other potential dinners are saved by the Scouts and the Irish cook. An entertaining play for 6th or 7th grade.

THE EMPEROR'S NEW CLOTHES. By Charlotte Chorpenning. French. 3 acts (1 int., 1 ext.). 8 men, 4 women, many weavers and citizens. One of the best plays for a children's theatre, appealing to every age. Though it is exciting and especially delightful when played by skilled adults, the lines and action are so good that a clever child cast can do it successfully.

Based upon the Andersen tale, the play elaborates on the story so that Zar and Zan, gay, adventurous young rogues, save the honest weavers and expose the treachery of the minister of the royal robes. By offering to weave cloth for the Emperor which can be seen only by those who are fit for the offices they hold, they make the vain Emperor ridiculous and bring upon the villain his just punishment.

THE ENCHANTED GARDEN. By Constance Mackay. In *The House of the Heart*. Holt. 1 scene, a garden, preferably a real one. Indefinite number of flower characters, also Prince Butterfly, Bumble Bee, and the Queen.

The Wild Rose, snubbed by the other flowers, is chosen by the Queen as her favorite. A charming little play for 4th grade or girls' camp.

THE EVIL KETTLE. By Lord Dunsany. In *Another Treasury of Plays*. Little, Brown. 1 act. (int.). 2 boys, 1 woman.

James Watt is first seen as the sensitive, dreamy child who fears the result from the invention of steam, and later as a thoughtful alert lad who is enthusiastic and determined to aid progress. The incident centers around the singing teakettle. An unusual play for 8th grade.

THE FAIRY AND THE DOLL. By Rose Fyleman in *Eight Little Plays for Children*. Doubleday Doran. 1 scene (ext.). 2 little girls.

An important conversation between a fairy and a squeaky little doll. For very young children this is widely used, and is suitable for assembly or auditorium programs. 3rd and 4th grades.

THE FAIRY RIDDLE. By Rose Fyleman. In *Eight Little Plays for
Children*. Doubleday Doran. 1 scene (ext.). 1 boy, 2 girls.

The Fairy Queen's silver cloak has been stolen and will not
be returned until she can answer the fairy riddle. Very young
children would delight in playing and seeing this played. 3rd
or 4th grades.

FATHER CHRISTMAS. By Rose Fyleman. In *Eight Little Plays for
Children*. Doubleday Doran. 2 scenes (int.). 2 boys, 1 girl.

Father Christmas gets stuck in the chimney. He "wishes his
way through the floor" and mysteriously disappears as he continues his Christmas journey. A delightful play for a puppet
show which can be adapted for playing by children. For 3rd
or 4th grades. To be played for little children.

THE FIFTEENTH CANDLE. By Rachel Lyman Field. In *The Atlantic
Book of Junior Plays* by Thomas. Little, Brown. 1 scene
(int.). 2 girls, 2 men, 1 woman.

Stella pleads with her father to let her younger sister continue with her art training, but he is determined that she must
leave school and work. A well-written and highly effective
little play with the child labor problem as its central idea.
For 8th grade assembly.

THE FIRST NOËL. In *Youth's Highway*. By Constance Mackay.
Holt. 2 short scenes (inn and stable). Many characters.

A lovely Christmas play in which a little boy begs that his
father will let Joseph and Mary sleep in the stable since there
is no room in the inn. The story of the Nativity with singing and pageantry. Highly recommended for churches and
schools.

FIVE GHOSTS. By Rowe Wright. In *Short Plays for Young Folks* by
M. Jagendorf. Brentano's. 1 act (int.). 7 boys, 5 girls.

Appearing as ghosts in a haunted house, a group of girls
frighten the boys away and thus win the building to be used
as a club-house. A good Hallowe'en play for 6th or 7th grades
as it is short with much humor and suspense.

THE FOAM MAIDEN. By Constance Mackay. In *The Silver Thread*.
Holt. 1 scene (a cottage int.). 3 characters.

A lad captures the Foam Maiden's scarlet cap which will

work magic for him, but he discovers that it is much better to do his own work than to rely on magic. 6th grade. Camp.

THE FOREST PRINCESS. By Constance Mackay. In *The Forest Princess and Other Plays*. Holt. 3 acts (1 ext.). Indefinite number of characters.

The Spirits of the Trees christen the Forest Princess with gifts of long life, constancy, purity, wisdom, and beauty. The Oak, who was not invited, becomes angry and bestows a curse on the princess. The spell is broken after many years by the kiss of a prince. 6th grade or camp.

THE FOREST SPRING. By Constance Mackay. In *The Silver Thread and Other Folk Tales*. Holt. 1 scene—a deep wood. 4 characters.

An old woman who desires to drink from the Forest Spring that she may live forever, discovers with the aid of the Spirit of the Forest that it is better to live fully each day than to dream of living forever. 5th or 6th grade. Camp.

GABRIEL AND THE HOUR BOOK. By Ethel Van der Veer and Franklyn Bigelow. French. 6 scenes (4 simple int.). 16 men, 10 women.

The story of a little boy in 15th century France who mixes colors for a monk in a monastery. Into the beautiful Hour Book which the monk has made, Gabriel slips a little prayer which is answered by the Lady of the Manor. The play is suitable for a group of children studying mediæval times and would be useful in supplying art projects. For 6th grade.

GAMMER GURTON'S NEEDLE. By Stuart Walker. In *Portmanteau Adaptations*. Appleton-Century. Permission from author, 824 N. Whittier Dr., Beverly Hills, Calif. 5 acts, prologue (simple setting).

An adaptation of this pre-Elizabethan farce which is suitable for Junior High School or older. Easily produced.

GEORGE WASHINGTON'S FORTUNE. By Constance Mackay. In *Patriotic Plays and Pageants*. Holt. No royalty. 1 scene. 8 boys.

Happy incidents during Washington's exploits as a surveyor. An excellent play for an assembly or other program celebrating Washington's Birthday. For 7th or 8th grade children.

THE GHOST OF MR. PENNY. By Rosemary Musil, author of *Seven Little Rebels*. Children's Theatre Press. 3 acts (2 int.). 3 men, 1 woman, 4 boys, 2 girls.

Five children and a mysterious stranger uncover a mystery and bring happiness to little Sally. Strange happenings, thrills, and refreshing comedy characterize this modern melodrama which is sure to be popular with a children's theatre audience.

THE GOLDEN TOUCH. By Alice C. D. Riley. In *Let's Pretend*. Baker. 2 scenes (int.). 7 characters.

A dramatization of the myth with a modern flavor. A property man explains the action, and two servants, Snip and Snap, add humor. For 5th or 6th grade or for a younger girls' camp.

GOLDTREE AND SILVERTREE. By Katherine Morse. Macmillan. Permission from author. 2 scenes (ext.). 5 boys, 7 girls.

The lovely little Goldtree is saved from the wicked stepmother's magic by the Blue Prince. This is a dramatization of the story, *Snow-White and Rose Red*. Children in the 4th and 5th grades greatly enjoy it.

GOOD KING WENCESLAUS. By Cloyd Head. Dramatic Publishing Co. 1 act. 8 men, 6 women, extras. Excellent for Junior High School.

Based on the familiar Christmas carol of that name, the play makes use of the carol in song and dialogue. An effective and dignified little play which if well-done would be both picturesque and impressive. The Poor Man of the carol turns out to be the King's friend and councilor who was believed dead. Singers may be an important part of the cast.

THE GOOSEHEAD AND THE GOBLIN. By Constance Mackay. In *The House of the Heart*. Holt. 1 scene (out of doors). 4 boys, 4 girls.

Conrad, the little gooseherd, discontented with his lot, has three wishes granted by Peterkin, a goblin. After experiencing the characters of the miser and the king, he is glad enough to be himself again. Suitable for children of 3rd or 4th grade.

GUTENBERG AND THE APPRENTICE. By Anne Deiss Fielden. In *Plays of Story and Legend*. Ed. by Sanford. Dodd, Mead. No royalty. 1 scene (int.). 10 men, 1 woman.

Early in the 15th century Johannes Gutenberg discovers a new method of printing as a result of the careless work of his apprentice. A short play for a Book Appreciation assembly. 6th grade.

HANS BRINKER AND THE SILVER SKATES. By Charlotte Chorpenning. Children's Theatre Press. 3 acts (4 scenes, 1 ext., 2 int.). One exterior with snow is difficult. Good production notes. 13 men, and boys, 1 woman, 5 girls.

An excellent dramatization of this popular book. Includes the exciting robbery scene at the inn, the cure of Hans' father, and the skating race. Should be acted by students of high-school age or older for a children's theatre.

HEIDI. By Lucille Miller. Children's Theatre Press. 4 acts (1 difficult ext. in the Alps, 2 int.). 3 men, 6 women, 4 children.

The best dramatization of this greatly loved story of the little Swiss girl and her grandfather, by Johanna Spyri. The spirit of the book has been well-kept in the play and it is very popular with children.

HELGA AND THE WHITE PEACOCK. By Cornelia Meigs. Macmillan. No royalty. 3 acts. (1 int., 1 ext.). 4 girls, 4 boys.

Helga, a mortal child, who has been stolen when a baby, is living with the Trolls. By the help of the White Peacock she is at last rescued by her brother whose purpose is stronger than that of the Troll's magic. A good play for a children's theatre, and interesting for 6th and 7th grades to present.

HILLTOP. By Louise Garnett. In *Three to Make Ready*. Doubleday Doran. No royalty. 1 act (ext.). 5 boys, 2 girls, 4 men, 1 woman.

At last Peter is content to search for the four-leaf clover on his own hilltop for he knows that industry, laughter, courage, and trustworthiness are the gifts for him who finds it. This little morality play is delightful in its fantastic treatment and is an unusual play for 6th or 7th grade. Music is included.

THE HOLE IN THE WALL. By Alice C. D. Riley. In *The Play's the Thing*. Winston. 2 scenes (no scenery), 12 men, 2 women.

The property man sets the stage and shows to the audience

the hole in the wall. Each character thinks the hole is his secret alone and they all use it as a hiding place, causing many difficulties and problems. A charming little play for 6th grade assembly or excellent for an older girls' camp.

THE HORNED BEASTS. By Rupert Sargent Holland. In *Plays of the American Colonies*. Harpers. No royalty. 1 scene (ext.). 10 men, 5 women.

In New Jersey in 1665 the English settlers receive word that the French are coming to take their new homes and they are regarded as horned beasts. The governor explains the misunderstanding and a happy time results. An excellent assembly play for 7th or 8th grade.

THE HOUSE OF THE HEART. By Constance Mackay. In *The House of the Heart*. Holt. 1 scene (int.). Cast of 12, boys or girls.

A morality play in which the virtues and vices living in the heart of the child are characterized according to their good or evil. Suitable for 6th grade.

HOW BOOTS BEFOOLED THE KING. By Sophie L. Goldsmith. In *Wonder-Clock Plays*. Harpers. Permission from Publisher. 3 acts, 7 scenes. 10 men, 10 women.

After many suitors have failed, Boots succeeds in fooling the king three different times, thus winning the princess as his bride. Much humor and suspense will appeal to children of the 5th and 6th grades for playing.

HOW THE PRINCESS'S PRIDE WAS BROKEN. By Sophie L. Goldsmith. In *Wonder-Clock Plays*. Harpers. Permission from Publisher. 3 acts (2 int., 1 ext.), 6 men, 10 women.

A young king fools the haughty princess by disguising himself as a swineherd, and thus wins her for his bride. Much action and rollicking humor. For 6th or 7th grade.

HUCKLEBERRY FINN. By Charlotte Chorpenning. Ms. 1504 Oak Ave., Evanston, Ill. 3 acts (4 scenes, 3 ext.). 8 men and boys, 8 women and girls.

This dramatization of Mark Twain's famous novel contains some of the most amusing episodes of the story, notably the scene in which Huck masquerades as Tom, forcing Tom to be Sid, and the one in which the boys confuse Aunt Sally when she is counting the silver. For adults and children to present for a children's theatre.

IN ARCADY. By Rose Fyleman. In *Eight Little Plays for Children*. Doubleday Doran. No royalty. 1 scene (ext.) 3 characters.

The Shepherd chooses to remain with the shepherds rather than follow the Dancer. A very short play suitable for a girl-cast. Good for camps.

THE INDIAN CAPTIVE. By Charlotte Chorpenning. Children's Theatre Press. 3 acts, 2 outdoor settings. 3 men, 3 women, 5 children.

An interesting story, based on history, of a little pioneer girl who is captured by the Indians. Distrusted by some of the Indians, she is about to be tested by fire when her courageous spirit wins their admiration, and she is adopted into the tribe. When at last her mother comes to search for her, the Indians, seeing their great love, let her go back to her home. For an adult and child cast to give for a children's theatre.

IN THE PATH OF THE CHILDREN. In *World Friendship Plays for Young People,* by Virginia Olcott. Dodd, Mead. 1 scene. Indefinite number of characters. The scene is laid in Germany. The play concerns a little girl who stayed behind during the Children's Crusade. For children of various ages, with several adult characters.

JACK AND THE BEANSTALK. By Charlotte Chorpenning. Children's Theatre Press. 3 acts (2 ext., 1 int.). 14 characters.

A charming and popular play based on the old fairy-tale. The Giant throws golden eggs at his whimpering little wife if she refuses to tell him anything he wants to know, and makes her dance to the music of his human harp. But she and Jack are too clever for him and all ends happily. The beanstalk is a difficult production problem, but many children's theatres have found it possible to produce the play.

THE JAPANESE TWINS. By Eleanor Ellis Perkins, 2319 Lincoln St., Evanston, Ill. Ms., 3 acts (1 set). 3 children, 6 men, 4 women, and a crowd of servants and relatives.

A quaint and charming play suggested by the story of the

same name by Lucy Fitch Perkins. The little girl twin, disconsolate that she cannot be knighted at the Samurai ceremony with her brother, proves in an exciting episode that she can be as valuable to her father as Taro.

JEANNE AND THE PEDDLER. By Anne Deiss Fielden. In *Plays of Story and Legend,* ed. by Sanford. No royalty. 1 scene (ext.). 2 boys, 1 girl, 1 man, 2 women.

A short play in which Jeanne, the Maid of France, hears the voice of St. Margaret and realizes that she is the chosen one to save her country. 7th grade assembly play.

JEANNE D'ARC. By Emma Gelders Sterne. In *Far Town Road.* Harcourt, Brace. 3 acts, 4 scenes (ext.). 10 men, 6 women and girls.

An excellent dramatization of the story of Jeanne D'Arc. Costumes and settings of the 15th century will add to the picturesque atmosphere. Suitable for a children's theatre.

JEAN VALJEAN AND THE CHRISTMAS DOLL. By Agnes Irene Smith. Dramatic Publishing Co. No royalty. 1 act (int.). 3 girls, 4 men, 1 woman.

A dramatization from Victor Hugo's *Les Miserables* in which Jean Valjean comes to the Inn of the Thenardiers on Christmas Eve. There he finds Little Cosette, the child for whom he has been searching, and makes her happy with the Christmas Doll and new clothes, for she is to go away with him. A good Christmas assembly play. 8th grade.

THE JESTER'S PURSE. By Nydia E. Minchin. Harcourt, Brace. 3 episodes (3 ext.). Indefinite number of characters.

A Jester starts to the fair with a penny in his purse. Seeing a Gypsy, he throws away his purse and runs, telling the people he has been robbed of a large sum. Can be done by the 7th grade.

KAI KHOSRU. By Dorothy Coit. J. J. Little and Ives. 3 acts, 1 setting arranged on levels. Indefinite cast.

A Persian King, frightened by the Magi's interpretation of his dream, orders his grandson Kai Khosru to be put to death. The boy is not killed but returns years later to claim the throne. As a correlated activity for children between the ages of 6 and 12, *Kai Khosru* would provide a rich experience. Unless the children are steeped in Persian lore, much of the sensitive delicacy and beauty of the play is lost.

KATRINKA. By Eleanor Ellis Perkins, Ms., 2319 Lincoln St., Evanston, Ill. 4 acts (2 int., 1 ext.). Indefinite number of characters.

A charming dramatization of the popular novel by Helen Haskell. Katrinka, heroine of this Russian story, wins the Czar's admiration by her beautiful dancing and secures a pardon for her parents who have been exiled to Siberia. Requires a leading character who can both act and dance well, and also a ballet of young girls. Can be done in coöperation with a good dancing school. Should be produced with grown-ups in the adult rôles. Thoroughly worth doing.

KINFOLK OF ROBIN HOOD. By Percy Mackaye. In *The Atlantic Book of Junior Plays,* ed. by Thomas. Atlantic Monthly Press. 4 acts (3 ext.). 15 men, 7 women.

Robin Hood and his merry men save Fair Alice, outwit the stupid Sheriff, and obtain pardon from the King and Queen. For a school play.

THE KING WITH THE IRON HEART. By Stark Young. In *Sweet Times and the Blue Policeman.* Holt. Also in *Another Treasury.* Little, Brown. 1 scene (int.). 7 boys, 3 girls.

The king's heart was bound with iron, but when he heard the song of the Old Woman of Dreams the iron bands burst and he pitied all. A short play. Good for 5th or 6th grades.

KINGS IN NOMANIA. By Percival Wilde. Appleton-Century. 5 scenes, simple settings, mostly imagined by the audience with the help of the Herald who sets the stage imaginatively. Indefinite number of characters.

A little bootblack, because he is a capable judge, shows the King his shortcomings and wins himself a pardon when he is unjustly condemned to die. An excellent play for 6th or 7th grade. May be presented at Christmas time or not. Costumes may be fantastic, adding to the delightful make-believe.

THE KNAVE OF HEARTS. By Louise Saunders. Longmans, Green. 1 act (royal kitchen). 6 men, 4 women, extras.

A charming and sophisticated version of the old rhyme in which the Knave steals the tarts because the Queen has made a failure of them. Can be done best by 8th grade or by older girls.

THE KNIGHTS OF THE SILVER SHIELD. By Elizabeth McFadden. French. Based on the Raymond MacDonald Alden story. 1 scene (int.). 12 men.

Sir Roland wins the star of knighthood by faithfully remaining at the gate and keeping it safely guarded. A very fine story. For 5th and 6th grades.

THE LANTERN. By Abbie Farwell Brown. Houghton Mifflin. 2 acts (int.). 4 girls, 5 boys, extras.

In the days of the American Revolution, Barbara holds a candle to the window to guide her father's boat safely through the Rocky Cove bearing a precious cargo of men to save the colony from the Redcoats. Suspense and excitement give this historical play a freshness that will appeal to 7th and 8th grades.

LANTERN LIGHT. By Olive Price. In *Short Plays from American History and Literature,* Vol. I. Also separately. French. No royalty. 5 scenes (3 int., 1 ext.). 7 boys, 6 girls.

The story of a near-disaster in early New England when a woman is accused of witchcraft. She is saved by the King's counselor who arrives just in time to administer justice. Best for a 7th grade assembly. The unfortunately large number of scenes means that it must be played with few properties and no scenery.

LITTLE BLACK SAMBO AND THE TIGERS. By Charlotte Chorpenning. Dramatists Play Service. 3 acts (all ext., which may have the same background and minor changes). Characters are Sambo, his mother, father, and monkeys and tigers.

An unusual dramatization of the Bannerman book, written with much imagination. There is a marked rhythm in the play, a strong feeling of the jungle, and very definite characterizations. A picturesque and entertaining play for children's theatres.

LITTLE LADY DRESDEN. By Olive Price. In *Short Plays from American History and Literature,* Vol. I. French. No royalty. 1 scene (int.). 4 men, 3 women.

Betty Warwick, called Little Lady Dresden, in her eagerness to dance the minuet with General Lafayette, confides her hopes to the kind stranger who is none other than the great general himself. A good assembly play for 7th or 8th grades giving much of the flavor of the early American period.

LITTLE LORD FAUNTLEROY. By Frances Hodgson Burnett. French. 3 acts (2 int.). 8 men, or boys, 3 women. Dramatization of the author's novel of the same name. Stilted and old-fashioned but interesting enough to be worth adapting.

Little Cedric Errol's father, who is heir to the Earl of Dorincourt, has been banished from home because he married against his father's wishes. After his death, the Earl sends for Cedric and is so charmed by the boy that he forgives the mother. For children's theatre.

THE LITTLE PRINCESS. By Frances Hodgson Burnett. French. 3 acts (3 int.). 5 men, 3 women, 14 children.

The story of plucky little Sara Crewe, rich and favored pupil of Miss Minchin's boarding-school, who becomes suddenly poor and outcast, then happy again, is one that children have always loved. It can be done simply and effectively for a children's theatre.

LITTLE SQUARE-TOES. By Rachel Field. In *Patchwork Plays.* Doubleday Doran. 1 act (ext.). 5 little girls.

A little pioneer girl, captured by Indians, gives up chance of returning because she is happier with them. Very simple. For 4th, 5th, or 6th grade. Rather charming Puritan play.

LITTLE WOMEN. By Marion De Forrest. French. 4 acts (int., ext.). 5 men, 7 women.

A dramatization of the famous story by Louisa M. Alcott, in which much of the humor and beauty of the story is retained. A good play for a children's theatre.

THE LITTLE YASHMAK (The Little Veil). In *World Friendship Plays for Young People.* By Virginia Olcott. Dodd, Mead. 1 scene. 1 man, 1 woman, 1 boy, 3 girls.

A play of new Turkey, showing the joy of a young Turkish girl at the order to cease wearing veils. For 8th grade children or older.

LOST CHILDREN. A Christmas play by Dorothy Nichols. Longmans, Green. 1 act (cottage int.). 4 boys, 4 girls, 2 women.

A fairy-tale type of play. Madge, who lives in the Woods of Lost Children, mothers all who come to her door. When one little family grows beyond the age of loving her simple Christmas, another group of children comes to take their place. Suitable for 7th and 8th grades, especially for a grown audience.

THE LOST COLONY. By Rupert Sargent Holland. In *Plays of the American Colonies*. Harpers. No royalty. 1 scene and prologue (ext.). 10 men, 3 women.

Early in 1591, Master John White, the leader of the Raleigh expedition, returns to Roanoke Island to visit his little granddaughter, Virginia Dare, but finds that the entire colony is lost. A good assembly play for Junior High School showing the hardships and courage of the early pioneers.

THE LOST PRINCESS. By Dan Totheroh. French. 1 act, 13 characters and extras.

A sequel to *The Stolen Prince*. It tells the story of the twin sister who is cared for by bandits. The nurse discovers her and she is reunited with her brother who has become emperor. Done in the Chinese manner. For 6th or 7th grade.

MAID OF THE NILE. By Clare Tree Major. In *Playing Theatre*. French. Permission from author, 480 Lexington Ave., New York. 4 scenes which can be set simply with Egyptian columns and a few other pieces. Indefinite number of characters. An interesting play based on Egyptian history. For children's theatre or school.

MAKE-BELIEVE. By A. A. Milne. In *Another Treasury*. Little, Brown. Prologue, 3 acts (4 sets). 21 men, 15 women. A charming play which is more thoroughly appreciated by adults than by children.

With the help of the butler, Rosemary is writing a play, and when the other children ask for a fairy-tale, an adventure story, a Christmas play, she puts all their ideas into one show. A children's theatre play best acted by adults and children.

THE MAN WITH ONE IDEA. By Gertrude S. Buckland. In *Let's Give a Play*. Crowell. No royalty if no admission. 1 scene (ext.). 1 boy, 3 men, extras.

Christopher Columbus was the man with one idea. At last through the efforts of the Padre his expedition is financed by Queen Isabella and he is determined to prove that the world is round. A good assembly play for Columbus Day. For 7th grade.

MARY POPPINS. By P. L. Travers. Dramatized by Sara Spencer. Ms., Children's Theatre Press. 3 acts, 5 scenes. 13 characters.

A dramatization of this very popular book which includes some of the best incidents of the story. Technically it seems difficult, though the Children's Theatre Press can supply practical solutions to the problems it offers. A delightful children's theatre play.

A MASQUE OF CHRISTMAS. By Constance Mackay. In *The Forest Princess*. Holt. 3 scenes (2 int.). Indefinite number of characters.

A mediæval play in which a little boy learns the difference between the Spirit of Giving and the Spirit of Getting. Giving proves to be Christmas Joy. For 6th grade.

MASTER SKYLARK. By Edgar White Burrill. Appleton-Century. Permission from author, 620 West 116th St., New York. 5 acts (2 ext., 2 int.). 2 boys, 1 girl, 7 men, 2 women, extras. Dramatized from the novel by John Bennett. Appleton-Century.

Nick Attwood, a young boy of Stratford, is taken by a company of players to London and becomes a famous singer. At last he appears before Queen Elizabeth and meets William Shakespeare whose efforts restore Nick to his parents. A very fine play for a children's theatre. A boy with a good singing voice is necessary.

THE MERCHANT GENTLEMAN (Le Bourgeois Gentilhomme). By Molière. Translation by Curtis Hidden Page. Putnam. No royalty. 3 acts, 1 setting. 14 men, 3 women, extras.

M. Jourdain, a rich retired merchant, resolves to be a gentleman, but is tricked by all and succeeds only in becoming a fool. To be played by 9th grade or older for a children's theatre. It can be elaborately produced, for the music, dances, and costumes provide an excellent opportunity.

MISS ANT, MISS GRASSHOPPER, AND MR. CRICKET. (With a special bow to Mr. Æsop.) *In Patchwork Plays.* By Rachel Field. Doubleday Doran. 1 act. Ext., showing quaint cottage. 3 characters. For 4th and 5th grade. An attractive little play following the story of the fable.

THE MISTAKE AT THE MANOR. By M. M. Frank. In *Short Plays About Famous Authors.* Holt. 1 act (int.), 4 men, 2 women characters.

Oliver Goldsmith when still a young boy spends the night at Featherstone Manor, which he mistakes for an inn. A good assembly play. 7th grade.

MR. BRAGG'S HEAD. By Rupert Sargent Holland. In *Plays of the American Colonies.* Harper. No royalty. 1 scene (int.). 10 men, 3 women.

The early colonists of South Carolina greatly feared the pirates along the Atlantic coast, and much excitement results when they demand drugs and medicine for the sick captain. An interesting assembly play for 7th or 8th grades with suspense and humor adding to its appeal.

MR. DOOLEY, JR. By Rose Franken and Jane Lewin. French. 3 acts (int.). 4 boys, 5 girls.

The action centers around Mr. Dooley, Jr., a little dog who is rescued from an unkind mistress by Tommy and Janie. A good modern play, very popular in children's theatres. A live dog is the star of the production.

MRS. WIGGS OF THE CABBAGE PATCH. By Anne Crawford Flexner. French. 3 acts (1 int., 1 ext.). 5 boys, 7 girls, 11 men, 3 women.

A dramatization of the story by Alice Hegan Rice including the wedding scene, Sunday School, and others that retain the humor and pathos of the story. For a children's theatre. Cutting is necessary for a child audience.

THE NATIVITY. By Douglas Hyde. In *Poets and Dreamers* by Lady
Gregory. Hodges, Figgis and Co., 20 Nassau St., Dublin,
Ireland. 1 act (ext.). 7 men, 3 women, extras.

A woman from the East and a woman from the West each
seeking pardon, meet at the door of Bethlehem's stable as
the kings and the shepherds come bearing their gifts. Within
they find the Babe in the manger, the King of the world. A
beautiful Christmas play. Junior High School or church program.

THE NATIVITY. By Phyllis Marschall. In *New Plays for Christmas*,
ed. by Sanford. Dodd, Mead. 8 scenes. 10 men, 3 women,
extras.

A good adaptation of a 13th-century miracle play of the
Nativity, presumably written by a French nun. For a Junior
High School production at Christmas time. Effective if played
by adults for children.

NEVERTHELESS. By Stuart Walker. In *Portmanteau Plays*. Appleton-Century. Permission from Author, 824 N. Whittier Dr.,
Beverly Hills, Calif. 1 act. (1 int.). 1 boy, 1 girl, 1 man.

An amusing little play in which a burglar surprises two
children who have just come across the word "nevertheless"
for the first time. The three of them have a thoroughly delightful time acting out the word. Children of 10 can play
the boy and girl if an older person takes the part of the
burglar.

ON CHRISTMAS EVE. By Constance Mackay. In *The House of the
Heart*. Holt. 1 scene. (int.). 5 boys, 7 girls.

A little girl's Christmas Eve dream of story-book characters; Wendy, Robinson Crusoe, and others. 4th or 5th grade.

ON THE TOWER OF THE SHADOWS. By Marion Brown. In *The Jester's Purse*. Harcourt, Brace. 3 acts (1 ext.). 8 boys and men,
5 girls and women, and extras.

An insight into the life of the Zuñi and Navajo Indian
tribes is gained from this play. "The only way to conquer
your enemy is to make him your friend," is the underlying
theme. A camp play. For 6th or 7th grade.

Once in a Hundred Years. By M. Jagendorf. In *One-Act Plays for Young Folks*. French. A fantastic comedy. 30 minutes. 2 boys, 1 girl.

Based on an ancient Japanese legend, this play tells the story of Goblins who appear once in a hundred years for a dance in the moonlight. Whoever dances with them can make some wish which the Goblins fulfill. Opportunity for dancing. Junior High School age. Camp.

The Orange Plume. By Rupert Sargent Holland. In *Plays of American Colonies*. Harpers. No royalty. 1 scene (ext.). 8 boys and men, 3 girls.

James Oglethorpe, the governor of Georgia, is saved from the Spanish spy by Tockahowi, an Indian boy, and the Indians and the colonists become good friends. For 7th and 8th grade assembly play. There is a freshness in the exciting treatment of the plot that will appeal to the older children.

The Patchwork People. By Alice C. D. Riley. In *The Play's the Thing*. Winston. 1 scene (ext.). 2 boys, 3 girls, extras.

Dame Patch who is very cross is unkind to the band of Gypsies, but later she finds that they can bring much happiness to her. An excellent play for a summer camp for girls of 5th and 6th grade age.

Peter Pan. By James M. Barrie. Scribners. Permission from Charles Frohman, Inc., New York. 5 acts, 4 sets. 14 boys, 2 girls, 2 men, 2 women.

A delightful fairy play of the little boy who did not want to grow up, and of Wendy the little girl who went with Peter to the Never Land. The finest of all plays for a children's theatre. It should not be produced, however, except by an experienced director, cast, and technical staff.

Peter, Peter, Pumpkin Eater. By Martha B. King, 225 Carey Ave., Highland Park, Illinois. Ms. 3 acts. 1 ext. (outside of Peter's farm home). Indefinite number of characters.

An unusual play based on the Mother Goose rhyme. Episodes woven together with music. The whole play is rhythmical and very picturesque. Peter's mother, grandmother, and two sisters dote on him. When he finds a wife, they do not receive her, and consequently she runs away. Peter builds a delightful little pumpkin house for her, and finally she comes back and they live happily ever after. Children's Theatre.

PETER SILVERLEG. By Rupert Sargent Holland. In *Plays of the American Colonies,* Harpers. No royalty. 1 scene (int.). 7 boys, 4 girls.

Peter Stuyvesant, governor of New Amsterdam, is successful in securing a young envoy to settle disputes between the Dutch and the Indians on the North River. Much suspense and excitement in this early American play. A good assembly play for 7th or 8th grades.

PINOCCHIO. By Adams T. Rice. French. 8 scenes, all different. 20 speaking parts, some of which can be either boys or girls. Many extras.

A good dramatization of Lorenzini's highly popular story of the little wooden puppet whose desire to become a real boy is finally realized when he acquires a good heart. Production problems are many, though the sets can be simplified and easily changed. An excellent play for a children's theatre.

THE PIRATE OF POOH. By Marjorie Barrows. Rand, McNally. One scene (ext.). 4 characters and extras.

G. Whiz longs to join the crew of retired pirates. When he finds the lost treasure by solving a cross-word puzzle (which contains the deed to the island), he is made a member. A play with an original turn—4th grade.

THE PLAY OF SAINT GEORGE. By J. M. Crum. In *The Atlantic Book of Junior Plays,* by Thomas. Little, Brown, The Atlantic Monthly Press. No royalty. 3 scenes. Indefinite number of characters.

Much humor and action result when St. George vanquishes the dragon in the accepted manner and wins the Lady Una. For a Junior High School assembly this play would provide rollicking entertainment.

THE PLAY'S THE THING. By Alice C. D. Riley. In *The Play's the Thing.* Winston. No royalty. 1 scene (ext.). 7 boys, 1 girl, extras.

The princess is restless and haughty. In a game the clever minstrel awakens her to the knowledge that she will find happiness if she will make others happy. For 5th or 6th grade. Easily produced. Suitable for an assembly program or a girls' camp.

POCAHONTAS AND JOHN SMITH. By Anna Jane Harnwell. In *Plays of Story and Legend,* ed. by Sanford. Dodd, Mead. 1 act (ext.). 1 girl, 7 men, 2 women, extras.

An historical play in which Pocahontas saves the life of John Smith. Much suspense. 7th grade assembly play. Summer camp.

POLLY PATCHWORK. By Rachel Field. In *Patchwork Plays*. Doubleday Doran. 3 scenes (2 int.). 2 boys, 7 girls, extras.

Polly is the winner of the spelling contest. The secret of her success lies in her queer little patchwork dress. For a 5th or 6th grade assembly program.

THE POOR LITTLE RICH GIRL. Eleanor Gates. French. 3 acts. 2 (int.), 1 (ext.). 15 men, 8 women.

A delightful play concerning a neglected rich child with a vivid imagination. An elaborate play which should be acted by adults for a children's theatre.

A POT OF BROTH. By William Butler Yeats. In *Plays for an Irish Theatre.* Vol. 2. Macmillan. 1 scene (int.). 2 men, 1 woman.

The cleverness of the beggar in outwitting Sibby and making a meal for himself results in a play of dramatic and literary merit that is appealing to older child audiences. For Junior High School.

THE PRINCE AND THE PAUPER. By Charlotte Chorpenning. Dramatists Play Service. 3 acts. 23 men, 12 women, extras.

A most satisfactory dramatization of the fascinating Mark Twain story, in which a little prince and a beggar-lad change places in life for a time. The acts are divided into a number of scenes, but plans are given for very simple changing of sets. A very fine children's theatre play. Most of the parts should be played by people of high-school age or older.

PRINCE FAIRY FOOT. By Maude Stewart Beagle. In *Plays for Autumn and Winter Holidays,* ed. by Sanford. Dodd, Mead.

4 short scenes—1 int., 3 ext.—which would have to be done very simply. Many characters.

A dramatization of the interesting Frances Hodgson Burnett story of the same name. To do justice to the story the play should be much longer and more elaborate, but this little dramatization would be usable for children from 9 to 11. Younger children would enjoy seeing it.

THE PRINCESS IN THE SLEEPING WOOD. By Hermon Ould. Baker. 4 scenes. 2 boys, 3 girls, 6 men, 10 women.

A delightful dramatization of the lovely old fairy-tale. Suitable for children's theatres.

THE PROUD PRINCESS. By Katherine Morse. In *Goldtree and Silvertree*. Macmillan. Permission from author. 3 scenes (int.). 14 boys, 7 girls.

The pride of the haughty princess is at last broken, and she cries. She is then chosen to reign as Queen with King Candour. Good play for younger children. Should be played by 5th and 6th grade.

THE PUDDING PAN. By Katherine Morse. In *Goldtree and Silvertree*. Macmillan. Permission from author. 1 scene (int.). 6 boys, 2 girls.

A cobbler and his wife argue over who is to return the pudding pan to the baker's wife. The play ends gaily. A good play to be done by 5th or 6th grade children. Suitable for an assembly program or for a club. Easily produced.

THE PUPPET OF PAPA 'TERO. By Emma Gelders Sterne. In *Far Town Road*. Dodd, Mead. 3 acts, 6 scenes. 14 men, 5 women.

By Pedro's clever use of a puppet, the Castilian soldiers are intrigued by the beautiful dancing lady and thus fail to capture the city of Catalonia. Much action and a fast moving plot that would be enjoyed by Junior High School students. A good play to present for an older audience.

RACKETTY-PACKETTY HOUSE. By Frances Hodgson Burnett. French. Also in *Another Treasury*. Atlantic Monthly Press. Prologue and 3 acts (int.). 16 boys, 17 girls.

The dolls' merriment in Racketty-Packetty House and Tidy Castle ends with the fairy-tale "and then they were married."

The appeal is for the younger children in that they enjoy seeing the dolls come alive. Intricate settings and mechanical business offer production problems. For children's theatre.

RADIO RESCUE. By Charlotte Chorpenning. Dramatists Play Service. 3 acts (including a corner of an attic, an old mill, a railroad embankment with a broken-down trestle seen only in the moonlight). 7 children, 4 men, 3 women.

An exciting modern melodrama of excellent quality, in which Sparky and his sister Jill save a train because of a message which comes over their home-made radio. The play is easy to act but rather difficult to stage. Requires many sound-effects made by means of a public address system and special sound records. (Gennett Records, Richmond, Ind.) Especially enjoyed by older children.

RAGGEDY ANN AND ANDY. By Eleanor Busch Cochrane. Ms. from French with music. Prologue and 4 acts (2 int., 3 ext.). 17 characters. A dramatization of the novel by Gruelle which is much liked by little children. Children's theatre.

THE RANSOM OF RED CHIEF. By Addison Geery Smith. French. 1 scene (int.). 3 men. A dramatization of the O. Henry story.

A rollicking comedy in which Johnnie, playing the part of Red Chief, is kidnapped, but he makes life so miserable for the kidnappers that they are only too glad to be rid of him. For a boys' camp. 8th grade.

REBECCA OF SUNNYBROOK FARM. By Kate Douglas Wiggin and Charlotte Thompson. French. 4 acts (2 int., 3 ext.). 1 girl, 4 men, 9 women.

Rebecca, a little country girl, comes to live with her aunts who are rigid and stern. At first she runs away, but returns and slowly wins her way into the hearts of her aunts as well as everyone else. Children's theatre.

RED SHOES AT PLYMOUTH. By Esther E. Olsen. Dramatic Publishing Co. No royalty. 1 act (int.). Cast of 11 children, 2 men.

Resolved White, a little girl of old Plymouth, gives up her bright red, new birthday shoes to an Indian child, and thus saves her colony from the horrors of an Indian attack. A good Thanksgiving play. 6th grade.

THE RETURN OF RIP VAN WINKLE. By Charlotte Chorpenning. Dramatists Play Service. 3 acts (parlor, mountain scenes). 10 men and boys; 11 women and girls.

One of the best dramatizations of Washington Irving's famous story. An excellent play for a children's theatre group. Production problems are not difficult.

RIP VAN WINKLE. By Hermon Ould. Baker. 5 scenes. 17 men, 12 women, extras. A dramatization of Irving's story with special regard for a large cast. Easily produced. Enjoyed by young children.

RIP VAN WINKLE. By Grace Dorcas Ruthenburg. In *Plays of Story and Legend*. Dodd, Mead. Ed. by Sanford. 3 acts (2 exts.). 10 boys, 3 girls, 9 men, and 9 women.

A good dramatization of Washington Irving's story which was first produced by the Children's Theatre of Charleston, West Virginia. For a children's theatre. No production problems.

ROBIN HOOD. By Owen Davis. French. 3 acts (2 exts., 1 int.). 2 women, indefinite number of men.

One of the finest dramatizations of the old ballad, with much action, adventure, and merriment. A good opening play for a childen's theatre. Requires much cutting for a child audience, but is highly effective when played for them by adults.

ROBIN HOOD. By Clare Tree Major. In *Playing Theatre*. French. Permission from author, 480 Lexington Ave., New York. 5 scenes (1 int., 4 exts.). 16 men, 2 women. A dramatization which is especially suitable to be played for children by adults.

THE ROSE AND THE RING. By Thackeray. In *Four Plays for Children*. Baker. 2 acts, 3 scenes. 3 boys, 4 girls.

The power of the rose and the ring to make the owner attractive in the eyes of the beholder causes many complications and much delightful comedy as the play progresses. Nonsensical and charming, and may be practically produced by 7th or 8th grade. Suitable for a children's theatre.

A ROSE FOR CAPTAIN BACON. By Rupert Sargent Holland. In *Plays of the American Colonies.* Harpers. No royalty. 1 scene (int.). 6 men, 3 women.

A rose with thorns sent to Captain Bacon is a secret message informing him of the unexpected action taken against him by the Governor of Virginia. A rather fresh and unusual assembly play for Junior High School.

RUMPELSTILTSKIN. By Charlotte Chorpenning. Ms., 1504 Oak Ave., Evanston, Illinois. 3 acts (1 set). 7 men and boys, 4 women.

A dramatization of the popular fairy story in which the power of the strange little dwarf is broken when the princess guesses his name. A good play for a children's theatre. Suggestions for production problems are given.

THE SAMPLER. By Rose Fyleman. In *Nine New Plays for Children.* Nelson. One short scene, 15 min. 1 man, 2 women, 1 little girl.

A quaint little playlet with a sampler as setting, and the people who live in the house as characters. The child who made the sampler neglected to finish the heart of Hetty so that she cannot love William with all her heart, but at last she works in the missing stitches and then all is well. Three characters must sing. Would be charming for girls' schools or clubs.

THE SCOTCH TWINS. By Eleanor Ellis Perkins. French. 4 acts (3 ext., 1 int.). 7 boys, 3 girls, extras. An excellent dramatization of the book of the same title by Lucy Fitch Perkins. Much liked as a children's theatre production.

THE SECRET GARDEN. By Clare Tree Major. Ms. Junior Leagues, Inc., Waldorf-Astoria, New York. 3 acts, 6 scenes (3 int., 2 ext.). 4 men, 4 women, 2 boys, 1 girl.

A dramatization of the well-liked story by Frances Hodgson Burnett, in which two children, a little girl with a temper, and a rich invalid boy, discover the secret garden, and with it the way to health and happiness.

THE SENTIMENTAL SCARECROW. By Rachel Field. French. Also in *Patchwork Plays.* Doubleday Doran. 1 scene, a cornfield. 3

boys, 5 girls. A sentimental scarecrow returns a fortune to Polly and finds romance. For children from 11 to 13.

SEVEN GIFTS. By Stuart Walker. In *The Appleton Book of Christmas Plays*. Appleton-Century. Permission from author, 824 N. Whittier Dr., Beverly Hills, Calif. 1 act, fantastic setting. 19 boys, 10 girls.

A fantasy in pantomime in which the sacrifice of a little girl proves to be the true gift. A good Christmas play. 7th or 8th grade, church or community.

SEVEN LITTLE REBELS. By Rosemary Musil. Children's Theatre Press. 4 acts (2 ints.). 3 boys, 5 girls of 10 or 11 years, 5 women, 2 men.

A highly popular modern comedy, the scene of which is a social settlement in a great city. It concerns the loyalty of seven children to the beloved head resident of Neighborhood House, and their rebellion against the woman who tries to close the settlement. The characters are delightfully real and interesting and the humor fresh and sparkling.

THE SHUTTING O' THE DOOR. By Wallace G. Dickson. In *Short Plays for Young People* by Webber and Webster. Houghton, Mifflin. Permission from author. 1 scene (int.). 4 men, 1 woman.

Suspense—who will speak first? A play based on the old ballad about the stubborn man and his wife. 8th grade assembly.

SIEGFRIED. By Constance Mackay. In *The Silver Thread*. Holt. 1 ext. a forest. 5 characters.

Because he is fearless and has a pure heart, Siegfried kills the dragon and sets out to conquer the world. For 6th grade.

THE SILVER THREAD. By Constance Mackay. Holt. Also in *A Treasury of Plays*. Little, Brown. 3 acts, 5 scenes (4 int.). Indefinite number of characters. Place: A kingdom west of the moon and east of the sun, yet not too far from the rockbound hills of Cornwall.

A folk play concerning the goblins who stole the Princess, and the Silver Thread that led the two children to safety. One of the best full-length plays for children to act. In both

literary and dramatic quality it is superior. Children in 6th
and 7th grade like to act it, but audiences of all ages enjoy it.

SIR DAVID WEARS A CROWN. By Stuart Walker. In *Portmanteau
Adaptations*. Appleton-Century. Permission from author, 824
N. Whittier Dr., Beverly Hills, Calif. 1 act (int.). 1 boy, 2
men, 4 women.

After David hides the queen and saves her life he becomes
Sir David Little Boy. In this sequel he is adopted by the King
and Queen and becomes heir to the throne. For 5th and 6th
grades.

SIR RICHARD SERVES HIS QUEEN. By Ida May Owen. In *The Jester's Purse*. Harcourt, Brace. 4 scenes (ext.). Indefinite number of characters.

The story of the loyalty of the favorite page of Queen
Eleanor of England to his Queen and to Robin Hood. The
chief episode concerns the shooting match at Nottingham. A
May Day festival offers wide opportunity for the inclusion of
special groups. 8th grade or camp.

SIX WHO PASS WHILE THE LENTILS BOIL. By Stuart Walker. In
Portmanteau Plays. Appleton-Century. Also in *A Treasury of
Plays*. Little, Brown. Permission from author, 824 N. Whit-
tier Dr., Beverly Hills, Calif. 1 act. 7 boys, 2 girls.

The Little Boy detains the six who pass while the lentils
boil and thus saves his Queen from the Headsman, for which
he is made Sir David Little Boy and has all of his wishes
granted. An unusual play for 5th or 6th grade. Fantastic and
beautiful.

THE SLEEPING BEAUTY. By Charlotte Chorpenning. Ms., 1504 Oak
Ave., Evanston, Ill. 5 acts (2 int., 1 ext.). Indefinite number
of characters.

Beauty's little page, because he is afraid of the fifth fairy,
does not give her the King's invitation to the christening. Because of Beauty's bravery and goodness, the first fairy is able
to change the fifth fairy's spell of death to sleep. And the
fairies grant the little page who loves the princess the power
to live the hundred years in order to direct the Prince through
the thorn-hedge to waken Beauty. For children's theatre.

SLEEPING BEAUTY. By Rose Fyleman. In *Nine New Plays for Children*. Nelson. Three parts (ints.). Indefinite number of characters.

The story of Sleeping Beauty is told by a narrator, and is partly pantomimed and partly spoken by characters. A chorus assists the narrator in commenting on the action. For use in a summer camp or school.

THE SLIPPERS OF CINDERELLA. By W. Graham Robertson. In *Another Treasury of Plays for Children*. Little, Brown. 1 boy, 6 girls, 2 women.

This delightful play, called "an impossibility in one act," tells of a fairy godmother who comes to a modern family, bringing each his heart's desire. So fantastic do her gifts prove to be that the children thank their lucky stars when they think of turning the clock ahead to twelve and causing the gifts to disappear! The play is very sophisticated and can best be done by young adults, though 8th graders have done it successfully.

SNICKERTY NICK. By Julia Ford. In *Ring Up the Curtain*. Little, Brown. 2 short acts (1 ext.). 12 characters with one boy or man much larger to play the Giant.

The author says that the play was suggested by the Oscar Wilde story of the Selfish Giant. The impish Snickerty Nick is, however, her own creation, though the plot is the story of the Giant whose garden will not bloom until the Little Boy plays in it. For a school play or children's theatre.

SNOW WHITE AND THE SEVEN DWARFS. By Edith Stebbins, 6537 Chabet Road, Oakland, Calif. 3 acts (3 ints., 1 ext.). 10 boys, 5 girls.

A delightful play of this beloved fairy-tale with much action and humor, and having a wide appeal to children of all ages. For a children's theatre.

SNOW WHITE AND THE SEVEN DWARFS. By Jessie Braham White. French. Indefinite number of characters. 6 scenes (3 ints., 1 ext.).

One of the most delightful of all plays for a children's theatre, combining the loveliness of the old fairy-tale with rare humor and imagination. The lines of the comical little dwarfs and the character of the sharp-tongued Witch Hex give the play distinction. Can be staged very simply if necessary, though it has fine possibilities for picturesque setting.

THE SNOW WITCH. By Constance Mackay. In *The Silver Thread*. Holt. 1 scene (int.). 6 characters.

An old woman, dissatisfied with her life, is given the power by the Snow Witch to change places with any one in the village; but after seeing the sorrow connected with the lives of the rich and the powerful, she decides that her happiness lies within her own life. For the 5th or 6th grade.

SOJOURNERS. By Harnwell and Meaker. In *Plays of Our American Holidays*. Dodd, Mead. 5 boys, 2 girls.

In Holland in 1620, we see the unrest of the English settlers, climaxing in their departure for America. Excellent for 8th or 9th grade.

SOME WITCH. By Lucy Barton. In *Plays for Autumn and Winter Holidays*, ed. by Sanford. Dodd, Mead. 1 int. 10 girls and a Negro waiter.

Hallowe'en play in which one of the girls disguised as a witch tells fortunes which come true during the party. Inconsequential but satisfactory for a Hallowe'en assembly in 8th grade.

SOUNDING BRASS. By Dorothy E. Nichols. Longmans, Green. 1 act (int.). 1 boy, 11 men, 7 women, extras.

Lord Baltasar, the rich man, and Anselm the priest, are jealous brothers who do many deeds for their fellow citizens prompted by a hatred between them. At last they learn that the true spirit of doing for others must be guided by charity and love. A good Christmas assembly play for 8th grade children.

SOUTHUMBERLAND'S YULETIDE. By C. A. Dean. French. 1 scene (int.). 20 men, 20 women, extras. This delightful festival is written in the spirit of the traditional Yule celebrations of olden days. An excellent Christmas play for a community, or an all-school play where a large cast is available.

THE STAFF AND THE FIDDLE. By Sophie L. Goldsmith. In *Wonder-Clock Plays*. Harpers. 3 acts, 8 scenes. 8 men, 4 women.

The little slaves of the fiddle and a magic staff were the rewards for the Fiddler's kindness. It was with the help of these that he was successful in winning the hand of the Princess. Much humor and excitement; however, there are many scene changes. For 5th or 6th grade.

THE STEADFAST PRINCESS. By Cornelia Meigs. Macmillan. No royalty. 2 acts. 11 boys, 3 girls, extras.

Ursula, who has been adopted by the Toymaster, learns that she is a princess and must rule a kingdom. She bravely keeps her promise, "To be a true queen, steadfast to the end." An excellent play for 6th or 7th grade.

THE STEADFAST TIN SOLDIER. By Dorothy Holloway. French. 3 acts (1 int., 1 ext.). Indefinite number of characters.

Peter's toys come to life and both the one-armed tin-soldier and the jack-in-the-box are in love with the crêpe-paper lady. Peter planned to give his toys away, but when he discovers that they can sing and dance and talk, he decides to keep them forever. Children's theatre.

THE STILL ALARM. By George S. Kaufman. In *One Act Plays for Stage and Study*. French. 1 act (int.). 5 men.

The hotel is on fire! The calm unconcern of the young men in one of the rooms provides sophisticated comedy which is very funny. For older boys' clubs or camps.

STOLEN FRUIT. By Paul Moffett. Dramatic Publishing Co. 1 act (int.). 4 men, 4 women.

Garrett Foster who has stolen corn from the fields of the early settlers finds that the Captain's men are after him. He jumps through the open window into the kitchen of Miles Standish and is hidden by Rose who is frightened for fear of his discovery. Suspense is heightened but rises to a happy ending. A good Thanksgiving play. For Junior High School or older.

THE STOLEN PRINCE. By Dan Totheroh. In *Short Plays for Young People*. Webber and Webster. Houghton, Mifflin. 1 act (simple Chinese int.). 8 men, 3 women, extras. A delightful play done in the Chinese manner.

Mistaken for his sister, the prince, when a baby, was put in a tub and sent down the river. Nine years later he is discovered by his exiled nurse. For children from 11 to 13.

THE STRANGER PRINCESS. By James Gardner Hellman and Lorna Williamson Talbot. French, 3 acts (2 int.). Many characters.

A charming version of Cinderella in which the transformation is achieved in an unusual manner. For children's theatre.

THE SUN GODDESS. By Constance Mackay. In *Pageant of Hours*. French. 3 acts, simple Oriental setting. 5 men, 11 women, extras.

The mirror which reflects the beauty of some little Japanese maidens so that they forget the approach of the Sun Goddess and fail to worship her, is used by the poet O Ku Re to entice the Goddess from her retreat, and induce her to restore sunlight to the earth. A beautiful pageant. For 6th or 7th grade.

SURPRISE. By Rose Fyleman. In *Nine New Plays for Children*. Nelson. 1 scene (ext.). 1 boy, 2 girls. In a garden at a masquerade party, Philip and Jennifer are surprised when they meet a fairy. For 3rd and 4th grades.

TEN MINUTES BY THE CLOCK. By Alice C. D. Riley. Doubleday Doran. 1 act (palace interior). 6 men, 2 women.

The Queen is tired of being a queen and rebels against convention. Insists on having her egg boiled ten minutes instead of the usual three. A good satire on useless convention. Dux and Dox, two little servants, are much liked by children. Suitable for Junior High School cast of 13, 14.

THE TESTING OF SIR GAWAYNE. By Marguerite Merington. In *A Treasury of Plays*. Little, Brown. 1 act (int.). 11 men, 3 women.

The story of how Sir Gawayne gives to his bride the thing that all women most desire—their own will. For a 7th and 8th grade assembly program.

THEORIES AND THUMBS. By Rachel Field. French. A museum fantasy. 1 act (a corner of a museum). An interesting little play about the sympathy of a scrubwoman for the mummy of a little Egyptian princess. For girls from 11 to 13.

THE THREE CITRONS. By Louise Housman and Edward T. Koeh-

ler. In *Footlights Up!* Harpers. No royalty. 4 short acts (2
int. and 2 ext.). 9 boys, 9 girls.

A delightful play from a fairy-tale of old Spain in which
the Prince is searching for his Princess. Amusing and entertaining for older children. To be played by 5th and 6th
grades.

THREE PILLS IN A BOTTLE. By Rachel Field. In *Six Plays*. Scribners. 1 act (cottage int.). 8 characters, several of whom can
be played by either boys or girls.

A little invalid boy plays with the souls of the people who
pass. A charming fantasy which may be played by children
from 11 to 14 but which is more effective done by young
adults.

THE THREE SPINNERS. By Florence Kiper Frank. In *Three Plays
for a Children's Theatre*. Vinal. 3 acts (2 int., 1 ext.). Indefinite number of characters.

A delightful version of the Rumpelstiltskin story in which
three queer old women spin straw into gold for the young
girl. The two funny little pages are very popular with children. Can be done by 6th grade. Younger children enjoy seeing it in the children's theatre.

THE THREE WISHES. By Constance Mackay. In *The Silver Thread*.
Holt. One simple cottage int. 3 characters.

A well-written dramatization of a poor couple who after
foolishly wasting their three wishes on a pudding, suddenly
realize that it is better to have enough of anything than too
much. For 5th and 6th grade.

TOAD OF TOAD HALL. By A. A. Milne. Based on the story "The
Wind in the Willows," by Kenneth Grahame. Scribner's. For
permission apply to Curtis Brown, Ltd., 18 East 48th St.,
New York. 4 acts, prologue and epilogue, 9 scenes (6 ext.,
3 int.). Fantastic settings. 2 girls, 3 women, 17 boys, and animal characters. A clever fantasy with charming and delightful
satire, making its appeal more directly to adults. For a children's theatre.

TOM SAWYER. By Sara Spencer. Children's Theatre Press. 12
scenes (3 ext., 5 int.). 18 men and boys, 9 women and girls.

A dramatization of the Mark Twain story in many short scenes. Children's theatre.

TOM SAWYER'S TREASURE HUNT. By Charlotte Chorpenning. French. 5 scenes (1 int., 4 ext.). Many characters.

An excellent dramatization of the Mark Twain novel, including the delightful white-washing, graveyard, island, funeral, and cave scenes. An unusually popular play for a children's theatre or Junior High School. Suggestions for production are included.

THE TOYMAKER OF NUREMBURG. By Austin Strong. French. Also in *A Treasury of Plays*. Little, Brown. 3 acts (2 sets). Indefinite number of characters.

A charming story of an old toymaker. With not too much stress of the romantic element, it is good for a children's theatre. Should have an adult cast.

THE TOYMAKER'S DOLL. By Marion Holbrook. Dramatic Publishing Co. No royalty. 1 act (a toyshop). Indefinite number of characters.

The toymaker has lost sight of the meaning of Christmas in his successful career. When his grandchild is changed into a doll, he sees many things in their true values. For 6th grade.

THE TRAVELING MAN. By Lady Gregory. In *A Treasury of Plays for Children*. Little, Brown. 1 act, 1 scene. Characters: a mother, a child, and a traveling man.

The traveling man comes to the house of the child and the mother. When he leaves, they discover by the fruit and flowers on the branch that he is the King of the World. An appealing play for Junior High School assemblies.

TREASURE ISLAND. By Jules Eckert Goodman. From the novel by Robert Louis Stevenson. In *Another Treasury of Plays for Children*. Little, Brown. For permission apply to Chas. Hopkins, Inc., 155 West 49th St., New York. 4 acts, 10 scenes (2 ints., 6 exts.). 23 men, 1 woman.

A very popular children's theatre play. Elaborate and difficult but highly dramatic and interesting. Should be played by an adult cast, though Jim Hawkins should be a youth.

THE TREASURE OF CARDONA. By Louise Housman and Edward T. Koehler. In *Footlights Up!* Harpers. No royalty. 3 short acts (3 ext.). 8 men.

Don Pedro solves the cipher in the old manuscript and so finds the treasure buried in the ancient tomb. A suitable assembly play for Junior High School. Staging and costume suggestions given.

TROLL MAGIC. By Constance Mackay. In *The Silver Thread*. One scene, a field bounded on one side by the deep troll forest. Indefinite number of characters.

A young girl is changed into an old woman by the evil trolls, but the fearlessness and the selflessness of her older sister breaks the spell. For the 5th and 6th grade.

TWO BIRTHDAYS. By Rupert Sargent Holland. *In Plays of the American Colonies*. Harpers. No royalty. 1 scene (int.). 7 men, 3 girls.

A new and worthwhile dramatization of the birth of our country and the writing of the Declaration of Independence. A good play for a summer camp to be given on the Fourth of July.

TWO SLATTERNS AND A KING. By Edna St. Vincent Millay. Appleton-Century. Also in *25 Short Plays (International)*. Appleton-Century. Also in *Three Plays by Millay*. Harpers. Permission from Baker, Boston. 1 act with prologue and epilogue. 2 men, 2 women.

A very clever little interlude in which the King chooses his wife by chance. Delightful play for girls' clubs and camps.

THE UGLY DUCKLING. By Alice C. D. Riley. In *Let's Pretend*. Baker. 30 minutes. A clever and unusual version of the Andersen tale which would not be easy to do, but which would be effective and humorous if well done. All characters are animals or fowls. Reminds one of *Chantecler*. Children of 6th or 7th grade.

UNCLE TOM'S CABIN. Ms. Children's Theatre of Evanston. No royalty. 4 acts. 7 men, 4 women, 2 children, extras.

A version of Harriet Beecher Stowe's famous story made for children's theatre production. Based on the novel and several old versions of the play. Opens with the singing of spirituals in Uncle Tom's cabin by the slaves on St. Clair's plantation. The play is especially liked by older children. Should be played by grown-ups in adult parts.

UNDERSTOOD BETSY. By Sarah H. Cleghorn. From the book of the same name by Dorothy Canfield Fisher. Harcourt, Brace. 6 acts (4 ints., 2 exts.). Indefinite number of characters, including children and adults.

Betsy is happier when she is allowed to live as other children do, and finds a happy home with her country cousins. Her many experiences are delightful and humorous. For a rural school or a small community, this play provides an excellent opportunity for a large cast. There are no production difficulties.

THE VALENTINE BOX. By Mirjane Strong. In *Plays for Autumn and Winter Holidays,* ed. by Sanford. Dodd, Mead. Scene: Inside of a Valentine Box. Indefinite number of characters who represent Valentines.

They come sliding into the box through a chute. The plain Valentine persuades the most beautiful one to exchange envelopes so that an unattractive girl will get the prettiest one. Rather charming, especially for a Valentine party.

THE VIOLIN-MAKER OF CREMONA. By François Coppée. In *The Atlantic Book of Junior Plays.* Atlantic Monthly Press. 1 scene (int.). 3 men, 1 girl, extras.

In the late 18th century a great music-master offered his daughter to the one who should make the finest violin. A little hunchback won her hand in marriage but nobly gave her to the man she wished to marry. Good for 8th grade.

WASHINGTON VISITS HIS SOLDIERS. By Gertrude Smith Buckland. In *Let's Give a Play.* Crowell. No royalty without admission. 1 scene (ext.). 5 men, extras.

The kindness of General Washington to his soldiers at Valley Forge is clearly shown. A good assembly play for Washington's Birthday. For 7th or 8th grades.

THE WEATHER CLERK. By Rose Fyleman. In *Eight Little Plays for Children.* Doubleday Doran. 1 scene (int.). 4 boys, 1 girl.

The Weather Clerk arrives at his office just in time to save the wicked Magician from stealing his "thunder." A short play, one of the best for the younger children. 5th or 6th grade.

WEST O' THE ALLEGHENIES. By Olive Price. In *Short Plays from American History Literature*. Vol. 2. French. No royalty. 1 act, Time, 1775. 1 boy, 1 girl, 7 men, 2 women.

The fugitive horse-thief leaves gifts for Daniel Boone and his family in the first pioneer Christmas on Wilderness Road. A good Christmas assembly play for 6th or 7th grades.

WHAT CHEER? By Rupert Sargent Holland. In *Plays of the American Colonies*. Harpers. No royalty. 1 scene (ext.). 6 men, 2 women.

Roger Williams and his colonists are greatly cheered when they find that they can settle in the new country of Rhode Island and be friendly with the Indians. A good assembly play for 7th and 8th grades.

WHAT EASTER MEANS. By Gertrude Smith Buckland. In *Let's Give A Play*. Crowell. No royalty without admission. 2 scenes (int., ext.). 3 boys, 1 girl, 2 women, 1 man.

An early Easter in Holland at the home of a poor family brings us the origin of the Easter Rabbit. An Easter play for the 5th and 6th grades.

WHAT MEN LIVE BY. By Virginia Church. From the story by Tolstoi. In *The Atlantic Book of Junior Plays*. Atlantic Monthly Press. 2 scenes (int.). 1 boy, 5 men, 4 women, 2 girls.

The angel sent by God comes to the home of the humble Russian shoemaker and learns of the three things by which men live. A beautiful play for the 8th or 9th grade.

WHEN LINCOLN WAS A BOY. By Gertrude Smith Buckland. In *Let's Give A Play*. Crowell. No royalty without admission. 4 scenes, prologue, epilogue (int.). 5 boys, 3 girls, 3 men, 1 woman.

Old logs from the cabin of Abraham Lincoln seen in a museum recall to one of the boys the outstanding incidents in Lincoln's life as were told him by his grandfather. These episodes are shown in four short scenes which are more interesting than many Lincoln plays. A good play for a Lincoln's Birthday program. 7th or 8th grade.

WHEN PAUL REVERE RODE. By Marion Holbrook. In *Plays of Story and Legend,* ed. by Sanford. Dodd, Mead. 1 scene (int.). 1 boy, 2 girls, 3 men, 1 woman.

In April, 1775, we see the loyalty and kindness of Paul Revere. He is at home with his family when he volunteers to make the dangerous ride to save his country. A short play. 7th grade assembly.

THE WHISKER. By Rose Fyleman. In *Nine New Plays for Children.* Nelson. 1 scene (ext.). 3 boys, 1 girl.

A freshly pulled whisker from the bunny's face assists the little goblin in breaking the spell and thus saving the Little Princess from the wicked magician. A short, fantastic bit of fun for little children. For 3rd or 4th grade.

THE WHITE CHRISTMAS. By Walter Ben Hare. In *The White Christmas and Other Merry Christmas Plays.* Denison. 1 act, 3 scenes, 8 men, 7 women, a concealed choir and extra children. About 1 hour.

A beautiful Christmas play with Mary and Joseph, the Shepherds, and the Wise Men. The songs and carols add to the spirit of the Nativity. A good Christmas play for Junior High School or a Sunday School group.

WHY THE CHIMES RANG. By Elizabeth McFadden. From the story by Raymond MacDonald Alden. French. 1 scene (int.). 3 boys, 1 woman, extras.

A beautiful, mediæval Christmas play in which the great chimes in the Church sound again because of the unselfish love shown by a little boy on the eve of Christmas. An excellent Christmas play for a Junior High School or a Church group.

WILL OF STRATFORD. By Louise Ayres Garnett. Baker. Prologue, epilogue, and 3 acts, 2 sets (one int., one ext.). Indefinite number of characters.

A story of Shakespeare at the age of 12, of his dreams and his ambitions. On New Year's Eve he dreams that he will find his fate on his own hearth. When he wakens, he finds on his hearth, a pheasant quill, "the pen with which to write the stories in men's eyes." Good for children's theatre.

THE WILLOW TREE. By Alice C. D. Riley. In *Let's Pretend*. Baker. 1 scene. 6 characters. A play done in the Chinese manner, similar to *The Stolen Prince*. Not as effective, however, but is suitable for a simple dramatization. For 5th or 6th grade. Suitable for a girls' camp program.

THE YEAR THAT WOULDN'T BE NEW. By Grace Dorcas Ruthenburg. In *Plays for Autumn and Winter Holidays,* ed. by Sanford. Dodd, Mead. 1 scene (The Hall of Day and Night). Indefinite number of characters.

A play for 5th grade or above which reminds one of the Kingdom of the Future in *The Blue Bird*. Father Time sends a box containing Hope with the little new year. The play has charm. For the New Year season.

YESI'S GIFT. By Jewell Bothwell Tull. In *Plays for the Changing World*. Abingdon Press. No royalty. 1 act (carpenter's workshop). 1 man, 1 woman, 4 little boys. An appealing little play with the boy Jesus as the leading character.

Yesi (Hebrew for Jesus) wishes to give the Magi's golden bowl to ransom a little black boy and his father. Forbidden by Joseph, he gives, instead, a little wooden cross he has made. Excellent for church schools.

YOUTH'S HIGHWAY. By Constance Mackay. In book by same name. Holt. 1 act (int.). 3 men, 5 boys.

A beautiful story of Michael Angelo's early boyhood and how he became a protégé of the Great Lorenzo. For 8th or 9th grade. It can be simply or elaborately staged and costumed.

For more inclusive play lists, consult the American Library Association or Junior Leagues, Inc.

PLAYS CLASSIFIED

CHILDREN'S THEATRE

Aladdin
Ali Baba and the Forty Thieves
Alice in Wonderland
The Black Knight
The Blue Bird
The Bubble Peddler
The Christmas Nightingale
Cinderella
Cinderella of Loreland
Darby and Joan
Dolls
The Emperor's New Clothes
Gammer Gurton's Needle
The Ghost of Mr. Penny
Hans Brinker and the Silver Skates
Heidi
Helga and the White Peacock
Huckleberry Finn
The Indian Captive
Jack and the Beanstalk
The Japanese Twins
Jeanne d'Arc
Kai Khosru
Katrinka
Little Black Sambo and the Tigers
Little Lord Fauntleroy
The Little Princess
Little Women
Maid of the Nile
Make-Believe
Mary Poppins
Master Skylark
Mr. Dooley, Jr.

The Merchant Gentleman
Mrs. Wiggs of the Cabbage Patch
Nevertheless
Once in a Hundred Years
Peter, Peter, Pumpkin Easter
Pinocchio
The Poor Little Rich Girl
The Prince and the Pauper
Racketty-Packetty House
Radio Rescue
Raggedy Ann and Andy
Rebecca of Sunnybrook Farm
The Return of Rip Van Winkle
Rip Van Winkle
Robin Hood
The Rose and the Ring
Rumpelstiltskin
The Scotch Twins
The Secret Garden
Seven Little Rebels
The Silver Thread
The Sleeping Beauty
The Sleeping Beauty in the Wood
Snickerty Nick
Snow White and the Seven Dwarfs
The Steadfast Tin Soldier
The Three Spinners
Toad of Toad Hall
Tom Sawyer's Treasure Hunt
The Toymaker of Nuremberg
Treasure Island
Uncle Tom's Cabin
Will of Stratford

SEVENTH- AND EIGHTH-GRADE ASSEMBLY

Around the Blue Wigwam
At the Spanish Court
The Babe at the Inn
Babouska Sees It Through
The Bellman of Mons
The Birdcage-Maker
The Birth of Old Glory
The Birthday of the Infanta
A Bit o' Shamrock
A Brewing of Brains
By Candlelight
Daniel Boone Blazed a Trail
The Evil Kettle
The Fifteenth Candle
The Horned Beasts
Jeanne and the Peddler
The Jester's Purse
The Knave of Hearts
The Lantern
Lantern Light
Little Lady Dresden
The Lost Colony
The Mistake at the Manor
Mr. Bragg's Head
Once in a Hundred Years

The Orange Plume
Peter Silverleg
The Play of Saint George
Pocahontas and John Smith
A Pot of Broth
The Puppet of Papa 'Tero
A Rose for Captain Bacon
The Shutting o' the Door
Sir Richard Serves His Queen
The Slippers of Cinderella
Stolen Fruit
The Testing of Sir Gawayne
Three Pills in a Bottle
The Traveling Man
The Treasure of Cardona
Ten Minutes by the Clock
The Violin-Maker of Cremona
Washington Visits His Soldiers
When Lincoln Was a Boy
When Paul Revere Rode
West o' the Alleghenies
What Cheer?
What Men Live By
Youth's Highway

FIFTH AND SIXTH GRADES

Alias Santa Claus
Alice in Wonderland
The Blue Prince
The Bubble Peddler
Cap o' Rushes
The Christmas Guest
The Cradle
Darby and Joan
Dick Whittington
The Dyspeptic Ogre
The Enchanted Christmas Tree
Five Ghosts
The Foam Maiden
The Forest Princess
The Forest Spring
Gabriel and the Hour Book

The Golden Touch
The Good Old Days
Gutenberg and the Apprentice
Helga and the White Peacock
Hilltop
The Hole in the Wall
The House of the Heart
How Boots Befooled the King
How the Princess's Pride Was
  Broken
In the Path of the Children
The King With the Iron Heart
Kings in Nomania
The Knights of the Silver Shield
Little Square-Toes
The Lost Princess

The Patchwork People
The Play's the Thing
Polly Patchwork
Prince Fairy Foot
The Proud Princess
The Pudding Pan
The Sentimental Scarecrow
Siegfried
The Silver Thread
Sir David Wears a Crown
Six Who Pass While the Lentils Boil
Sleeping Beauty
The Snow Witch
The Staff and the Fiddle

The Steadfast Princess
The Stolen Prince
Theories and Thumbs
The Three Citrons
The Three Spinners
The Three Wishes
The Toymaker's Doll
Troll Magic
The Ugly Duckling
The Valentine Box
The Weather Clerk
What Easter Means
The Willow Tree

THIRD AND FOURTH GRADES

Cabbages and Kings
The Enchanted Garden
The Fairy and the Doll
The Fairy Riddle
Father Christmas
Goldtree and Silvertree
The Gooseherd and the Goblin

Miss Ant, Miss Grasshopper, and Mr.
   Cricket
On Christmas Eve
The Pirate of Pooh
Surprise
The Test
The Whisker

SCHOOL PLAYS FOR PUBLIC PERFORMANCES

Cap o' Rushes
The Christmas Nightingale
Cinderella of Loreland
The First Noël
Good King Wenceslaus
Hilltop
Kai Khosru
Kinfolk of Robin Hood
The Knights of the Silver Shield

Lost Children
Maid of the Nile
Snickerty Nick
Snow White and the Seven Dwarfs
Southumberland's Yuletide
The Three Spinners
Understood Betsy
The White Christmas
Why the Chimes Rang

SPECIAL DAYS

At the Spanish Court
The Birth of Old Glory
A Bit o' Shamrock
The Boy Who Discovered Easter
Five Ghosts
George Washington's Fortune

Gutenberg and the Apprentice
The Man With One Idea
Red Shoes at Plymouth
Sojourners
Some Witch
Stolen Fruit

SPECIAL DAYS (cont'd)

Two Birthdays
The Valentine Box
Washington Visits His Soldiers

What Easter Means
When Lincoln Was a Boy
The Year That Wouldn't Be New

CHRISTMAS PLAYS

Alias Santa Claus
The Birds' Christmas Carol
The Black Knight
The Christmas Guest
The Christmas Nightingale
The Cradle
Dolls
Father Christmas
The First Noël
Good King Wenceslaus
Jean Valjean and the Christmas
    Doll

Kings in Nomania
Lost Children
A Masque of Christmas
The Nativity
On Christmas Eve
Seven Gifts
Sounding Brass
Southumberland's Yuletide
The Toymaker's Doll
West o' the Alleghenies
The White Christmas
Why the Chimes Rang

CHURCH SCHOOL

The Babe at the Inn
Babouska Sees It Through
The Bellman of Mons
The Boy Who Discovered Easter
The Christmas Guest
The Christmas Nightingale
The Cradle
The Enchanted Garden
The Fifteenth Candle
The First Noël
Gabriel and the Hour Book
Good King Wenceslaus
The Gooseherd and the Goblin
Hilltop
The House of the Heart
In the Path of the Children
Jeanne and the Peddler
Jean Valjean and the Christmas Doll
The King with the Iron Heart
The Knights of the Silver Shield
Lantern Light
The Little Yashmak

A Masque of Christmas
The Nativity
On the Tower of the Shadows
Red Shoes at Plymouth
Seven Gifts
Siegfried
The Silver Thread
Sojourners
Sounding Brass
Southumberland's Yuletide
The Steadfast Princess
Theories and Thumbs
Three Pills in a Bottle
The Traveling Man
What Easter Means
What Men Live By
When Lincoln Was a Boy
The White Christmas
Why the Chimes Rang
The Year That Wouldn't Be New
Yesi's Gift
Youth's Highway

Girls' Camps and Clubs

Ali Baba and the Forty Thieves
The Arrow-Maker's Daughter
Around the Blue Wigwam
The Bubble Peddler
The Enchanted Garden
The Foam Maiden
The Forest Princess
The Forest Spring
The Golden Touch
The Hole in the Wall
In Arcady
The Jester's Purse
Kings in Nomania
The Knave of Hearts

Little Square-Toes
The Little Yashmak
The Sentimental Scarecrow
Sir Richard Serves His Queen
The Sampler
Sleeping Beauty
The Slippers of Cinderella
The Sun Goddess
Surprise
Ten Minutes by the Clock
Theories and Thumbs
Three Pills in a Bottle
Two Slatterns and a King
The Willow Tree

Boys' Camps and Clubs

The Crowsnest
Daniel Boone Blazed a Trail
Dick Whittington
The Dyspeptic Ogre
George Washington's Fortune
Gutenberg and the Apprentice
The Knights of the Silver Shield
The Man With One Idea

On the Tower of the Shadows
Once in a Hundred Years
Pocahontas and John Smith
The Ransom of Red Chief
The Still Alarm
Two Birthdays
What Cheer?
Youth's Highway

NON-ROYALTY PLAYS

Indicates no royalty if no admission.

Around the Blue Wigwam, Price
Arrow-Maker's Daughter, Smith and Knevels
*Babouska Sees It Through, Buckland
Birdcage-Maker, Housman and Koehler
*Birth of Old Glory, Buckland
*Bit o' Shamrock, Buckland
Blue Prince, Riley
By Candlelight, Holland
Cap o' Rushes, Housman and Koehler
Cradle, Vinton
Dick Whittington, Housman and Koehler
George Washington's Fortune, Mackay
Gutenberg and the Apprentice, Fielden
Helga and the White Peacock, Meigs
Hilltop, Garnett
Horned Beasts, Holland
In Arcady, Fyleman
Jeanne and the Peddler, Fielden
Jean Valjean and the Christmas Doll, Smith
Lantern Light, Price

Little Lady Dresden, Price
Lost Colony, Holland
*Man With One Idea, Buckland
The Merchant Gentleman, Molière
Mr. Bragg's Head, Holland
Orange Plume, Holland
Peter Silverleg, Holland
Play of Saint George, Crum
Play's the Thing, Riley
Red Shoes at Plymouth, Olson
Rose for Captain Bacon, Holland
Steadfast Princess, Meigs
Three Citrons, Housman and Koehler
Toymaker's Doll, Holbrook
Treasure of Cardona, Housman and Koehler
Two Birthdays, Holland
Uncle Tom's Cabin, Stowe
*Washington Visits His Soldiers, Buckland
West o' the Alleghenies, Price
What Cheer?, Holland
*What Easter Means, Buckland
*When Lincoln Was a Boy, Buckland
White Christmas, Hare
Yesi's Gift, Tull

322

COLLECTIONS OF PLAYS

A TREASURY OF PLAYS FOR CHILDREN. Edited by Montrose Moses. Little, Brown. Contains: *The Little Princess; The Silver Thread; The Testing of Sir Gawayne; Pinkie and the Fairies; Punch and Judy; The Three Wishes; The Toymaker of Nuremberg; Six Who Pass While the Lentils Boil; Master Skylark; Alice in Wonderland; The Traveling Man; The Months—A Pageant; The Forest Ring; The Seven Old Ladies of Lavender Town.*

ANOTHER TREASURY OF PLAYS FOR CHILDREN. Edited by Montrose Moses. Little, Brown. Contains: *Treasure Island; The Slippers of Cinderella; Don Quixote; The Racketty-Packetty House; The Evil Kettle; The Dame School Holiday; Abraham Lincoln; The Birthday of the Infanta; The Mikado; Snow White and the Seven Dwarfs; Make-Believe; The King with the Iron Heart.*

BEHIND THE MAGIC CURTAIN.—Folk Scenes—National Theatre Conference, Theatre Arts, Inc. Contains: *Adventures of Olle; Kolyada; The Mummer's Revel; The Masque of the Apple; Mascaiada; Fleur et Blanchefleur; Fêtes in Paris; Harnsaki.*

EIGHT LITTLE PLAYS FOR CHILDREN. By Rose Fyleman. Doubleday Doran. Contains: *Darby and Joan; The Fairy Riddle; Noughts and Crosses; The Weather Clerk; The Fairy and the Doll; Cabbages and Kings; In Arcady; Father Christmas.*

FOOTLIGHTS UP! Edited by Housman and Koehler. Harpers. Contains: *Cap o' Rushes; The Treasure of Cardona; Dick Whittington; The Birdcage-Maker; The Man Without a Country; The Three Citrons;* Directions for Staging; Costumes; Bibliography.

FOREST PRINCESS AND OTHER MASQUES. By Constance Mackay. Holt. Contains: *Forest Princess; Gift of Time; Masque of Conservation; Masque of Christmas; The Sun Goddess.*

House of the Heart and Other Plays. By Constance Mackay. Holt. Contains: *House of the Heart; The Gooseherd and the Goblin; The Enchanted Garden; Nimble-Wit and Fingerkin; A Little Pilgrim's Progress; A Pageant of Hours; On Christmas Eve; The Elf Child; The Princess and the Pixies; The Christmas Guest.*

Jester's Purse. By Nydia E. Minchin. Harcourt, Brace. Contains: *Jester's Purse; On the Tower of the Shadows; Sir Richard Serves His Queen; Coming of Summer; The Birthday Cake.*

Kai Khosru and Other Plays for Children. By Dorothy Coit. Theatre Arts, Inc. Contains: *Kai Khosru; Theseus; Aucassin and Nicolette; Nala and Damayanti; The Tempest.*

Let's Give A Play. By Gertrude S. Buckland. Crowell. Contains: *When Lincoln Was A Boy; Washington Visits His Soldiers; A Bit o'Shamrock; What Easter Means; The Right Kind of Remembering; The Birth of Old Glory; A Man With One Idea; Thanksgiving Up to Date; Babouska Sees It Through.*

Let's Pretend. By Alice C. D. Riley. Baker. Contains: *Bubble Peddler, a modern version of Little Red Riding Hood; Golden Touch; The Willow Tree; The Ugly Duckling.*

More Portmanteau Plays. By Stuart Walker. Appleton-Century. Contains: *Lady of the Weeping Willow Tree; The Very Naked Boy; Jonathan Makes a Wish.*

Nine New Plays for Children. By Rose Fyleman. Nelson. Contains: *The Whisker; The Moon; Cinderella "At Home"; The Sampler; Three Naughty Imps; Surprise; The Test; Sleeping Beauty; Father Christmas Comes to Supper.*

One-Act Plays for Everyone. By Dan Totheroh. French. Contains: *The Stolen Prince; The Lost Princess; Good Vintage; In the Darkness; The Breaking of the Calm; Pearls; The Great Dark; While the Mushrooms Bubble; The Widdy's Mite; A Tune of a Tune; Mirthful Marionettes.*

Patchwork Plays. By Rachel Field. Doubleday Doran. Contains: *Polly Patchwork; Little Square-Toes; Miss Ant, Miss Grasshopper, and Mr. Cricket; Chimney Sweeps' Holiday; The Sentimental Scarecrow.*

Playing Theatre. By Clare Tree Major. French. Contains: *Cinderella; *Aladdin and His Wonderful Lamp; The Prince's Secret; The Maid of the Nile; Michio; Robin Hood.*

PLAYS OF THE AMERICAN COLONIES. By Rupert Sargent Holland. Harpers. Contains: *A Rose for Captain Bacon; What Cheer?; Two Birthdays; An End to Witchcraft; The Lost Colony; Mr. Bragg's Head; The Orange Plume; The Horned Beasts; Peter Silverleg; By Candlelight.*

PLAYS FOR AUTUMN AND WINTER HOLIDAYS. Selected by A. P. Sanford. Dodd, Mead. Contains: *The Earth Is Flat; At the Spanish Court; Some Witch; Prince Fairy Foot; Far Voices; Odysseus and Circe; Mulligan, the Mouse, Tells All; Toy Symphony; Music Hath Power; Why We Give Thanks Today; The Well; The Three Bears' Merry Christmas; The Crookedy Christmas Tree; Christmas Eve; The Holy Hour; The Year That Wouldn't Be New; Even As You and I; The Valentine Box.*

PLAYS OF STORY AND LEGEND. Selected by A. P. Sanford. Dodd, Mead. Contains: *Gutenberg and the Apprentice; Jeanne and the Peddler; When Paul Revere Rode; Virginia Dare; Pocahontas and John Smith; The Minute Man; A Meeting On the Bounty; Daniel Boone Blazed a Trail; The Sword with the Golden Hilt; Roland; Rip Van Winkle.*

PORTMANTEAU ADAPTATIONS. By Stuart Walker. Appleton-Century. Contains: *Gammer Gurton's Needle; The Birthday of the Infanta; Sir David Wears a Crown; Nellijumbo.*

PORTMANTEAU PLAYS. By Stuart Walker. Appleton-Century. Contains: *The Trimplet; Nevertheless; The Medicine Show; Six Who Pass While the Lentils Boil.*

RING UP THE CURTAIN. Edited by Montrose J. Moses. Contains: *Ten Minutes by the Clock; The Land of Nod; Nimble-Wit and Fingerkin; The House Gnomes; Aladdin; Little Black Sambo; The Dragon; The Talking Chair; Jeanne D' Arc; Snickerty Nick; A Masque of May Morning; Princess Tenderheart.*

RITUAL AND DRAMATIZED FOLKWAYS. By Ethel Reed Jasspon and Beatrice Beeker. Appleton-Century. A collection of rituals and dramatized folkways for use in camp, club, religious assembly, settlement and school. Practical and of excellent quality. Part I. Ceremonies and Devotional Plays; Part II. Dramatized Folkways; Part III. Allegories.

SEVEN LITTLE PLAYS FOR CHILDREN. By Rose Fyleman. Methuen and Co., Ltd., 36 Essex St., Strand, London, WC2. Contains: *The Princess and the Pirate; Butcher, Baker, Candlestick-Maker; The Mermaid; Peter Coffin; The Arm Chair; Mother Goose's Party; Coming of Father Christmas.*

SEVEN TO SEVENTEEN. Edited by Alexander Dean. French. Contains: *Ring Leader; Star Dust; What's a Fixer For?; Th' 'Nitiated; The Palace of Knossos; The Reunion; The Moon for a Prince; The Forks of the Dilemma; A Woman of Judgment; Toast and Tea; At the Fountain; The Brand; Mrs. Magician's Mistake; Breakfast; The Thursday; Six; The Very Sad Unicorn; The Fatal Quest; The Rival Peach-Trees; The Next-Best Man; Moon Magic.*

SHORT PLAYS FOR JUNIOR AND SENIOR HIGH SCHOOLS. By Webber and Webster. Houghton, Mifflin. Contains: *The Prince of Stamboul; The Toy Shop; The Stolen Prince; The End of the Rainbow; The Princess on the Road; Goodnight, Babette; The Raggle-Taggle Gypsies; Pyramus and Thisbe; Miss Burney at Court; John Silver Off Duty; The Little Boy Out of the Wood; The Legend; Saint Dorothy; In the Good Green Wood; The Lion's Whelp; Benjamin Franklin, Journeyman; The Boston Tea Party; The Little King.*

SILVER THREAD AND OTHER FOLK PLAYS. By Constance Mackay. Holt. Contains: *Silver Thread; Forest Spring; Foam Maiden; Troll Magic; Three Wishes; Brewing of Brains; Siegfried; Snow Witch.*

TEN MINUTES BY THE CLOCK AND OTHER PLAYS. By Alice C. D. Riley. Doubleday Doran. Contains: *Ten Minutes by the Clock; The Blue Prince; Tom Piper and the Pig; The Poet's Well.*

THE APPLETON BOOK OF CHRISTMAS PLAYS. By Frank Shay. Appleton-Century. Contains: *Dust of the Road; The Littlest Shepherd; Christmas Eve; A Christmas Tale; A Modern Viking; The Boy on the Meadow; Exile; The Enchanted Christ-*

*mas Tree; The Duquesne Christmas Mystery; A Christmas
Carol; The Seven Gifts.*

THE ATLANTIC BOOK OF JUNIOR PLAYS. Edited by C. S. Thomas.
Atlantic Monthly Press. Contains: *What Men Live By; Kin-
folk of Robin Hood; Nerves; The Violin-Maker of Cremona;
The Dyspeptic Ogre; The Fifteenth Candle; The Bellman of
Mons; A Marriage Proposal; Jephthah's Daughter; A Minuet;
The Play of St. George; The Birthday of the Infanta; The
Christmas Guest.*

THE CHILDREN'S KING. By Elisabeth Edland. The Abingdon
Press. A collection of very short ethical plays based on the
idea of building friendship for other peoples. Also chapters
on dramatizing stories. Includes: *The Children's King; Cotton Roses; Red-Top; Falling Leaf; With the Watermelon
Seeds.* For a church school.

THE PLAY'S THE THING. By Alice C. D. Riley. Winston. Contains:
*The Pool of the Wilful Princess; The King's Great Toe; The
Patchwork People; The Prize Zinnias; The Hole in the Wall.*

THREE TO MAKE READY. By Louise Ayres Garnett. Doubleday
Doran. Contains: *Hilltop; The Pig Prince; Muffins.*

WONDER-CLOCK PLAYS. By Sophie Goldsmith. Harpers. Contains:
*Master Jacob; How the Princess's Pride Was Broken; The
Staff and the Fiddle; How Boots Befooled the King; How
One Turned His Trouble to Good Account.*

YOUTH'S HIGHWAY AND OTHER PLAYS FOR YOUNG PEOPLE. By
Constance Mackay. Holt. Contains: *Youth's Highway; In
the Days of Piers Ploughman; A Calendar of Joyful Saints;
The Pageant of Sunshine and Shadow; The First Noël;* Play-
shop Practicalities.

SELECTED BIBLIOGRAPHY

This very short reference list of books is recommended as a selection of books of most direct help for those who are preparing to produce children's plays.

ALBERTI, Mme. Eva—*A Handbook of Acting* (New York, Samuel French, 1932).

BAIRD, John—*Make-Up* (New York, Samuel French, 1931).

BARTON, Lucy—*Historic Costume for the Stage* (Boston, Walter H. Baker Company, 1935).

BOLESLAVSKY, Richard—*Acting: The First Six Lessons* (New York, Theatre Arts, Inc., 1933).

BROWN, Corinne—*Creative Drama in the Lower School* (New York, D. Appleton-Century Company, 1929).

BROWN, Gilmor and GARWOOD, Alice—*General Principles of Play Direction* (New York, Samuel French, 1936).

BURRIS-MEYER, Harold, and COLE, Edward C.—*Scenery for the Theatre* (Boston, Little, Brown and Company, 1938).

DEAN, Alexander—*Little Theatre Organization and Management* (New York, D. Appleton-Century Company, 1926).

GRIMBALL, Elizabeth, and WELLS, Rhea—*Costuming a Play* (New York, D. Appleton-Century Company, 1925).

HEFFNER, Hubert, SELDON, Samuel, and SELLMAN, Hunton D.— *Modern Theatre Practice* (New York, F. S. Crofts and Company, 1935).

HIETT, Harry L.—*Screen Process Production* (Cincinnati, Signs of the Times Publishing Company, 1936). (Supplies for silk screen posters may be had from Prairie State Products Co., Chicago.)

HUME, Samuel, and FOSTER, Lois—*Theatre and School* (New York, Samuel French, 1937, New Edition).

MACKAY, Constance—*Children's Theatres and Plays* (New York, D. Appleton-Century Company, 1927).

McCANDLESS, Stanley—*A Method of Lighting the Stage* (New York, Theatre Arts, Inc., 1932).

MERRILL, John, and FLEMING, Martha—*Playmaking and Plays* (New York, The Macmillan Company, 1930).

NORRIS, Herbert—*Costume and Fashion* (New York, E. P. Dutton and Company).

SELDON, Samuel, and SELLMAN, Hunton D.—*Stage Scenery and Lighting* (New York, F. S. Crofts and Company, 1930).

SMITH, Milton—*A Book of Play Production* (New York, D. Appleton-Century Company, 1926).

WARD, Winifred—*Creative Dramatics* (New York, D. Appleton-Century Company, 1930).

WEBSTER, Glenn R., and WETZEL, William—*Scenery Simplified* (Franklin, Ohio, Eldridge Entertainment House, 1934).

YOUNG, Agnes Brooks—*Stage Costuming* (New York, The Macmillan Company, 1927).

ADDRESSES OF PUBLISHERS

Abingdon Press, 150 Fifth Avenue, New York City
D. Appleton-Century Co., Inc., 35 West 32nd St., New York City
Atlantic Monthly Press, 34 Beacon St., Boston, Mass.
Walter H. Baker Co., 178 Tremont St., Boston, Mass.
Brentano's Book Stores, Inc., 1 West 47th Street, New York City
Children's Theatre Press, South Hills, Charleston, W. Va.
Thomas Y. Crowell Co., 432 Fourth Avenue, New York City
Denison and Co., 203 N. Wabash Ave., Chicago, Illinois
Dodd, Mead and Co., 449 Fourth Ave., New York City
Doubleday Doran and Co., 14 West 49th St., New York City
Dramatic Publishing Co., 59 E. Van Buren St., Chicago, Ill.
Dramatists Play Service, 6 East 39th St., New York City
Samuel French, Inc., 25 West 45th St., New York City
Harcourt, Brace and Co., 383 Madison Avenue, New York City
Harper and Brothers, 49 East 33rd Street, New York City
Henry Holt and Co., 239 West 39th Street, New York City
Houghton Mifflin Co., 2 Park Street, Boston
Alfred Knopf, 730 Fifth Avenue, New York City
Little, Brown and Co., 34 Beacon St., Boston, Mass.
J. J. Little and Ives, 435 E. 24th St., New York City.
Longmans, Green and Co., 114 Fifth Avenue, New York City
Macmillan Co., 60 Fifth Avenue, New York City
Thomas Nelson and Sons, 381 Fourth Ave., New York City
Oxford University Press, 114 Fifth Ave., New York City
G. P. Putnam's Sons, 2 West 45th Street, New York City
Rand McNally, 536 S. Clark St., Chicago, Illinois
Charles Scribner's Sons, 597 Fifth Avenue, New York
Theatre Arts, Inc., 40 East 49th St., New York City
John C. Winston Co., 1006-1016 Arch St., Philadelphia, Pa.

INDEX

(1)